RETURN
of THE GODDESS

Edward C. Whitmont

RETURN
of THE GODDESS

CROSSROAD • NEW YORK

ACKNOWLEDGMENTS

I would like to give my thanks to Sylvia Perera for her helpful comments and suggestions, especially regarding feminine psychology and the scapegoat complex, and for drawing my attention to the figure of Gawain as Grail Hero.

I would also like to thank Diana Lee James, curator of ARRAS, for her unstinting help in finding suitable illustrations and for permitting me to use them. I am grateful too to Mitchell Hall and Paul Walsh for their editorial help.

Above all I want to thank my analysands, students, and workshop participants for their uncounted contributions in raising questions and challenges, for permitting me to use their material, and for offering their feeling reactions and thoughts in the course of therapy sessions, supervisory seminars, and workshops.

1984

The Crossroad Publishing Company
370 Lexington Avenue, New York, NY 10017

Copyright © 1982 by Edward C. Whitmont

Library of Congress Cataloging in Publication Data

Whitmont, Edward C., 1912–
   The return of the goddess.

   Includes bibliographical references and index.
   1. Goddesses. 2. Aggressiveness (Psychology)
3. Grail. 4. Women and religion. 5. Psychoanalysis and religion. I. Title.
BL325.F4W44 1982   150.19'54   82-13075
ISBN 0-8245-0536-0
ISBN 0-8245-0643-X (pbk)

Contents

Introduction   vii

Part 1   THE MODERN DILEMMA   1

Chapter 1   A Modern Theophany   3
Chapter 2   Desire, Violence and Aggression   11
Chapter 3   Myth and Psychological Functioning   28

Part 2   CONSCIOUSNESS IN EVOLUTION   37

Prologue to Part 2   39
Chapter 4   The Magical Phase   41
Chapter 5   The Mythological or Imaginal Phase: Dionysus
and Apollo   49
Chapter 6   The Mental Phase   69

Part 3   THE PATRIARCHAL MYTHS   77

Chapter 7   The Divine Kingship: Superego and Ego   79
Chapter 8   The Human Exile; Paradise Lost; The Death of God   98
Chapter 9   The Scapegoat   105
Chapter 10   The Feminine and Its Repression (Femininity and
Masculinity)   121

Part 4   A MYTH FOR OUR TIMES   147

Chapter 11   The Grail   149

Part 5   VISION FOR A NEW AGE   181

Chapter 12   New Models of Orientation   183
Chapter 13   Individuation and Destiny   205
Chapter 14   Ethics   214
Chapter 15   On Ritual   235
References   259
Index   268

THE SECOND COMING
W. B. Yeats

Turning and turning in the widening gyre
The falcon cannot hear the falconer;
Things fall apart; the center cannot hold;
Mere anarchy is loosed upon the world,
The blood-dimmed tide is loosed, and everywhere
The ceremony of innocence is drowned;
The best lack all conviction, while the worst
Are full of passionate intensity.

Surely some revelation is at hand.
Surely the Second Coming is at hand.
The Second Coming! Hardly are those words out
When a vast image out of Spiritus Mundi
Troubles my sight; somewhere in the sands of the desert
A shape with lion body and the head of a man.
A gaze blank and pityless as the sun,
Is moving its slow thighs, while all about it
Reel shadows of the indignant desert birds.
The darkness drops again; but now I know
That twenty centuries of stony sleep
Were vexed to nightmare by a rocking cradle,
And what rough beast, its hour come round at last,
Slouches toward Bethlehem to be born?

Introduction

Clearly, mythology is no toy for children. Nor is it a matter of archaic, merely scholarly concern, of no moment to modern men of action. For its symbols (whether in the tangible form of images or in the abstract form of ideas) touch and release the deepest centers of motivation, moving literate and illiterate alike, moving mobs, moving civilizations. There is a real danger, therefore, in the incongruity of focus that has brought the latest findings of technological research into the foreground of modern life, joining the world in a single community, while leaving the anthropological and psychological discoveries, from which a commensurable moral system might have been developed, in the learned publications where they first appeared. For surely it is folly to preach to children who will be riding rockets to the moon a morality and cosmology based on the concepts of the good Society and of man's place in nature that were coined before the harnessing of the horse! And the world is now far too small and men's insanity too great, for any more of those old games of Chosen Folk (whether of Jehovah, Allah, Wotan, Manu, or the Devil) by which tribesmen were sustained against their enemies in the days when the serpent still could talk.

J. CAMPBELL, *The Masks of God**

At the low point of a cultural development that has led us into the deadlock of scientific materialism, technological destructiveness, religious nihilism and spiritual impoverishment, a most astounding phenomenon has occurred. A new mythologem is arising in our midst and asks to be integrated into our modern frame of reference. It is the myth of the ancient Goddess who once ruled earth and heaven before the advent of the patriarchy and of the patriarchal religions.

* Vol. I, p. 12.

The Goddess is now returning. Denied and suppressed for thousands of years of masculine domination, she comes at a time of dire need. For we walk through the valley of the shadow of nuclear annihilation, and we do fear evil. We long for love, security and protection, but there is little to comfort us. Violence within our own society threatens to overwhelm us. Mother Earth herself has been pressed to the limits of her endurance. How much longer can she withstand the assaults of our rapacious industrial and economic policies? The patriarchy's time is running out. What new cultural pattern will secure for humanity a new lease on life on earth?

Amidst tremendous transition and upheaval, the Goddess is returning. Traditional male and female roles in society are being challenged. The feminine call for a new recognition arises simultaneously with the violence that threatens to get out of hand. This strange coincidence eludes our understanding. Here mythology unexpectedly comes to our aid. It reveals an ancient pattern that points to the significance of this coincidence. The oldest deities of warfare and destruction were feminine, not masculine. Listen to their all but forgotten names: Inanna in Sumer, Anath in Canaan, Ishtar in Mesopotamia, Sekhmet in Egypt, the Morrigan in Eire, Kali in India, Pallas in Greece and Bellona in Rome. These archaic goddesses had dominion over both love *and* war. They were credited with both chastity and promiscuity, nurturing motherliness and bloodthirsty destructiveness. But they were not at all concerned with conquest and territorial expansion. Those were male obsessions. Rather, these goddesses monitored the life cycle throughout its phases: birth, growth, love, death, and rebirth. Evidently today our endangered life cycle again needs divine monitoring. In the depths of the unconscious psyche, the ancient Goddess is arising. She demands recognition and homage. If we refuse to acknowledge her, she may unleash forces of destruction. If we grant the Goddess her due, she may compassionately guide us toward transformation.

The reader is forewarned that this is a complex book. In calling attention to the Goddess's return, we will have to consider several interrelated issues. A primary focus is on aggression. In our nuclear age, for the sake of survival, we *must* learn new ways of dealing with conflict and aggression. Hence, in the first chapter we look closely at the story of a woman who was on the brink of violently harming her only child. Through a successful course of therapy, she was able to transform those threatening energies by responding to the implications of the archetype of the Goddess pressing forward toward consciousness in her dreams. The next two chapters will consider the problem of aggression and need in more general terms. Human aggression, human rights and needs are the dilemma of our times. We are all caught on its horns. If we look deeply, we will discover that the horns are on the head of Dionysus. He is the Goddess's consort. He embodies need and aggressive violence. She never appears without him.

To gain perspective on where we are, we need an orientation concerning where we have come from. Consequently, the second part of the book gives an overview of the evolution of consciousness through three phases: magical, mythological and mental. While our rational conditioning leads us to assume we have gone beyond the first two layers, they are ever with us not too far beneath the surface. For our further evolution, we will have to integrate them anew. In charting our course through these three phases, we will be especially concerned with how the masculine ascendancy has been accomplished and how aggression and need have been channelled or contained in these past phases.

Part 3 examines the chief myths whereby the patriarchy has maintained its control: the divine kingship, the human exile, the scapegoat, the repression of the feminine. It is these myths we need to go beyond, if we are to survive.

Part 4, therefore, reveals the Quest for the Holy Grail as the key myth to the transformations desired of our times. It underlies all our striving for liberation, for need fulfillment, and our urge to discover the secrets of existence, whether through scientific research or religious contemplation. It inspires our hopes to restore a golden age of human dignity. The psychosis of Hitler and National Socialism expressed a perversion of the Grail myth. This too, though in negative terms, shows its centrality.

Part 5 explores the psychological, ethical, and social implications of the Grail myth and the Goddess's return. Those looking for easy recipes to be followed literally will not find them here. Our problems are too serious, too complex, too individually patterned. Solutions cannot be concocted out of one person's head. I would caution the reader to be wary, in fact, of any utopian promises from any source whatsoever. Jung has rightly pointed out:

The serious problems of life are never fully solved. If ever they should appear to be so, it is a sure sign that something has been lost. The meaning and purpose of a problem seem to lie not in its solution but in our working at it incessantly. This alone preserves us from stultification and petrification.

The Goddess is guardian of human interiority. The patriarchy regulated the externals of human behavior but devalued individualized instinct, feeling, intuition, emotion, and the depth of the feminine, except in the service of the collective. How significant that "effeminate" was coined as a pejorative term. In the new orientation, each individual needs to discover the indwelling source of authentic conscience and spiritual guidance, the divinity within. Jung called this transpersonal center the Self. It is being born amidst much suffering. In trying to get their bearings, individuals are being torn between passion and reason, desire and obligation, the personal and the collective, the call of the new and the demand of the old. Many who have rejected the collective norms fall into moral nihilism, cynicism, or outright antisocial behavior. The miscarried search for interiority is behind the much-decried contemporary narcissism. The Goddess's coming does not mean a rejection of ethics though, but a new ethics, more deeply rooted in individual conscience.

I am hoping for readers willing to enter a dialogue with me and personally work through their reaction to the material. The kind of change that I am signaling is so major that we will encounter many inner resistances to recognizing it, let alone responding.

A note on terminology is appropriate here. Our Western languages lack words equivalent to the Chinese Yang and Yin. These denote cosmic or archetypal principles of polarity. The biological sexual genders are but special instances. Being reluctant to invent new words, I am using *masculine* and *feminine* as synonymous with Yang and Yin whenever I speak of archetypal, psychological principles. *Male* and *female* will indicate overt sexual distinctions.

The modern mind might find references to gods and goddesses peculiarly archaic or pagan. They are, however, archetypal and compelling ideals. Although not literal objects, these symbolic representations are real and powerful. Although not persons, they are personalities. They arise as energetic configurations from very deep levels within us and can elicit tonifying responses not possible through mere abstract thought.

Some readers may wonder what right a man has to be speaking of the Goddess and of feminine dynamics. Let us remember that both sexes have what are called male and female sex hormones. Jung was the first to demonstrate an analogous situation psychologically. Above and beyond these formal justifications, there is a more concrete one. This book has a personal corollary in the inner experience and development of my life. Some aspects of my own Quest for the Goddess and the Grail can be described.

I was raised in Austria in an Orthodox, parochially narrow Jewish family, with a rigid rule and law system. My ineffective and yielding father was concerned only with the traditional, moralistic, religious standards, dietary and behavior regulations. Without any brothers or sisters, I learned from early years on to go my own lonely way. Any mishap or difficulty was interpreted as God's punishment for the breaking of a taboo. This led to my early estrangement from anything religious. In fact, I began to hate anything religious. At the same time, however, I was attracted by myths and fairy tales. I imbued myself in them. The Germanic myths impressed me very much. One of my earliest memories is of two pictures, one of Siegfried, the other of Tristan and Isolde. These had been picture postcards that a friend and I cut out and hung on the wall. Consequently, I was also impressed by the Germanic hero worship. Later on I recognized that this reflected the very same rigid rule system as the religious parochialism, but this time in terms of honor and pride.

At an early age I became deeply involved with music. I started playing the piano at age four or five. Up to the age of fifteen or sixteen I lived entirely in the world of Wagner. I knew the scores of *The Ring* and *Parsifal* practically by heart. With a friend I played a game. One of us would play a few passages on the piano, and the other would have to indicate exactly where it came from in *The Ring*. People were judged by how well they understood *The Ring*.

To me the whole theme of *The Ring* pointed to the failure of power striving. This can be resolved only through unselfish dedication, the motive of Brunhilde's self-sacrifice to make Siegfried's birth possible. That led directly to *Parsifal*, where the Grail is the answer to human striving. Still it was seen as an allegorical, artistic statement of a social or even national issue. In view of the stupidity and destructiveness of the power urge, as demonstrated to me by *The Ring*, I thought the Grail could be sought through social liberation. So I became a dedicated socialist. According to the social gospel of liberation, I wanted to enlist in the heroic battle for the betterment of mankind. For that reason, I turned away from my earlier goal of becoming a musician and conductor. I put aside the many years of music study I had started. Instead, I chose medicine. In that way, I hoped to be of service. Moreover, the example of my always sick and neurotic mother made me determined to fight her chief weapon, disease.

Eventually, I discovered the unsatisfactory wasteland and power strife within the leftist movement itself. I got the first glimpse of what in its extreme form later emerged as Stalinism. I saw the absolute denial of personal and feeling values for the sake of fanatical dedication. The goal of liberation was used to justify any means. This paralleled what I perceived again in the same form in National Socialism. Increasingly, I abhorred what I came to regard as the secularization of the "sacred goal."

For a time I became involved with Adlerian counseling and the asso-

ciated communal sense, which I assiduously tried to cultivate. There
again I found power strife. It was just covered up: "I am more communally striving than you" was a common attitude.

In medical school, I was struck, on viewing a cadaver, that this was
not the human being. Something was missing. Our life is not just a
matter of chemistry. At the same time, I realized I was being taught to
dissect frogs, rabbits and people, but not how to cure a living human
being. It was the high point in medical nihilism in those days. All we
could do was to diagnose and then shrug it off as nothing could be done.
In this purely materialistic approach, there was no sense of a soul.

Subsequently, in seeking answers to this dilemma, I was led, in turn,
to Christianity, Anthroposophy, homeopathy, psychosomatics, alchemy, and then Jung. Jung confirmed for me the relevance of myth
and dream to a transpersonal, almost objective, realm of meaning. I met
the Grail again in the alchemical symbolism.

I had first come in contact with Nazism at the age of seventeen. For
the following nine years I was in constant touch with it. I even knew
some Nazis personally. One of them, to protect me, would send me
warnings when a fight was coming. With respect to Germanism and
music, we were on the same wave length. I witnessed something else
that was peculiar. Among socialists, communists, Marxists and Nazis,
there was a constant coming and going. One day many of them were
this, another day that. All these variations were the projection of the
religious dedication externally onto a cultic liberation creed. This observation gave me a profound suspicion of fanaticism, no matter
whether I found it in myself or in others. Most of these people were
really highly idealistic. More recently, we have seen the Yippies, the
antiwar and liberation movement guerillas and terrorists, the moral
rearmament movement, the resurgence of the Ku Klux Klan and born-
again Christians. Such people have the same blind expectation that
radical answers to the human situation are to be found in societal
changes or simple determination of will. Political changes avail us little
without greater psychological awareness of the unconscious power and
destruction urges which slumber in our souls, good intentions notwithstanding. In "The Great Day," Yeats ironically commented on this:

> *Hurrah for revolution and more cannon-shot!*
> *A beggar up on horseback lashes a beggar on foot.*
> *Hurrah for revolution and cannon come again!*
> *The beggars have changed places, but the lash goes on.*[1]

In 1938, at the age of twenty-six, I emigrated from Austria to
America to escape from the Nazis. By the quota system, I, having been

born in Vienna, could leave, but my parents, who were originally from Poland, could not. They were murdered in the Nazi gas chambers.

In the United States, I was again thrown back onto the heroic model, with a lot of restless seeking of "the answers" in the various spiritual and intellectual currents. Eventually I became settled domestically, financially and professionally, and somewhat contained in the inertia of the practice of medicine. At this time, dreams began to appear, pointing to what I lacked.

There were dreams of living in empty, decrepit houses, of everything falling to pieces, of bearded, old fuddy-duddies looking vainly for answers on dusty shelves. These dreams I found puzzling at first. Then I began my own analysis. Gradually there appeared images like a numinous Goddess that pointed to a deeper connection to emotions which the heroic culture had repressed. They implied the need to relate to woman as if she were a goddess, that is, to revere qualities, feelings, and emotions previously repressed.

I came to see now that in opposition to parents, under the influence of the heroic tradition, and in response to the emigration, I had learned to rely only upon pushing, heroic strength, and self-reliant challenging of obstacles. Will, reason and understanding, honor and responsibility—rather than feeling—were the guiding impulses for me. The heroic ideal which helped me maintain a sense of identity in an early environment that was so unsupportive of a rebellious, curious, and musical child had hardened me into an armor of responsibility, duty, and combativeness. I loved as well as feared to fight teachers and later adversaries, such as Nazis. I began to realize that during my childhood there had been a lack of a woman who could accept my idealization. I felt the same fear of women around me as I had felt as a child. The only women I had known as a child were my hysterical, neurotic mother and my grim, Puritanical governesses and nursemaids, who were as harsh and unsupportive as could be. So I had learned to fear women primarily for their power to reject and to make me feel guilty. There had been no one to admire as strong or in touch with the ecstasies of life and death. Music had been my compensation for these lacks. But in my teens I had already started to view music as an escape from economic and heroic realities. It seemed at the time a "cop out" from dedicating myself to the Grail search for outer liberation. Nowadays, music is for me the primary connection to the psyche, the soul, the spirit, and the unconscious. Whenever I want to know how I feel, I go to the piano.

At one time when, contrary to my conscious intentions and rational judgment, I felt strongly attracted to a woman and feared that this would raise serious complications and troubles, I had the following dreams. (Although not under my name, these dreams were previously published in *The Symbolic Quest.*)[2] While walking across the country-side, I was suddenly attacked by a herd of blue geese. I called for help. The mistress of the geese appeared. She resembled the woman I was in love with, but was a much more beautiful and numinous figure. With a magic wand she appeased the geese. I knelt down before her and offered her my fealty. She bestowed upon me graciously a bouquet of flowers. The dream has remained in my memory until now, because those blue geese were terribly scary. I later found out that geese are among the oldest images of the Earth Mother. They were the animals of Hera and Aphrodite in Greek mythology. When Rome was almost overwhelmed by an attack of the Gauls who stealthily crept in at night, the geese awakened the defenders and warned them. They represent a conscious-ness of the night and instinct. This aspect is emphasized in my dream by the dark blue color which conveyed a sense of night and mystery. It was as though the spirit of the dark mystery of earth life and emotion were to attack and threaten me unless I served its mistress through honoring my feeling for that concrete person who then embodied her to me. In doing so, in turn, I was to receive flowers, a new blooming.

In a later dream, I prayed to have the divinity revealed to me. Sud-denly, like a curtain parting, the divinity appeared with a blast of light. I saw a cave, and within the cave, the nativity. There was a hare holding a baby hare in its hands. Shattered, I fell on my face and wor-shipped. I woke up with a jolt, rather scandalized, and wondered: "Why a hare?" For I knew the hare only as the animal of fertility, sexu-ality, and promiscuity. Should this be my image of divinity? Only thirty years later I discovered that the hare is the original animal sym-bol for the zodiacal sign of Virgo: the Virgin Goddess, Mother of the Divine Child, reconnected again in the symbolism of this dream with instinct and sexuality, the forces of the earth and the body, from which Christian tradition had severed her.

In another dream, I saw my mother imprisoned in a castle, bewitched by an evil power magician. To deliver her, I had to submit to the fero-cious animals in the castle. My doing so changed her into an attractive Goddesslike figure. In terms of my mother, this made no sense. All I could then understand was the need to encounter passionate emotion. Again, later I noted the similarity between this dream and the adven-tures of Gawain in Wolfram von Eschenbach's *Parzival*. While Parzi-fal, having failed in his first encounter with the Grail, is lost sight of, Gawain—his other, perhaps more earthly, side—delivers the women imprisoned by a power-hungry magician in the *Castel merveil*. He does so by encountering the onslaught of a wild lion. As will be discussed in the Grail chapter, Gawain's adventure constitutes the hidden, esoteric aspect leading to the restoration of the Grail by honoring the Feminine aspect of existence. Also, this dream's message was that feeling and emotion have to be struggled with as part of a quasi-religious quest and dedication for the sake of liberating the imprisoned Mother, the Goddess.

The significance of my own encounter with this material was confirmed to me when gradually I came to see the same or similar motifs coming up in the unconscious productions of my patients. So I was not alone, at least, with my "crazy" notions. Something was coming up in the collective unconscious to which in my own life I had to make my own contribution. Struggling with my own problems, I could help my patients better. I discovered new experiential and emotional ways of working, incorporating body, imaginal, group, and Gestalt methods into my Jungian frame of reference which at first had been relatively abstract and theoretical. Revalidation of the basic instinctual energies I discovered to be necessary for an opening of the way to the spirit.

The following book, which I have worked more than ten years to prepare for publication, presents the perspective I have gained through my own life experience and analysis, through working with my patients, and through my studies.

Aphrodite on a goose. Terra cotta Boeotia, classical period,
Louvre, Paris.

Part 1

THE MODERN DILEMMA

May you be born in an interesting time.
TRADITIONAL CHINESE CURSE

CHAPTER 1

A Modern Theophany

All ages before ours believed in gods in some form or other. Only an unparalleled impoverishment in symbolism could enable us to discover the gods as psychic factors, which is to say, as archetypes of the unconscious. No doubt this discovery is hardly credible yet.

C.G. JUNG*

"A downtrodden . . . housewife, devoid of place and purpose, and filled with poison . . ." as she called herself. She was on the verge of a dangerous breakdown. For over a year she had been hearing a voice that commanded her to take a knife and stab and dismember her only child, a five year old boy. She resisted but was terrified. The voice kept insisting. It went on calling until she felt that she had to use every ounce of strength and willpower to resist. She dared not look at sharp objects or go near her child lest her resistance weaken and she do him harm. Frightened and desperate, she sought psychiatric help. Her first therapist explored with her the major events of her childhood and marriage. She had grown up in a small town; her family was middle class and conservative. There was little genuine affection, of which even less was allowed to be overtly expressed. In place of love there was pressure to be bright and cheerful, to conform, and to do one's best (as spelled out by the lifeless rules of her mother, church, and school). The children learned to hide their feelings. Expressions of individual needs and sex

---

* *Collected Works,* Vol. IX, p. 72.

were taboo. Her parents had forced her to break off a passionate early
love affair because there was "no future in it." She had then married an
"intelligent and sophisticated" high school teacher whom she regarded
as boring and ineffectual.

Her first therapist had correctly diagnosed a great deal of repressed
anger, first at her domineering mother who had frustrated her emotional and sexual development, and second at her life circumstances,
particularly her marriage which continued her bondage and, so she felt,
stultified any hopes of finding herself as an authentic human being. She
was angry also at the men in her life: her absentee father and her weak
(at least in her view) husband. It was obvious also that the restrictive
atmosphere and value system of her childhood had produced a sort of
psychological paralysis. Where traditional religion and morality had
failed to give her an effective sense of herself as an individual person or
to give a meaning to her life, the emerging threat of destruction from
dangerously pent-up violence became very real.

An intelligent woman, she understood the reasons for her predica-
ment, and the hate and resentment it engendered, but her understanding of the crisis, and the reasons for it, did not help. The voice continued telling her to murder her son.

She came to me when, in despair, she decided to try a different form
of therapy. Since rational explanations had no effect, I felt an answer
had to come from nonrational sources, specifically from some wellspring of creative energy within the patient herself. I suggested therefore that the next time the voice spoke to her she put her feelings down
on paper, uncritically, with crayons or paint. I asked her also to try to
remember and write down any dreams she might have.

This soon produced dramatic results. After a severe spell of anxiety
she painted a yellow sunlike disc with rays spreading out in all directions. One ray shot down to the ground like a tail (her own description). To her surprise, she felt considerably calmer after she finished
the painting. She also was able to recall several dreams, the most significant of which I shall discuss here.

In the first dream she saw a six-pointed star made up of two inter-
locking triangles. The star was distorted: the top triangle, which
pointed upward, was excessively large; the lower one, which pointed
downward, was shrunken and small.

In the second dream she saw what she called a "music master." He
had a goat's body and a bright halo around his head. She tried to chase
him away, whereupon he turned into a violent and angry demon.

The third dream showed her a gigantic snake with a bull's head,
cooped up in the attic of her house. This bull-snake was starving and

threatened to break out of its confines and destroy the house, dreamer, and child if she did not care for and feed it.

In the fourth dream, she was in a museum where a stone cat came to life and asked her what she sought. She answered that she needed to learn the forgotten secret of the ages. The cat then led her down to a cellar where she met ancient figures with torches. They asked her if she really wanted to become one of them. She said yes. She then had to swear to dedicate herself fully to the initiation that would follow.

In a fifth dream she found herself ranging over mountain tops in what she called a higher atmosphere. There she was suddenly engulfed by terrible thunderstorms and powerful lightning flashes. In order to avoid destruction she had to come down and seek refuge in a dark cave or grotto, in the back of which there was a dark, mysterious pool of "living" water in which she felt she needed to submerge herself in order to be safe.

Dreams are symbolic as well as symptomatic. A symptom expresses a variation from a supposedly healthy normal state. A symbol points beyond itself to a meaning that is out of reach of the familiar words of our language. The dream language of the psyche is archaic: spontaneously, regardless of our conscious awareness, it produces fragments of myth, legend, and fairy tale in the form of personal dramas. These are concerned with one's relationship to one's own deepest reality, and can acquaint us with sources and meanings whereby we may relate our lives to our own personal mythic structures.

I suggested to my patient that the images in her dreams and in her painting were of a religious nature and deserved to be taken seriously; that suprapersonal needs can be as important to the organism as biological urges. It did not matter that these images could not readily be translated into rational terms. They were designed not to explain, but to expand her awareness and, perhaps, impel her towards some focal point of significance in, and perhaps beyond, her concrete personal existence.

The six-sided Star of David is one of our oldest symbols. The up-pointing triangle expresses the dynamism of upward striving: towards the heavens, towards light, air, spirit, abstraction, expansion, and rationality. In short, it points toward the archetype of maleness.

The down-pointing triangle represents the drive of spirit towards earth, towards inwardness and incarnation, organic experiencing rather than rational explanation. It points toward the archetype of the feminine. As stated in the Introduction, neither of these terms is to be confused with male and female in the ordinary sense. They are archetypal forces which are alive in both sexes, albeit in different proportions. Men are not merely masculine, nor women merely feminine. Both have to integrate the other into themselves; man his unconscious femininity, or *anima* as Jung called it, and woman her unconscious masculinity, her *animus*. When these forces are in balance, the personality likewise achieves balance.

In this woman's dream the star was severely distorted. The down-pointing triangle that represented the feminine, instinctual, and emotional sides, her attunedness to natural urges, rhythms, and needs, was atrophied and repressed. The upward-pointing triangle, symbolic of order, discipline, and willful rational control, was overly large. She had no adequate access to the depth of her femininity.

In the second and third dreams the aggressive threat is personified, rather surprisingly so, as music teacher or a goat with a halo and a bull-snake. Who or what is this strange figure? How is he also a snake and a bull? The music teacher with a halo alludes to a divine or semidivine mythological figure concerned with cultivating music. Apollo, Hermes, Krishna, and Dionysus were such archetypal divinities, but only Dionysus has been depicted also as goat, bull, stag, stallion, and serpent. In the myth, he turns with destructive rage against those who fail to honor him. These he strikes with madness. He was, in fact, known as the "mad god," and he forced the women who resisted him to slay their children. The patron of music, drama and intoxication in ancient Greece, the god who dies and is ever reborn, the entity he represents was known under many names among different people: the Horned God, Osiris, Pan, Dumuzi, Azazel, Attis, and Tammuz are examples. The most familiar of these to us is the Greek Dionysus. His rites abounded with orgiastic and emotional rapture, with dance and violent abandonment. In the context of the dreamer's life, however, it is important to be aware that the Dionysian rites expressed more than just an acting out of sexuality, desire, and violence. Indeed, the Dionysian cults used music and ritual as means of integrating violence and desire into the whole personality. Of Orpheus, the humanly incarnate form of Dionysus, the legend says that he tamed wild beasts and even the furies with his music. Likewise, the religious ceremonies and rituals of the Dionysian cults may be presumed to have been aimed at taming and harmoniously integrating the hungry and needy beasts and furies in man.

The ritual enactment of the drama of the god, who here represents orgiastic violence, served to tame the potentially destructive urges into socially acceptable channels. Practice of a religious ritual, in the past, provided a dynamic equivalent to the aggression-control ritual of animals, to be discussed in the next chapter. As this "divine" power and its ritual are refused (the music teacher is chased away and the bull-snake is imprisoned and starved), a destructive potential is released. In the myth of Pentheus, the king of Thebes was torn to pieces by his own mother in menadic frenzy because he refused homage to Dionysus.

But an additional and perhaps even more unexpected and surprising factor presses for consideration in terms of this strange material. The disregard of Dionysus is associated also with a disregard and repression of femininity in its archetypal dimension. The Dionysian rites were first and foremost women's rites. The down-pointing lower triangle denoting the feminine is atrophied; the cat goddess (the dreamer's associations pointed to a cat goddess she had seen in the Egyptian section of the museum) leads her to the religious services of the ancient, forgotten rites; the refuge from the lightning bolts of patriarchal Zeus or Jupiter is to be found in the feminine grotto or cave, and in the dark water, the womb of the Earth Goddess.

In Egypt, the cat was sacred to Bast, Sekhmet and Isis. In medieval lore, like the goose, it was the *familiaris* of witches, the worshippers of the old Mother religion, and of Pan. Dionysus, like Pan, Dumuzi, Attis, etcetera, was a god of women.[1] Nothing less than a reemergence of a feminine religious attitude, ancient, repressed, and forgotten, a new relationship to the Goddess and her consort, to archetypal femininity and its active expression is offered here as an approach that might stave off the threat of destruction.

That this is indeed what is called for is summed up and emphasized in the vision of the painting. At first the painting was puzzling. After she had completed it, the patient felt strangely relieved. She did not understand why, nor did the painting have any meaning to her. I too was at a loss until I suddenly remembered a case history that Jung had described many years earlier.

Jung described the hallucinatory fantasy of an uneducated laborer, a schizophrenic patient at the Zurich Burgholzli. This man would stand all day at the window and excitedly call the hospital physicians to come and look at the sun. He insisted that if they moved their heads back and forth, they could see the tail or penis of the sun moving to and fro. This tail, he said, was the source of the solar wind. (At that time, the concept of a solar wind had not yet been enunciated by science.) Years after this patient's death, Jung came across a translation of a newly discovered Greek papyrus called "A Mithras Liturgy." This obscure work described the experience of a Mithraic initiate:

For you will see in that day and in that hour the divine order, the ruling gods ascending to heaven and the others descending; and the path of the visible gods will appear through the disc of the sun, my father, the god; similarly also the so-called tube, the origin of the ministering wind. For you will see as it were a tube hanging from the disc of the sun and toward the regions of the west, limitless like an east wind if the other is appointed to blow toward the regions of the west. . . .

Obviously the Zurich patient could not have known of this Mithraic material, and neither did my patient. The Mithraic version reminded me of a similar Judeo-Christian motif, the dream of Jacob who saw "a ladder set up on the earth, and the top of it reached to heaven: and behold the angels of God ascending and descending on it." God's voice promised the covenant "I am with thee, and will keep thee in all places whither thou goest, and will bring thee again into this land; for I will not leave thee until I have done that which I have spoken to Thee of." After the dream, Jacob was awed and relieved of his anxiety. His reaction was "Surely the Lord is in this place; and I knew it not" (Gen. 28:16).

In our patient's case however—and therein lies its newness—the deity involved is feminine, and assertively feminine. She is even solar rather than receptively lunar, as has been the case with the traditional feminine symbolism throughout the patriarchal period. By virtue of the Egyptian cat-Bast association, it points to the mythologem of Sekhmet, the solar aspect of Bast, who was depicted with the powerful but graceful body of a human female and the head of a lioness. A solar disc with a serpent crowned her head. Sekhmet was addressed by such titles as Lady of the Beginning of Time, Lady of Flame, Lady of the Lamp, and Great One of Magic. Her name, according to Sir Wallis Budge, is likely to be derived from the root *sekhem,* to be strong and mighty, both in aggressive, destructive fierceness (Sekhmet was a violent goddess of war) and in desire, sexual power, love and healing.[2]

What our patient's unconscious was presenting, then, as the alternative to destruction and as a way of healing, was nothing less than the renewal of a religious attitude, long repressed collectively, hence previously inaccessible to our patient. This religious attitude was expressed symbolically as though pertaining to the ancient Goddess of life and sexual and emotional intoxication, and to her consort, lover, and victim who ever dies and ever is reborn. They represent and call for an attitude to life which reemphasizes femininity and yet can constructively channel our patient's fierce aggressive needs for assertion as well as her needs for more adequate emotional and sexual self-expression. Healing is promised through channels which under the influence of the patriarchy were repressed and branded as evil, particularly in women.

Through emotionally accepting and—over a three- to four-year period of psychological work—experiencing and integrating into her own personal psychology the powerful, previously repressed impulses and needs represented by the mythological material in her dreams, our patient was freed from the murderous urge to harm her son, and enabled to make basic, highly constructive changes in her own life and outlook.

From a "downtrodden housewife devoid of place and purpose and filled with poison" (as she described herself at our first meeting), she changed into a person who felt herself guided by an internal source of wisdom coming from a deep instinctual wellspring of her femininity. She learned to honor her own needs in a responsible fashion. She found her own standards, her sexual and emotional values, and a new capacity for self-assertion and self-respect. Eventually a satisfying career in addition to child and home opened for her. The conscious relation to the power of the Goddess in terms of a psychological reassessment of herself as a woman served to inhibit and redirect the destructive threat of violence into creative activity. This transformation of her personality and outlook on life came about not as a result of rational or theoretical understanding on her part, nor by indiscriminate acting out of sexual or violent urges, nor by joining a church or cult, but by working through the material in personal, experiential forms in the course of therapy.

I have described here the dangerous problem of one particular woman. Yet her dilemma is typical of the anger and unsatisfied longing for self-validation that fills the souls of millions of women and men the whole world over. All too often individuals and communities seem to be driven to acts of irrational anger and destruction, regardless of rationality and intentions, which wreak havoc in our individual lives. In their extreme form they may thus even ultimately destroy us and our children in a worldwide holocaust.

Like sexuality and the need of care and dependable support, anger, aggression and the drive to violence are also basic urges of autonomous archetypal character. In Victorian days, they were considered evil, selfish, indeed Satanic urges, neither to be admitted nor even to be allowed to be parts of the personality of a "good" person. Psychologically speaking they were repressed from consciousness. Since the days of Freud, sexuality has been admitted to the rank of a psychological drive. But aggression and neediness are still largely repressed and looked askance at as sexuality was during the Victorian days. Therefore, like sexuality then, they now threaten to invade and poison our conscious lives. And denied the dignity of a *daimonion*, even a Satanic one, sexuality, neediness and aggressive violence cannot be controlled by rationality and good will alone.

Thus the impasse of our patient reflects the impasse of our culture.

Might her individual experience also help us with our individual and even collective problem? Might it show us the way to a new ethic?

Before we can attempt to answer that question, a closer look at the way in which aggression and need operate in our culture and minds will be called for.

CHAPTER 2

Desire, Violence and Aggression

He who ... learns to surmount the promptings of desire and
anger finds Brahman and is happy.

Bhagavat Gita, 5.

War is both father and king of all ... It shall be understood that
war is the common condition, that strife is justice and that all
things come to pass through strife.

HERACLITUS

Man is a wolf to man.

Ancient Roman Saying

Our patient's problem could be called thwarted authenticity.
Achieving authenticity necessitates honoring one's emotional needs
and desires. Need is the basic urge to biological, emotional and spiritual
satisfaction. It functions for the sake of survival, group or personal
identity and self-validation. In its most primitive form, it manifests as
vague wanting, hunger, greed, envy, dependency, fear, hostility, and
the urge to violence. Personalized and channelled responsibly toward
specific objects, these primitive modes can be refined into longing, desire, love, self-appreciation and self-assertion. Our human problem lies
in the fact that our basic instinctual urges are polarized; they include
both social and antisocial drives: the desire to give and receive mutual
support as well as the tendency to envy, greed and hostile destructiveness.

Theoretically, at least, we are prepared to admit that wholesome human functioning should be based on self-authentication. To be one's authentic self is probably the most fundamental human right. But what are we then to do with our antisocial urges? Are we to act them out in the name of "authenticity"? Past cultures have dealt with that question without even considering human rights, let alone authenticity. Instead, for the average person, conformity, obligations and duties were stressed. Today, we believe in human rights. But by and large, we still limit their definition to biological, social and political standards. We are largely unaware of their psychological implications and give little value as yet to individual feeling needs. For the sake of social conformity with the masculine ideal of bravery, we still repress and teach our children to repress their subjective feminine sides, their affects, feelings and neediness. Thus our culture collectively replicates the pathology of that individual woman patient. It represses rather than sensitively integrates the Goddess's realm of birth, death, the tides of inwardness, moods, and emotions. Likewise, it represses Dionysus's domain of desire, joy, aggression, and destruction. This results in a widespread sense of depersonalization, frustration, resentment, hate, incapacity to love and insensitivity to the humanness of others and of self. Primeval envy, greed, and destructive hostility increasingly dominate the scene. We have not yet confronted the paradox of the need for individual authenticity versus the demands of social ethics.

Having been exposed firsthand to the grim spectacle of National Socialism, I see these trends as more than theoretical issues. They are a reminder and warning of where we might be heading if we do not wake up to the depth of the problem. For it would be optimistic self-deception to assume that the passing of one or the other dictator solves our dilemma. After Hitler came Khomeini, after Vietnam came Poland and El Salvador. And then what? What about the climate of crime, terrorism, racial polarization and exploitation in our own midst and daily lives?

Probably there is no more violence and brutal oppression or exploitation nowadays than in the past. But they are no longer compatible with our moral conscience, nor with our hopes for the survival of the human race. With our present state of technological development, uncurbed violence may mean the disintegration of social structure, nuclear holocaust, and collective suicide. Yet we have no satisfactory cure for this threat. Attempts to regulate violent aggression or for that matter greed, by law, Christian charity, ethical principles, social reform, and good will are no longer adequate. We need religio-cultural systems capable of defusing aggression, anger, and violence, and directing them into constructive channels. Yet we have none. Our traditional patriarchal religions no longer help us to contain them. Our cultural code has made us view anger, hostility, aggression and desire as evil, unnecessary, and avoidable. Often, therefore, we are naively unprepared for each new assault. We are shocked. Or worse, we are not even shocked, because we expect it.

Narrow, ruthless self-interest prevails among individuals and social groups. Violent political crimes, guerilla warfare, banditry, kidnappings, and terrorism are ever increasing, and ever justified by their perpetrators in the name of good causes. We take nationalism for granted as a politically motivating force, and as a self-evident basis for ethics. Yet it became a significant factor only after the French Revolution. To this development, Grillparzer, the Austrian poet and playwright, responded about one hundred and fifty years ago with the prophetic verse: "The ways of modern erudition: From humanism / through nationalism / to brutalism."

In the past, violence was more successfully contained within socially sanctioned channels. It was not, as in our time, looked upon as almost always wrong. Given scope for legitimate expression, its prohibition within the body social could also be enforced. The hero of the past combined physical and spiritual bravery with a muscular ability to butcher the opponent. Achilles, Samson, and the medieval knight are examples. Today, we are in a schizophrenic state: despite conscious protestations, we still unconsciously regard violence and aggression, no less than greedy exploitation, as admirable. Witness our media. Television and the movies glorify violence, horror and explicit sex to the point where these performances are almost ritualistic. Their appeal seems to rest upon the cathartic effect of drama. These violent contemporary dramatics are secularized, indeed decadent, caricatures of the solemn presentation of ancient tragedy. In Greek, *trag-odia* meant the "song of the goat," referring to Dionysus. Originally, this was a cathartic presentation of the rise, violent destruction, and glorification of the human protagonist who embodies the fate of Dionysus, the sacrificial goat, the ever-dying and reborn power of life, the needy child and self-sacrificing god. The tragedy of life was represented as an inexorable struggle, albeit in vain, against the god-ordained fate which decreed destruction for the sake of rebirth or as the punishment for hubris.

As long as aggression and violence were considered an expression of the power of a tutelary deity (such as Dionysus, Ares, Shiva, Thyr, Sekhmet, and the Morrigan) or served the greater glory of emperor, church or fatherland, they were integrated into a morally and ethically functioning system. By virtue of belonging to a deity, violence and aggression could be related to as part of a self-regulating cultural balancing system. And neediness was offered up to a deity who was served by careful observance of the rules and taboos, impulses and inhibitions inherent in its mythology. Even warfare had its rules and rituals. It had to be declared, originally, by invoking the god. In the code of chivalry, the weak and helpless were to be spared, and those asking asylum, even though they were enemies, were held inviolable. It is ironically significant that the last vestiges of the various codes of chivalry have met their ultimate demise in the fanatical violence of our own "enlightened" and "peace-loving" modern warfare, fought for purportedly sacred causes and for the betterment of the human lot. Along with the demise of God in our day, the last shred of respect for the order imposed by the old god has also ceased. Law and rule no longer protect us from violence.

Anger, hate, aggression, greed, and violence are *officially* considered to be unconditionally evil. At the same time, they have become a prerogative of the modern ego, to be used at its most arbitrary discretion, uninhibited by any personal concern for the powers thus abrogated. In our time the horrors of genocide and concentration camps have confronted us with the face of unalloyed evil, a madness our proud civilization thought it had disavowed. The divine command, "Thou shalt not murder,"[1] has fallen victim to our loss of transpersonal guidance. We lack a credible ethical system by which to integrate desires and aggressive urges. We feel ourselves more and more endangered by the violent forces that we piously deplore but cannot stop indulging. The contradictoriness of this schizophrenic attitude is as acute a threat to our sanity, individual as well as collective, as was the attitude toward sex in the Victorian days before Freud.

The patriarchal ego (to be discussed later) abhors change and surrender. It wishes for life and consciousness in unaltered, unchangeable perpetuity. Hence it fears any threat to its own continuity. Yet it is willing, nay compelled, to repress and destroy what stands in the way of its hunger and security. The patriarchal ego wills life but creates the very death and evil which it fears and denies.

What we fear we consider evil. We fear violence because we have come to expect life to be orderly, rational, peaceful and perpetual. We fear change because our sense of personal identity in time and space rests upon the illusion of sameness, of psychic stability and permanence.

Jung observed that "Nothing arouses so much panic among primitives as something out of the ordinary; it is at once suspected of being dangerous and hostile."[2] The same is equally true of civilized man.

Change is a threat to our present state of consciousness and to our accustomed sense of identity. Hence we dread death, the ultimate change, as the greatest evil of all. Dionysus, the dark god of change, represents such a threat. He had to be cast out in the name of the God who is *I am,* the God who separated the evil from the good, the above from the below. As a result, paradisiacal oneness was lost. This theme, in one way or another, runs through all patriarchal mythologies.

The creative abyss of the maternal ground, the Feminine or Yin, was split off and rejected. The violent, ecstatic urge to death and destruction that is such an important part of the Yin principle was denied and repressed. The abysmal ground and origin of being is felt as sacred, dangerous and overpowering, all-in-one. Its attraction is passionately desired, yet also dreaded by the gradually emerging individual identity which came to fear it as chaos. Hence taboo and repression were needed to prevent regressive merging and assure order and rationality.

Our rational consciousness and a seemingly viable social order of respect for individual rights have been built on this rejection of the Dark Mother and of Dionysian violence. But society is not so orderly as it seems. The rejection of violence is ambiguous and half-hearted. We believe that our definition of order is built on rational expectations. More often it is based on bias and wishful thinking.

In trying to establish social and political systems that will be absolute and eternal, we try to banish the disorder for which we have left no place. Yet sooner or later the banished shadow side, by way of compensation, prevails and manages to undermine the credibility of the established cultural values. Thus the way is opened for the structuring of new, equally temporary, cultural accommodations. Yesterday's god tends to become today's devil.

It has always been thus. The Greek democracy fell through demagoguery. Rome—the mother of law, order, and national pride—fell through lawlessness, corruption, and national indifference. Christian medieval cultures, whose kings ruled by God's grace, fell through loss of faith in divine power. The moralistic Victorian culture fell through lack of awareness of its intrinsic immorality and hypocrisy.

Likewise, our rejection of greed and violence is at best half-hearted and of but limited value in controlling their destructive power. In fact, we have been extremely skillful in devising innumerable righteous justifications for our own violence. We consider it evil when it threatens us but glorious and admirable when we ourselves inflict it.

Our moralizing side considers violence and the taking of life reprehensible; an evil and a threat. Unconsciously, however, our whole being is pervaded by this love of violence for its own sake.

This dichotomy is reflected in the legal order of the Decalogue. It commands, "Thou shalt not kill." At the same time, it enjoins the extermination of nonconformists and the ruthless genocide of conquered nations.[3] This contradictory tradition has remained at the heart of the

Christian culture of the West. The love of God and of one's enemies is preached, but pagans, Jews, heretics, dissenters, and national enemies have been put to the sword and the stake, and thrust into torture chambers and concentration camps. The most effective and acquisitive war leaders are glorified as heroes.

The unpleasant fact is that the ego's striving for permanence, and its rejection of the urge for violence, is opposed by the persistence of the Dark God (or demon, if you will) in the recesses of the psyche. Violence, the urge for the destruction of form and the inflicting of bodily harm and death, continue to exert a forceful, exciting, and invigorating attraction upon the ego. This is the basis of the archetype of the hero as warrior, a butcher of his opponents, which is indispensable to ego building at an early phase. To an increasing extent, violence nowadays is perpetrated indiscriminately and without cause against the young, the old, and in everyday, ordinary situations. It seems to be unleashed neither in anger nor out of economic necessity, but purely for the intoxication of satisfying a sadistic power urge.

Movies featuring murder and violence find even greater acceptance and tolerance than overt sexual pornography, since they appeal to the traditional, hallowed sense of the heroic. For the same reason, people continue to be energized by the spectacle of boxing, football, bull fights, gory accidents, and executions. They are "turned on" by violence and enjoy it as a cathartic experience. We are talking now of the average citizen of either sex, not just so-called perverts or sex criminals. If we are but willing to look, we may discover that sado-masochism is a common phenomenon. What we call perversion or criminality is a matter of degree and of the lack of capacity for dealing with the urge within socially acceptable limits.

This latter point is crucial: it does not help to deny or rationalize the seemingly insatiable bloodlust of *homo sapiens* by putting the blame only on frustration and economic deprivation. We do so, apparently, because we find it impossible to accept these transpersonal, autonomous energy patterns of aggression, sexuality and need for what they are: the basic, primordial forces of attraction and repulsion which constitute the two poles of life. They are aspects of our human authenticity.

To be sure, all kinds of frustrations intensify the violent urge. Yet repressive denial and moralistic devaluations of a natural drive and of individual needs constitute frustrations of the first order in themselves. Far from being helpful, they aggravate the problem and block the possibility of adequate and appropriate channels of expression. The condemnatory preachiness against dependency needs, aggression, and anger in our present culture closely parallels the Victorian attitude toward sexuality: self-righteous condemnation coupled with unadmitted fascination. We profess one thing and practice another. Like the Victorians, we attempt to deal with the issue by means of respectable commercialization. "National interest" and economy require selling billions of dollars worth of arms—not to mention nuclear capability—to anyone who professes to be against the feared and hated enemy. Sexuality is sold as a necessary, hence useful activity to further love, family, and recreation. Aggression and acquisitiveness are praised as essential for getting ahead in business, and for achieving economic, political, or military dominance, individually or as a nation.

But these attempts to commercialize the gods merely make them more demonic. The price we pay is obsession, cynicism, brutality, and smut. The lost divinity continues to make its presence felt through pornography.

The unreadiness to relate to the transpersonal, daimonic quality of aggression tends to increase its demonization.[4] The cynical inhumanity of modern violence, rationalized by political, social, or commercial justification, exceeds even the callous exploitation of sensuality in the TV, film, and news media. Yet many psychologists still wishfully insist that aggressive urges are no more than reactions to fear and frustration. They claim that the need to express hostility can be forestalled by social change, by creating a non-frustrating environment, free of fear. This is analogous to the idea that passions and emotions are undesirable disturbances of rationality. Yet the lack of something to fight against would itself be a frustration. And a total lack of fear is a threat to survival.

Aggression is indispensable for adequate ego functioning and for the capacity to love and to relate. Ares, the God of war and strife, and Eros, the God of love and desire, are twin brothers psychologically.

In the development of the child, the "warrior phases"[5] which constellate father-son and brother conflicts have been shown to be necessary for the development of masculinity and animus functioning. Ego consolidation and the sense of personal identity are based upon individual acceptance and the capacity to affect others. The absence of fighting experience makes for a wishy-washy personality devoid of thrust, motivation, and self-confidence. Differentiation from others, and hence self-definition, occurs through struggle.

Though we may find it unpalatable, violence, far from being merely a response to frustration, is one of mankind's most profoundly moving experiences. It is fascinating as well as terrifying, and closely akin to sexuality and creativity.

Stanislav Grof has described the close association of birth and rebirth experiences with violence, upheaval, and death as they emerged in LSD research.[6] He describes the arousal of feelings and urges of violence during the passage through the birth canal. The subject experiences overcoming a state of deadlock and inertia, of feeling oppressed and hemmed in. Subsequently, urges of violence and aggression are likely to be aroused by any stagnating or deadlocked life situation which calls for the need for regeneration, a *new* birth. This is true collectively as well as individually. We need only remember the feelings of jubilation and relief felt by all participating nations at the outbreak of World War I, or by the German people at the beginning of Nazism, to say nothing of the explosive violence upon which revolutions rest.

These joyous feelings have little if anything to do with a rational understanding or intelligent appraisal of the situation by the people involved. They are like the outbreak of a tempest in response to the accumulation of stagnant air. The explosion of joy at the prospect of war betrays an elementary need for shaking up and wrecking existent structures to make space for a change, regardless of rational planning, and even at the risk of self-destruction. Aggression and violence, in one way or the other, are essential for the development of self-assertion and the expansive feeling of being alive, as well as for psychological change and growth. These considerations explain the inevitability of outbreaks of seemingly senseless violence when things are getting too quiet, and people are feeling hemmed in or impotent. Experienced camp counselors and school teachers know they have to be prepared for sudden explosions when things have been quiet for too long. When he got bored, one of my children used to call, "Let's have a fight." World War One exploded into a world of seeming prosperity, German terrorism into the *Wirtschaftswunder* ("economic miracle"). Many random snipers or Sons of Sam turn out to have been shy, well-mannered types who minded their own business and helped little old ladies with their groceries, before they went on their rampage.

Ethologists have come up with impressive evidence that aggression is phylogenetically pre-programmed in the biological organism of animals and, hence, probably also of humans.[7] It is counterbalanced by and intermingled with equally deep-rooted urges for dependency and love which call for mutually supportive social behavior. Aggressive and sexual or erotic pathways are interlinked in the lower brainstem.[8] In the course of aggressive behavior, some animals exhibit the erect phallus in order to demonstrate superiority, or engage in homosexual rape gestures.[9] With humans, too, violence and sexuality are closely linked. Soldiers at the moment of killing[10] and people legally executed[11] have been observed to have seminal emissions at the moment of inflicting or suffering death.

Aggression intends to separate, yet ends by drawing together through the desire to make oneself felt by the other. The urge is to hit, hurt and even destroy. The end result, however, is a binding and connecting. The urge of Eros, on the other hand, is to unite with, to satisfy one's own or the other's needs, penetrate or be penetrated by—as the case may be. Yet the result is often separation and falling apart in satiety, and frequently in hurting and destroying. Who, in fact, could enumerate the multiplicity of interplays that take place under the name of love and violence? Violence passionately aims to destroy its object, but so does Eros in its desire to unite with, satisfy one's needs and dissolve the separateness of the other.

Love drowns all too easily in boredom, resentment or indifference. Passion fades away in any relationship which is devoid of difficulties, problems, crises, and fights. Therefore, frequently women, more sensitive to the needs and workings of Eros, are instinctively driven to stir up conflicts and trouble in relationships, in order to keep the spark alive. Our *joie de vivre*, too, depends upon a sense of victory over adverse circumstances or antagonists as much as it depends upon supporting love and dependency needs. For that reason, hate that is unrequited and not fought out, which is inhibited in its means of expression, can lead to destructive violence as well as can unhappy love, unsatisfied neediness, and a sense of rejection. In "A Poison Tree," Blake insightfully showed the insidious path of unexpressed anger:

> *I was angry with my friend.*
> *I told my wrath; my wrath did end.*
> *I was angry with my foe.*
> *I told it not, my wrath did grow.*
>
> *And I watered it in fears*
> *Night and morning with my tears*
> *And I sunned it with smiles*
> *And with soft, deceitful wiles.*
>
> *And it grew both day and night*
> *Till it bore an apple bright*
> *And my foe beheld it shine*
> *And he knew that it was mine*
>
> *And into my garden stole*
> *When the night had veiled the pole*
> *In the morning glad I see*
> *My foe outstretched beneath the tree.*[12]

In order to personalize violence and to taste the possibility of victory in aggression, there must also be an object to be vanquished. The psychology of the personalizing of violence through aggression expresses the fact that victimization and submission demand to be experienced actively but also passively. One cannot win and be strong and independent all the time. Victor and victim, the stronger and the weaker, are inseparable partners, necessary to each other for the playing out of the urges to aggression and dependency in human interrelationships. Everywhere life pairs desire with the possibility of satisfaction, but also with frustration and resistance. Without the tension of a resistance that calls upon us to overcome it, there is no genuine satisfaction, no sense of identity, of "I can"—only boredom. Without surrender there is endless tension. Without joining there is only loneliness.

When aggression is repressed, for instance by having learned not to reveal one's anger or by having everything made too easy as a child, the result can easily be frustrating impotence. The lack of necessity to achieve anything through one's own effort brings about a sense of stagnation and hopelessness, and a dangerous build-up of unexpressed and nonpersonalized violence, including self-destructive urges and an inability to love. The urge to violence, when lost sight of by consciousness through repression, is as dangerous, perhaps even more so, than violence and aggression overtly expressed. Indeed, repression makes the control of violence difficult or impossible. The question then arises of the possible or appropriate forms by which aggression can be controlled and personalized.

To approach this problem only in terms of sociology is inadequate. While not denying its importance, the mere sociological understanding of aggression and need is insufficient without an appreciation of the underlying archetypal dynamics.

The Industrial Revolution and periods of great economic depression, such as between the World Wars, did not per se increase the incidence of outer-directed violence. Frustration factors that contribute to the intensification of violence are not so much economical as they are psychological. Human need and longing are not only for food and physical comfort but *also* for social dignity, interpersonal relatedness and some form of self-authentication. The feelings of stagnation, impotence, lack of value, personal power and a sense of unfulfilled self-value and longing render the natural aggressive instinct destructive, and uncontrollably so. But *even they* do not of themselves *cause* aggression. They only call it forth or aggravate it.

Behind the various rationalizations of aggression, including the urge for territorial protectiveness and the response of fear, lies a much more basic life force. This is a form of self-assertion and self-transcendence based upon the capacity to destroy others and oneself, in the service of life renewal. This is the real *daimonion* of violence, dangerous when denied and secularized. It is experienced as a powerful surge of sadomasochistic, lustful, and ecstatic destructiveness, which, strange to say, aims at the ecstasy of reunion with the maternal sourceground of being.

Through the exercise of this Dionysian power, self-fulfillment, a sense of "I can" potency, is experienced. It is for this reason that a sense of impotence, the absence of "I can," calls forth destructive aggression as a sort of compensatory panic reaction.

Aggression cannot be gotten rid of. It is absolutely necessary for survival and a basis of ego strength and self-confidence. It is an essential part of us and will remain with us to be reckoned with, any educational and social reform attempts notwithstanding. Neediness can balance it as a social factor of support when accepted, but aggravates it as envy and greed when denied.

The acceptance of this fact is not an expression of pessimism or fatalism, but a realistic appraisal that could enable us to find a less destructive integration of violent urges into our cultural needs. The way to achieve this goal would be through transforming violence and aggression into assertion by personalizing it. This conversion seems to be the way the individuation urge has chosen for the purpose of bringing about psychic differentiation of the personality, and for the promotion of interpersonal relatedness.

The real danger of aggression, psychologically speaking, comes from its repression and denial, which in our culture are caused by a one-sided image of human nature as basically good, law-abiding, and devoid of the ecstatic surge of destructive impulses. Rousseau's model of the noble savage substituted a sentimental and idealized image of man for the more realistic medieval view, which still allowed Dionysus a continuing existence, even though in the degraded role of devil.

Every culture of the past has taken into account the fact that aggression cannot be aborted but must be respected and given space in such a way that its blind violence is restricted and redirected into positive channels. The ancient propitiatory rites and mystery celebrations offered channels of substitution and sublimation for the archetypal force of Dionysus and Azazel, the Middle Eastern goat god, the scapegoat.[13] When denied or repressed, what belongs to the god is appropriated by the devil, who acts out the demonic urge in such activities as the Black Mass and witch burning, bloody inquisitions, and crusades.

Aggression, sexuality, and the need to be cared for, then, are archetypal, transpersonal powers, irresistible and fascinating. As such, they are in need of appropriate observances or rituals to contain them. We can accomplish this, however, only when we stop viewing these forces as inherently good or bad, useful or useless. What is needed is to try to discover their inherent archetypal meaning and evolutionary trends, their place in the wholeness of organic functioning.

What then is the nature of that strange triple force of aggression,

need, and erotic frenzy? Since it is a life force, why have we been unable
to relate to it in a more constructive fashion? Shunning it as unconditionally evil, have we deprived ourselves of its life-sustaining benefits?
Have we instead provoked it into assailing and obsessing us with the
darkest and beastliest side of our nature? Why did Dionysus have to
become Satan?

How can we make peace with this strange force of potential madness,
evil and destruction and embody it into new ways of human interaction
and ethics?

In seeking answers to these questions, we will have to look not only at
the conscious and unconscious dynamics of human behavior, but at
basic drives and evolutionary patterns as they operate in animal behavior as well.

The Natural History of Aggression

In discussing the relevance of animal behavior to human psychology,
Konrad Lorenz, the ethologist, postulates that animals act like emotional humans who do not have, or use, much intelligence. Their behavior represents relatively pure drive-expression. Hence, it may serve as a
model for behavioral patterns of the aggression archetype.

Lorenz differentiates intraspecific aggression from predatory or defense aggression. The former is found among animals of the same species, a fight or "competition between near relatives." He points out that
animals of different species generally tend to leave each other alone.
This is surprising since we would expect near relatives to love and protect each other and aggression to be turned outside against other species.

The next insight is even more surprising. The ability to form something akin to a personal bond and mutual support occurs in proportion
to the degree of intraspecific aggression. *The bond and the aggression
are part of the same pattern.*

Furthermore, Lorenz shows that the aggressive drive is built-in a
priori. It does not occur solely as a reaction to a stimulus but is capable
of erupting spontaneously in the absence of a provoking factor. If an
enemy is unavailable, one will be found or created. Interestingly, this
applies to the sexual urge also. Lorenz observed that animals who do
not have a love or fight partner (which seems to amount to the same
thing) will show the eruption of the urge first by becoming restless. In
the absence of a partner, they may attack or make love to a broomstick
or a wall or even the focal point where two lines divide on the floor.
Fear, too, erupts spontaneously in the absence of a provoking agent.

The term *Leerlauf* or "dry run" has been coined for this restless activity without a provoking factor. If a certain amount of time has elapsed since the last outbreak of sexual or aggressive behavior, the energy is recharged and spontaneous restlessness begins to ferment. Hence the most likely time for an outbreak of aggression is when everything is going smoothly and the situation seems under control. Lorenz remarks that

it is the spontaneity of the instinct that makes it so dangerous. If it were merely a reaction to certain external factors as many sociologists and psychologists maintain, the state of mankind would not be as perilous as it is—for in that case, the reaction eliciting factors could be eliminated with some hope of success.[14]

Little as we may like it, as students of the human capacity for spontaneous and even joyful brutality we must agree with Lorenz. Here, however, we encounter the great paradox of transformation: among many animals aggression turns at this point into relationship and partnership. This occurs in three basic ways: (1) the attack is redirected to another object; (2) a propitiatory gesture is made which exposes the creature's most defenseless part; (3) a ritualization of both these elements occurs: i.e., an acceptable form of redirected attack is developed, whether as a reaction regardless of the exposure of the defenseless part or as a reaction to it, which now acts as a symbol of both.

Psychologically, the significance of these rites is that, although aggression is expressed, it is expressed *only in part*. When cut off, aggression goes underground where its explosive quality increases, and its chance for transformation decreases; on the other hand, when it is allowed full sway, it may destroy us as well as its object. *Regulation of aggression demands both expression and inhibition.* Here, again, animal behavior can teach us something.

Some animals expose their unprotected side, an act which we find extremely difficult. Yet admitting to oneself or to someone else that one feels hurt or that one was wrong or a fool is often crucial. Whoever has made such an admission knows its disarming effect.

We may assume that the transformation of the aggressive act into a relationship in animals corresponds to archetypal movements on the human level which fashion personal relationships out of aggressive encounters. We can read this passage from Lorenz in terms of Jung's idea of the archetype:

Like the performance of any other independent, instinctual act, that of the ritual has become a need for the animal, in other words, an end in itself. Unlike the autonomous instinct of aggression out of which it arose it cannot be indiscriminately discharged at any anonymous fellow member of the species, but demands for its object the personally known partner. Thus it forms a *bond* between individuals.[15]

The hidden element striving for manifestation in such confrontations is a quality of Eros. This is impressively demonstrated in the following episode:

I once watched two strong old male Hamadryas Baboons assaulting each other in real earnest. . . . Unable to escape, the loser took refuge in the submissive gesture, whereupon the winner turned away and walked off . . . Upon this, the loser ran after him and presented his hindquarters so persistently that the stronger one eventually "acknowledged" his submissiveness by mounting him. . . . Only then was the submissive one apparently satisfied that his rebellion had been forgotten.[16]

Two significant conclusions can be drawn from these observations: first, that transformed aggression is the raw material of relationship; second, that the transformation occurs by virtue of ritualization, to which idea we shall now turn.

As Lorenz points out, ritual is as necessary to the animal as any other instinctual act. It cannot be indiscriminately discharged. Man has evolved a similar inborn need for ritual. But we cannot achieve a ritual by mere rational planning. Like genuine religion, it cannot be imposed by intellect, but must arise from unconscious depths, to be structured secondarily into conscious action. Thus the allusion to past rituals came in our patient's dreams. How to make them real in her concrete life of today became the task of psychotherapy. The creation of a ritual or a liturgy is like the creation of a work of art. Indeed it often is a work of art, and a collective cultural value, while at the same time channeling and integrating otherwise destructive urges. Tribal dances and the Christian Communion and Mass are instances of rituals that represent blood sacrifices. The therapeutic effectiveness of such practices is increasingly appreciated in modern psychotherapy, where the ritualization of everyday experience is proving to have transformational effects. Ritualization is being attempted in art therapy, psychodrama, nonverbal sensory awareness procedures and various Gestalt techniques. Its use for human aggression channeling is the subject of Chapter 14.

Ritualization aims at the conscious enactment of archetypal drives, or emotional urges in ways that are socially and personally acceptable, while expressive, at least symbolically, of the intent of those urges. Although verbalization brings the drive to conscious expression, concrete,

nonverbal expressions carry consciousness more deeply into the sub-
strata of the drive and are essential for clarification and transformation. When deliberately expressed, aggression carries its own inhibitory force. We can become aware of this only by risking the aggressive
experience; risking it, for instance, in a consciously formalized way
within a group. Then we discover the unprotected side of the other and
its inhibitory effect upon our aggression. A slight gesture of hand or
face may serve for the whole feeling of aggression; in face of the helplessness of the other, one is compelled to go with him, not against him.

At first it strikes us as incomprehensible that love and relationship
could be merged with aggression. The aggressive encounter, however, is
developmentally a necessary first experience of the involvement of an *I*
with a *You*. It establishes them as separate identities. In order to maintain this separate identity necessary for love, relationship contains
varying degrees of resistance and even rebellion against the urge to
dissolve in the other. As we shall see later, relationship rests indeed
upon the tricky balance between loving opening and dependency on the
one hand and aggressive closing and individual separation on the other.
Love without strife readily results in boredom and indifference because
the challenge needed for growth is lacking. Love is not static peace but
active involvement with and against one another. Genuine enemies do
not strive to annihilate their antagonists; they would be left without a
sounding board whereby they could feel their own strength. The concealed intent is to humble, to bring one's power to bear, to be acknowledged by the other as effective. We cut the other down to our size in
order to enlarge our own self-image. If the other is completely destroyed, or the problem solved, we are bereft of the antagonist who gives
us stature. We are familiar with the sense of anticlimax after complete
victory.

Our strength comes from wrestling with the problem or partner. It
grows from holding our own rather than from finally destroying the antagonist. The picture of Jacob wrestling with the angel serves as illustration. Jacob said: "I will not let you go unless you bless me" (Gen.
32:26). We can better understand the secret, mutual appreciation and
attachment of antagonists, who can live neither with nor without each
other. Lovers, siblings, and competitors, in their constant squabbles,
are wrestling with this sense of identity. We can also better appreciate
resentment against an opponent who does not uphold his end of the
struggle: one eggs him on to greater battle. A desire to penetrate a
closed front in relationship is also a desire for greater involvement. The
vulnerability and fear of hurt in strife is similar to that in love.

The opposite pole of love is not so much hate as indifference. The latter is more painful than hate. Even in its most destructive form, hate

springs from frustrated emotional involvement. It is unwise therefore, indeed unsafe, to disregard those factors that would help to transform the head-on clashing, antagonistic movement into the side-by-side partnership movement.

Yet the inhibitory and transforming factor in aggression depends upon ritualized, individual, face-to-face encounter. A. Storr specifies the foremost elements that interfere with the inhibiting impulse in human aggression: the tendency to paranoid projection (ascribing one's undesirable aggressive traits to the *other*); the invention of artificial weapons that depersonalize combat and prevent a face-to-face encounter with the enemy as vulnerable human beings; the aggregation into large societies which submerges individuality; the effects upon hostility of crowding.[17] To these trends can be added the one-sided, heavy-handed reliance upon the repressive "Thou shalt not," which is an intrinsic part of the patriarchal tradition. Harsh discipline and repression of desire—without simultaneously honoring the sense self-entitlement as an individual who has the task of finding alternative ways of need fulfillment—enhance frustration, resentment and bring about a sense of emptiness. They increase and depersonalize natural aggression into primitive violence. All these trends increase the danger that our aggressive impulses cannot be adequately integrated into social functioning. Thus we must face the alarming fact that present-day man, unlike the animal, cannot rely upon the automatic functioning of instinctive aggression inhibition. His reactions have become inadequate. Unlike the animals, he cannot prevent hurt, injury and destruction. When contact with the partner is inadequate, when confrontation is lacking, we are especially susceptible to uninhibited destructive aggression.

As our aggression cannot be adequately discharged in the personal encounter, and as we deny our need in order to be heroic or at least altruistic, inner resentment builds to destructive proportions. This is significant in a culture of bodily distance where aggression has little physical outlet in touching and body contact such as jousting, wrestling, or even a box on the ear. We release our aggression with push buttons and remote control bombing where the *other* is a mere abstraction, rather than a human being. Moreover, the inhibitory function will not work in the face of the collective prejudices of mob psychology. To the lynchers and the posse, the *other* is not a *person* but a collective *concept*, a "nigger," "kike," or "rapist." Here we are not as fortunate as the animals, whose rites are instinctive.

How can we humanely relate to those situations when, owing to the absence or failure of this inhibitory function, aggression ends in hurt, pain, death, and destruction? Unlike animals, we are faced with the *question of meaning.* What is the meaning of inescapable aggression and its grim results, the tragedies of open warfare, the ravages of predatory competition and possessiveness in social and personal relations? But most importantly, how can we structure or find equivalents to the instinctual, inhibitory, and transforming rites of animals? We know too well by now that our conscious rationality, our traditional ethics and goodwill have proven all but helpless in the face of the dark onslaught. Therefore our human instinctual inhibitions, if they exist at all, would have to be sought in the form of new ethical attitudes. Perhaps these are about to arise from the depths of the unconscious psyche, in terms of mythological or religious fantasies such as our patient had.

And indeed the motif of the return of the Great Goddess and her consort is encountered over and over in the dreams and unconscious fantasies of people who seek psychological help to overcome the deadness of their lives. Art, films, literature, and political upheavals also reflect increasingly the same dynamics. The changes they demand entail new understandings of masculinity and femininity in both men and women and the relations between the sexes, as well as new views of reality. To understand how these new approaches could help us to "contain" and rechannel aggression, violence, and needy desire, we will, however, have to look deeper into the mythological roots of these *new* archetypes as well as the significance of myth and mythmaking for psychological functioning.

CHAPTER 3

Myth and Psychological
Functioning

Archetypes ... are psychic forces that demand to be taken
seriously, and they have a strange way of making sure of their effect. Always they were the bringers of protection and salvation
and their violation has as its consequence the "perils of the soul"
known to us from the psychology of primitives. Moreover, they are
the infallible causes of neurotic and even psychotic disorders, behaving exactly like neglected or maltreated organs or organic
functional systems.

C.G. JUNG, "Essays on a Science of Mythology"*

There is increasing evidence that personal and cultural belief systems
have a profound effect upon psychological and even biological functioning. Beliefs that give hope and meaning can see us through severe
difficulties. Belief in the curative power of a placebo has relieved symp-
toms. Belief in a meaning to their suffering and lives has kept concentration camp inmates alive.[1] Loss of meaning and hope results in depression and illness. Yet where do our beliefs originate? Doubtless, to a
large extent they are culturally engendered; but how do they get into
the culture? Even our so-called rational convictions, like all of our as-
sumptions and viewpoints, rest upon productions of the unconscious

* *Collected Works,* Vol. IX, p. 105.

psyche. They arise as spontaneous fantasies and are secondarily explained, rationalized and interpreted by the conscious mind. Often enough they are misinterpreted and then lose their ability to help. Our outlooks, thoughts, and convictions are products of a mythmaking stratum of the psyche (to be discussed in a later chapter as the Mythological Dimension). This stratum functions like our dreams. As our example has shown, when we are able to attune ourselves to its imaginal and symbolic language, this stratum can provide us with helpful insights about facts and dynamics which transcend our conscious awareness and informational resources.[2]

The images produced by the psyche may be highly personal, but the drama on our inner stage often enacts the general human drama as well. Artists and sages have always understood this. Our personal problems—birth, death, relationship, conflict and the search for meaning—are human problems. An individual facing one of these problems is apt to perceive the experience as a version of the grand images that symbolize the way mankind has always experienced this problem. Jung called these timeless images *archetypes*. They provide patterns of behavior, emotion, and perceptual experience that transcend personal history.

Unrecognized archetypes have the power to destroy, not just individuals, but whole nations. This was demonstrated in Germany by the bloody reemergence of the Grail myth in the guise of Nazism. For, as Jung said, when an archetype is unconsciously constellated and not consciously understood, one is *possessed by it* and forced to its fatal goal.

The fact that an archaic God formulates and expresses the dominant of our behavior means that we ought to find a new realization of our dependence upon superior dominants. I don't know how this could be possible without a renewed self-understanding of man, which unavoidably has to begin with the individual . . .[3]

Myths could well be considered the ever-recurring collective dreams of mankind. To our rational outlook they are as unreal as dreams, and yet as uncannily effective when carefully considered as indicators and directors of psychic development. We ought not to forget the ravaging effects of the reemergence of the Grail myth under Nazism. Similarly destructive has been the revolutionary Marxist version of the Jewish messianic myth of salvation of the downtrodden, lowly and despised, via one last battle between good and evil. The myth of divinely derived commandments establishing eternal standards vested in the collective structure and its representatives—be it church, Holy Roman Empire, pope, king, or emperor by God's grace—has led us through the convulsions of the religious wars as well as through the revolutionary upheavals that swept away the monarchical structures of the past. These are examples of myths writing bloody history. On the other hand, individual dreams may be seen as personalized forms of myth. They indicate ways in which the dreamer has to realize and test the potency of the myth's directions for action and meaning. Thereby the grand themes that structure the particular culture are tested in terms of the person's own realities. Cultural questions and conflicts are lived by individuals. Joseph Campbell has concisely summed up the psychic and cultural functions of myth:

The first (function) is what I have called the mystical function, to waken and maintain in the individual a sense of awe and gratitude in relation to the mystery dimension of the universe, not so that he lives in fear of it, but so that he recognizes that he participates in it, since the mystery of being is the mystery of his own being as well.

The second function of the living mythology is to offer an image of the universe that will be in accord with the knowledge of the time, the sciences and the fields of action of the folk to whom the mythology is addressed.

The third function of the living mythology is to validate, support, and imprint the norms of a given specific moral order—that, namely, of the society in which the individual is to live.

And the fourth is to guide him, stage by stage, in health, strength, and harmony of spirit, through the whole foreseeable course of a useful life.[4]

The integrity of an individual life, no less than of the collective life that is culture, depends upon the myths. Their archetypal themes give form and meaning. Falling out of meaning, out of touch with archetypal structuring, means disintegration.

Essentially the same thematic trends arise and transmute in individual as in collective developments and their potential pathologies. Thus individual psychological and psychopathological trends may allow the drawing of conclusions about cultural dynamics, provided they can be shown to correspond to generally predominant themes and their changes.

The unconscious psyche is the source of conflict and pathology as well as of psychological and spiritual guidance. The individual, once touched by the power of the archetype, must be moved to change, to integrate the dreams and legends of the autonomous complex into life. My patient was transformed as therapy progressed. She managed to find her own standards and emotional values. Even more importantly, she came to experience the meaning of Dionysian sacrifice: not the resigned or grudging giving-in to restrictive oppression, but the joy of offering her capacity to creative effort and herself to loving surrender.

I have described her case at length as an example of a modern version of a myth at work in shaping an individual's destiny. It is typical, but not unique. As an example, however, it is not yet necessarily a proof of the thesis I intend to develop. It is typical, however, inasmuch as the prevailing motif, the return of the Goddess and of her consort occurs over and again in the utterances of the psyche in our time of both men and women. For simplicity's sake, I shall call that consort by his Greek name, Dionysus.

For instance, I recall an early dream in the analysis of a businessman. He lived entirely by will power and rational control, devoting his whole life to success and to providing for his family. He was plagued by unaccountable anxiety all the while. He dreamt that he had offered his cut-off penis to a solemn group of patriarchal elders dressed in business suits. Later on, as he became more in touch with his instinctual nature and began to consider questions such as what was the point and meaning of living, he dreamt that he had received a living phallus to be held in his hands, like a scepter for benediction. From it streamed blessings, strength and peace onto those around him and into the world. (Dionysus has been depicted as phallus-like, particularly as a giant phallus planted at the doors of Hades, the place of death and renewal.)

Equally relevant is the dream Jung described as the earliest one he remembered from childhood.

In the dream I was in this meadow. Suddenly I discovered a dark, rectangular, stone-lined hole in the ground. I had never seen it before. I ran forward curiously and peered down into it. Then I saw a stone stairway leading down. Hesitantly and fearfully I descended. At the bottom was a doorway with a round arch, closed off by a green curtain. It was a big, heavy curtain like brocade and it looked very sumptuous. Curious to see what might be hidden behind, I pushed it aside. I saw before me in the dim light a rectangular chamber, about thirty feet long. The ceiling was arched and of hewn stone. The floor was laid with flagstones, and in the center a red carpet ran from the entrance to a low platform. On this platform stood a wonderfully rich golden throne. I am not certain but perhaps a red cushion lay on the seat. It was a magnificent throne, a real king's throne in a fairy tale. Something was standing on it which I thought at first was a tree trunk, twelve to fifteen feet high, and about one and a half to two feet thick. It was a huge thing reaching almost to the ceiling. But it was of a curious composition. It was made of skin and naked flesh. And on top there was something like a rounded head with no face and no hair. On the very top of the head was a single eye, gazing motionlessly upward. It was fairly light in the room although there were no windows and no apparent source of light. Above the head however was an aura of brightness. The thing did not move, yet I had the feeling that it might at any moment crawl off the throne like a worm and creep toward me. I was paralyzed with terror. At that moment I heard from outside and about me my mother's voice. She called out "yes, just look at him. That is the man eater." That intensified my terror still more and I awoke sweating and scared to death. For many nights afterward I was afraid to go to sleep because I feared I might have another dream like that. This dream haunted me for years. Only much later did I realize that what I had seen was a phallus. And it was decades before I understood that it was a ritual phallus.[5]

It is noteworthy that in a relatively recent collection of articles on Satan by Catholic editors,[6] the cover picture presents a phallic image, a fleshy thing with one eye that closely fits Jung's description, but here it is represented as Satan personified. The phallus indeed, in its manifestations as Pan and Dionysus, personified the devil in the Christian Middle Ages.

Another example is the case of a businessman, described in the *Symbolic Quest*. For sexual arousal, he had to prostrate himself before his partner, caress and kiss her feet, and gradually, as it were, work his way upwards. Any attempt to avoid this path of approach always resulted in sexual impotence. He had the following dream:

I saw a dagger, sickle-shaped and silvery, and I was told that this was a weapon that would kill or had killed Siegfried, the dragon-slaying hero of the *Nibelungenlied*. And there was the implication of a threat that this weapon might also kill me.[7]

He also was a very aggressive man, independent, self-reliant and overly rational. He expected every situation and every person to heel to his driving will, and insisted on his own way in everything. While successful in business, he was impoverished in feeling, in interpersonal relationships, and especially in any orientation toward a higher meaning in life. The dream also showed him that his heroic stance, which arose from his need to fortify his ego position through a reliance upon aggressive courage, was vulnerable. It might succumb to an element, a force likened here to the moon, or to a sickle-shaped weapon. The moon crescent and the sickle-shaped sword occur repeatedly in mythological imagery. They refer to the rising power of the feminine. The crescent moon is symbolic of Artemis (Greek goddess of the moon, wild animals and hunting), or Diana (Roman goddess of hunting and virginity), of the virginal, as yet unrevealed, mystery of emotion, of love, generativeness, renewal, and change. Symbolically, the moon weapon points to the fact that the force of the moon, the force of the psychic tides of life, of emotion rather than rational functioning, represents an energy not to be disregarded by him. It might destroy him if his one-sided attitude of ego and hero-identification should prevail.

As I reviewed the manuscript of this book, another unconscious eruption of the ancient myth and ritual of the Goddess occurred. A young man, raised in a devout, fundamentalist Christian family, attempted to assassinate President Reagan. According to the reports in the media, he had nothing against Reagan personally or politically. He shot Reagan because Reagan happened to be the president: he felt that he had to kill the president, whoever that happened to be. He had at first stalked Carter, but could not get near him. So he tried to get Reagan. He was motivated to do this to gain the "love" of a young actress he had never met personally but had seen in the role of a prostitute in the film "Taxi Driver."

This bizarre motivation becomes understandable when seen as an acting out of the obsessive invasion of the archaic archetype of *The King Must Die*, first described in Frazer's *Golden Bough*.

The movie figure of the adored prostitute evidently activated the fantasy image of the ancient Goddess who was mother but also young virgin and harlot. Sacred prostitution was part of her cult. Her priestesses were hierodules, sacred prostitutes. At regular intervals, the ruling king or tribal head who embodied her consort, the Dionysian god who must ever die and be reborn, was slain for the sake of renewal. The slayer became the new king and hero, the new Tammuz, Attis or Adonis, beloved of the Goddess. As if to defy the conscious Christian attitude into which it could not be integrated, this split-off pagan, Dionysian violence drove this man first to seek affiliation with the American Nazi party and then to the direct murderous acting out.

The common archetypal lines running through all these contemporary materials are aspects of the *lower triangle* of our patient's dream: earthliness, cave, femininity, animal instinctuality, need and need satisfaction, and the phallic power of aggression and assertion devoted to the feminine, to life universal.

It is virtually a reawakening of a long-forgotten pagan world with its religious mysteries, and nonrational secrets. We have become aware of this counter-cultural trend in our time. It is approved by some, deplored by others.

What I wish to stress, however, is the seriousness and significance of the new theophany. A meaningful new orientation to the secrets of existence is arising from the very depths of the psyche from which religions are born. It stresses the feminine, earthly, instinctual, and sensual aspects. The cultural development of the West has consistently controlled, repressed and denied these through the last five thousand years. Their disregard threatens to unleash untold violence and destruction. Their assimilation in turn may redirect these otherwise threatening energies into new forms of culture, consciousness and aggression-control.

Yet, one may argue, these are all private cases and problems. What evidence if any points to a *real*, not just *fantasy* or dream relevance of the repressed Feminine and Dionysus-Pan, to the crisis of our collective existence? Is our collective problem really best understood in religio-psychological rather than sociological terms?

In our patient's case, we had to recognize the threat of violence as arising from repression of what the unconscious psyche spontaneously depicted as feminine and Dionysian power. This repression is culturally, not just personally, conditioned. A cultural attitude which poses a threat of destructive violence to one individual must be assumed to be a threat, likewise, to the many.

The Great Goddess and her phallic Dionysus-Pan consort were representative of a world soul and of its inherent power of destruction and renewal. They stood for a continuity of life and existence in which birth, love, aggression, violence, destruction, and rebirth were like pulsebeats. We have lost sight of this aspect of reality. Consequently, our present views and our relation to existence have become warped, absurd and unrealistic. Collectively we are in an existential deadlock of estrangement from nature and from ourselves. However, this cultural end phase with all its decadence is not exclusively negative. It heralds the beginning of a new phase as well.

How and why have the feminine and Dionysian been repressed? How can they be restored? By what rituals could violence be transformed into aggressive assertion and personal relatedness?

Maenad.

Part 2

CONSCIOUSNESS IN EVOLUTION

An old pond—
The frog jumps in.
The sound of the water.

BASHO

I died to mineral and plant became
Died from the plant and took a sentient frame
Died from the beast and donned a human dress
When by my dying did I ere grow less?

RUMI

Prologue

In his path-breaking *Origins and History of Consciousness,* Erich Neumann was the first to describe the evolution of consciousness from the matriarchal to the patriarchal level, collectively and individually. Written more than thirty years ago, his work concludes with the achievement of patriarchal consciousness. Neumann does not deal with the return of the archetypal Feminine. He did not go on to forecast the reappearance of the Goddess and her Dionysian companion who embody desire, neediness, and aggression in both their destructive and consciousness-expanding possibilities. In the light of the dynamic developments of the three decades since his book was published—especially those brought about by the Women's Movement—this study picks up where Neumann left off.

Since there is a high probability that the human species has developed through evolution, it makes little sense to assume this biologically but disregard it psychologically. Indeed, concerning the human brain itself, Maclean has described its structure as historically layered—"triune."[1] It consists, first, of the "neo-mammalian," cortical areas; second, beneath that operates the affect-generating limbic system; third, the still more primitive reptilian brain is concerned primarily with adaptation and survival. Neumann,[2] Gebser,[3] and Van Scheltema[4] have postulated an evolution of consciousness that culminated in post-Renaissance modern rational culture. Analogous premental and preverbal functioning has been described in recent psychiatric and psychoanalytic case studies.

Hence we may assume that the psychological development of the individual replicates the evolutionary history of mankind. This repetition, however, is not an exact replication. For we cannot say that a child of three or four is a primitive savage. It does not use magic for antelope hunting. In fact it does not go antelope hunting at all. But it does weave fantasies similar to those of early humans of the magical age and in these fantasies may stage magical hunts.

Most importantly, though, beneath our rational modern mind lie dormant the earlier ways: the matriarchal, magical, and mythological perception and concept formations, the limbic and reptilian affects, aggression, defense, and survival adaptations. From the standpoint of our most recently acquired neo-mammalian awareness, these earlier strata appear unconscious. In fact, however, they show a sort of consciousness, and even intentionality, of their own. Ever and again they prove capable of opposing the rational stance. Jung has shown that the conscious and unconscious dynamics operate in a kind of dialectic polarity. Optimally, this makes a complementary system of compensation and cooperation. But all too often, particularly in periods of transition when the depths begin to stir, their relationship is fraught with conflict and mutual sabotage. This may result in psychopathology. The history of the evolution of consciousness, therefore, is in part a history of ever-new longings, of conflict and struggle. The externalization and projection of the inner struggle upon our fellow human beings gives rise to what we call the *historical process.* How we perceive and experience our psychological makeups, idiosyncrasies, and conflict-tensions determines how we interact as social (or antisocial) beings. Our unawareness of the opponent within causes us to fight him without. This dialectic of polarity and conflict is the dynamic, evolutionary movement of life. It is not likely to cease in the future. No social paradise, no classless, perfect society or world organization is likely to bring permanent peace or put an end to the awesome convulsions and struggles of the life current.

Every major transition period, then, unleashes conflicts and aggressions as the status quo is challenged.

While old values are breaking down, a new consciousness is also being born. The eternal problems and themes of mankind are to be wrestled with in new ways. We seek new forms of self-validation and of relating to our emotional and instinctual urges. Yet paradoxically these new ways require a retrieval of old, seemingly discarded and repressed modes of functioning. The *magical, mythological,* and feminine ways of dealing with existence, left behind thousands of years ago, must now be reclaimed by consciousness. But compared to the past, the new consciousness will have to be endowed with greater clarity, freedom, self-awareness, and a new and different capacity to love.

CHAPTER 4

The Magical Phase

Once sat Idisi
Sat here and there
Some grasped the grip
Some hurt the host.
Some culled
Knee bend of willow.
Foe's fetters unbend!
Enemy's grip elude!
                    Merseburg magic spell

Tree runes must learn
Who healer would be
And know how to care for the wound,
Carve them on bark and leaves of the tree
Eastward the branches must bend.

Victory runes shall bring you success
When carved on the hilt of your sword
Wisely engraved on handle and blade
Then twice call on Tyr for support.
                    Edda

I am she that is the nature mother of all things, mistress and governess of all the elements, the initial progeny of worlds, chief of the powers divine, queen of all that are in hell, the principal of them that dwell in heaven, manifested alone and under one form of all the gods and goddesses. At my will the planets of the sky, the wholesome winds of the seas, and the lamentable silences of hell are disposed; my name, my divinity is adored throughout all the world, in divers manners, in variable customs and by many names.

Address of the Goddess, APULEIUS, *The Golden Ass*

As far as we can trace, consciousness developed from an early gynolatric, matriarchal, and magical orientation to a later androlatric one. By *magical* is implied the preverbal, unitary symbiotic identity level of existence or consciousness prior to the arising of mythological imagery or rational thought. The terms gynolatric and androlatric denote the reverencing of respectively, the feminine or the masculine. They describe psychological rather than sociological value standards, and precede the positions of mother and father in matriarchal or patriarchal rule. The social position of either parent is seen here as a secondary expression of a more basic perception of the value of the archetypally feminine or masculine in general.

This transition from a predominantly gynolatric to an androlatric world has been marked by stages; from Goddess to God, from pantheism to theism, and then to atheism or nontheism. It entails more than a change in cultural outlook. Consciousness itself has evolved through changes in the quality of self and world experiencing. This may even parallel changes in the structural adaptation of the brain.

The gynolatric period probably extends from the gray past of the Stone Age into the Bronze Age. A shift to a decisive predominance of male values occurred possibly sometime during the second millennium B.C. This is the onset of the heroic age when iron gradually replaced bronze. It also marks the decline of what shall later be described as the mythological age, when male divinities replaced the image of the Great Goddess as the central object of worship. In the gynolatric period, the world is magical.[1] It is ruled and encompassed by the power of the Great Goddess. She is mother and daughter, maiden, virgin, harlot and hag all in one. She is mistress of stars and heavens, the beauty of nature, generating womb, nurturing power of earth and fertility, fulfiller of all needs, but also the power of death and the horror of decay and annihilation. From her all proceeds, and to her all returns. The latter aspect was graphically represented in some ancient burial mounds which were built in the shape of a reclining woman. The corpse was buried through the opening into the womb cavity of the figure. The Goddess is attended by or includes a male counterpart, a phallic or double horned goat stag or bull god, often split into twin figures of maleness who fight, slay and succeed each other. In later representations, such as the Oedipus myth, they appear as a father-son pair.

Eventually they are depicted as twin animals, e.g., two serpents. They complement and serve her in the roles of child, lover, partner, play-mate, and sacrificial victim. Their cycles of birth, death and rebirth embody the endless tides of physical life.

The total figure depicts the androgynous wholeness of natural exis-tence: growth and decay, life and death, are both opposites and yet con-tained, even embraced, by a continuum. The male experience is one of discontinuity, contrast, and opposition. This is subordinate to the femi-nine continuity just as the ephemeral is to the eternal. The Great God-dess represents being and becoming. The Feminine is not concerned with achieving or ideating. It is not heroic, self-willed and bent upon battling against opposition. Rather, it exists in the here and now and the endless flow. It values the vegetal dimension of growth-decay, the continuity and conservation of natural orders. It expresses the will of nature and of instinctual forces rather than the self-will of a particular person. The feminine form of consciousness is global, field, and process oriented. It is functional rather than abstract and conceptual. It is de-void as yet of the strict dichotomy of inner-outer or body-mind.

The cult of the Great Goddess becomes fully developed in the mytho-logical Bronze Age. The divine forces, intrinsic to nature and the object world, are worshipped and seen as manifest in human and animal bodies, plants, stones, earth, sky and stars. "The ancients, as Socrates remarked, had no pretensions to cleverness and were quite prepared to listen to a rock or oak tree if only it spoke the truth."[2] This cult is a cul-mination of animism and pantheistic nature religion. The root word *man* referred in its ancient usage to what we now call *hu-man*. It was not yet reserved for the male sex exclusively. Because historical and ar-cheological documentation is inadequate we can only approximate the likely attitudes of the early *magical* epoch. For our reconstruction, we make use of myths and cult and art objects. Further, we can look at the comparable stages of contemporary primitive psychology and cult forms, and the development of the child up to the age of approximately three or four.[3]

It is tempting to regard any approach to reality that is not rational, in our accepted sense, as inferior. A magical world view certainly in-vites such judgement. However, the discoveries of physics in our cen-tury have taught us that our rational, *"commonsense"* view of reality has been naive. We know as little what matter and nonmatter *really* are and how they interrelate as the mystic or the shaman. Our minds are structured to approach reality in a particular way. This creates our mental version of things. But it is no more valid than the reality of a different way of perception. The ancient magical and mythological levels of our being, although "unconscious" to our current *modus oper-*

andi, need to be recognised as vital capacities of ours. If we fail to integrate them with our rational world view, we are likely to regress into a new barbarism rather than take the next step of conscious evolution.

The concept of *magical* as used in this context needs some clarification. It is not to be understood in terms of Webster's definition as "the art which claims or is believed to produce effects by the assistance of supernatural forces or by a mastery of secret forces of nature." This definition limits magic to a manipulation of force, rather than to a particular form of consciousness and dynamics. The magical consciousness historically expressed the dynamic of instinctual and affect energies in the context of a field of unitary reality.

At the magical or instinctual level only the *here and now* exists. It is all-encompassing. Past, present, and future are not differentiated. Neither are *within* and *without;* body, mind, or psyche; selfness or otherness. What our rational consciousness has separated into inner and outer worlds is psychologically still equivalent. J.C. Pearce reports on an amusing example of the magical level of consciousness.

Jean MacKellar told me of her years in Uganda, where her husband practised medicine. Local mothers brought their infants to see the doctor, often patiently standing in line for hours. The women carried the tiny infants in a sling, next to their bare breasts. Older infants were carried in the back, papoose style. The infants were never swaddled, nor were diapers used. Yet none of them were soiled when finally examined by the doctor. Puzzled by this Jean finally asked some of the women how they managed to keep their babies so clean without diapers and such. "Oh," the women answered, "we just go to the bushes." Well, Jean countered, how did they know when the infant needed to go to the bushes? The women were astonished at her question. "How do *you* know when *you* have to go?" they exclaimed.[4]

This illustrates the continuity of consciousness between the mothers and their children, whom we would normally consider separate subjects. The infants' needs automatically *are* the mother's urges. Such a continuity is not to be found only between humans, however. On the magical level, it may operate between humans and animals as well. Pearce again reports:

Farley Mowat, a Canadian biologist, relates the story of how an Eskimo friend of his, the "minor shaman" Ootek, gained an uncanny knowledge of and rapport with wolves. Ootek's father had been a full shaman (a kind of spiritual leader, medicine man, and mediator for his people, who communed with the spirits and rulers of nature). When Ootek was five years of age, his father left him with a wolf pack for twenty-four hours. After an initial thorough sniffing, the adults ignored the child, but the cubs played with him, roly-poly, the entire time. Then the father returned, walked into the pack, and retrieved his son. As a result of this experience and the general tutelage of his father, Ootek could interpret all wolf calls for the tribe. For instance, at one point he heard quite distant wolves howling, then a nearby pack answering the distant signals. Ootek announced that a caribou herd was so many hours north, heading west. The hunter of the group immediately left, returning the next day with ample meat, having intercepted the caribou just where Ootek had indicated. On another occasion, Ootek heard distant wolves, delightedly leaped up, excused himself to prepare for a short trip. The wolves had informed him, or rather he had eavesdropped on their signals, that people were some certain hours away, heading toward Ootek's camp. Ootek knew, somehow, that these were his cousins and, according to protocol, hastened to meet them. The next day he returned, happily introducing his cousins to Mowat.[5]

Furthermore, the magical continuum has been observed between animals and our earthly environment itself:

A naturalist specializing in the study of foxes described his long-term study of a particular fox family located near a creek in a ravine. One beautiful, sunny afternoon, he observed the mother doing something he had never seen a fox do. She suddenly left her burrow and kits, went up the hillside some thirty yards and began busily digging another burrow. She then carried each of the kits up the hill to the new den. Several hours later, the reason for this atypical act became clear. Although the weather remained beautiful and clear, a flash flood cascaded down, flooding the ravine; a cloudburst many miles upstream proved the culprit. Had the family remained where they were, they would surely have been drowned.[6]

In terms of observed animal behavior, Uexkull describes this magical world: "Subject and object are dovetailed into one another to constitute a systematic whole. . . . all animals from the simplest to the most complex are fitted into their unique worlds with equal completeness. A simple world corresponds to a simple animal, a well-articulated world to a complex one."[7]

Uexkull expresses the fact that our particular structure of consciousness determines the world we live in and how we perceive and understand it. Through the magical structuring of perception we live in a magical world. Jung spoke of the *Unus mundus* and Neumann of *Unitary Reality*. In such a biopsychic organismic system, the single personal unity is contained like a cell in an organism. It is viable functionally only by virtue of being contained in and sustained by the total system. To be cut off from such a system, voluntarily or otherwise, is to be separated from the source of existence, expelled from paradise. The ancient Greek word *idiotes* ("idiot") means one who does not participate in public endeavors whether involuntarily or willfully. While voluntary sacrificial death for the sake of the community was felt to guarantee rebirth and continued participation in the biopsychic social, life-sustaining organism, ostracism was felt as equal to, if not worse than, death. In primitive, that is decadent, magical societies still surviving in our time, the deathspell or the casting out by the medicine man is felt to be a real and deadly actuality. No amount of modern medical know-how will convince the victim otherwise. Similarly, small children deprived of caring human companionship wither and even die, in spite of adequate nutrition. At this level the integrity of family and tribal bonds; the "purity of blood" of clan and family bonds and traditions, taboos, and rituals, are still vitally important.

It is often shocking to discover, contrary to rational protestations, that magical blood tribalism continues to operate also in our *modern* unconscious psyche. It intrudes into the conscious functioning of modern man, and is no longer safely to be disregarded. Every psychotherapist gets his fill of incest stories. (I recall a patient who, while suffering from an undiagnosed, depleting ailment, was advised by a friend with magical leanings to have sexual intercourse with his mother. He did, and according to his story, was cured. If we call this suggestion or faith healing, we merely affirm the magical character of the ritual.)

Incest continues to occur among peasant, working- and even upper-class populations, contrary to professed conviction, and to religious and moral precepts. Among the aristocracy and would-be aristocratic upper classes, the archetype of incest continues as a matter of conscious conviction, even though the actual incestuous act is outlawed. The blood lineage of princes has been a traditional concern and standard throughout history. Although changing times have diminished the power of royalty, concern for its purity still exists. Intermarriage with commoners is a contamination. The reemergence of blood ritual wrote the history of the last world war. Racism as hatred between whites, blacks, Jews, Italians, Hispanics, Aryans and non-Aryans is far from being a mere socio-economic problem. It will undoubtedly concern us on a worldwide scale for a long time to come. Its roots lie in the instinctual, magical layer of the unconscious.

From the magical point of reference, events are not *caused* and cannot be rationally planned. They happen as *fated* manifestations of powerful and unknowable forces beyond man's control. They express inexorable natural forces. They are inevitable, not subject to challenge, change, responsibility, or understanding. One can only invoke, accept, propitiate, and adapt to one's fate.

In the gradual process of mythologization these blind and anonymous forces are personified. Only thus can the *powers* be directly related to by appropriate magico-religious ritual. Propitiation and invocation for magical man is a matter of anxiety versus trust, trust in the supporting world and trust in his gradually developing skill to adapt, to utilize what is available, to will and to plan. The communal structure was not necessarily matriarchal. But it was either gynolatric or androgynous (giving equal value to both sexes). Survival was the dominating need.

The life and death cycles of nature also meant life and death for the chief of the clan and his retinue, for he embodied the god who must die to be reborn so that life may go on. Though ruler and doer, he was still subject to sacrifice to the goddess, the giver and the taker-away of life.

With the beginning of trust in our own capacities comes the responsibility for our judgments and a sense of ethics, together with the resulting shame, guilt, and anxiety. The next step in the evolution of consciousness brings the gift of the serpent, the knowledge of good and evil. Yet the temptation is great to forfeit responsibility as a way of avoiding anxiety.

On the archaic magical level, then, ethics and personal responsibility as we know them are absent. As with the young child, this stage is amoral. Within the containing organic group, family, or clan, the single person functions like a cell in a larger mother organism. Activities are coordinated by instinct, fixed action patterns, ESP-determined *knowing,* and by imitation. Rule, law, and individual ethos do not yet exist. This "Golden Age" morality was romanticized by Ovid and Rousseau. The former, in the first poem of his *Metamorphoses,* describes it as the age where "without law or punishment everyone did the right thing spontaneously." The latter celebrated it in his vision of the "noble savage" (natural man). From a less poetic viewpoint, human behavior of this epoch, like a small child's, can be seen as cruel, brutal, destructive, and hence immoral. Of course, neither judgment is fully valid. Magical behavior is premoral or amoral just as it is preconscious by our standard of consciousness. The single person is a herd member, a participant in a group-patterned, nonpersonal process, beneficiary or victim as the case may be. The contingencies of life are dealt with by the group. Consciousness is a group consciousness. Will is the will of the group. What we call *good* or *right* is simply what propitiates terror and danger, what benefits and sustains the life of the group. What we now consider individual needs or rights are irrelevant, indeed unimaginable on this level.

The child exists in this magical stage approximately until the age of three or four. Throughout that time he or she functions in a state of symbiotic identity with surroundings, mother and family. The influences imprint themselves unconsciously and indelibly upon the child's psyche. They are basic conditioning factors, and modify the inherent mental, emotional, and behavioral response potential. The young child learns by psychic identity-participation and imitative behavior, which is, to quite an extent, automatic.

In addition to the parents, the containing group is endowed with numinosity and suggestive power in the child's magical state. Loss of group containment means loss of soul and identity, if not of life. In brainwashing, personality changes can be induced by forcefully regressing the victim to the infantile need and symbiotic identity stage. Under hypnotic regression to the magical level, psychological and even biological effects such as second degree burns or anesthesia can be produced.

It is important for us to realize that the magical dynamics, far from being left in the past, are merely overlaid and repressed by our rational mind. Yet they continue to function and to influence our feelings and behavior. The blood-race magic is reemerging from the depths of the unconscious. It must be dealt with, not by repression, but by integration. Primitive group dynamics emerge in the various *isms* of our time, unconsciously and compulsively invading our minds with paranoic obsessions. What may have been natural and acceptable on earlier levels of evolution becomes beastly regression when it invades a collective or individual consciousness that is further along the road of differentiation. The power of the group archetype emerges via particular ideological rationalization. Examples are Hitler's assertion, "Good is what benefits Germany," the Ayatollah Khomeini's ideology, infringements upon individual unfoldment in the name of the rights of the state, or the dogmatic Madison Avenue logic that "ten thousand buyers can't be wrong." This archetypal demand of submission and our archaic willingness are rooted in regions of the old brain and experienced as an urge to abdicate personal responsibility ("I merely obeyed orders"). Unless we consciously confront the magical archetype it threatens us with regression into primordial primitivity, into an ontologically outdated, hence inferior, level. What is ontologically inferior is evil, says Teilhard. The danger of the modern *isms*—social, political, religious, or scientific—lies precisely in their challenge to the hard-won achievements of consciousness and moral responsibility, which were developed during the mythological and mental ages. Yet this challenge is also a call toward finding the next step to integration. We must use our hard-won rationality to make sure that the emerging Goddess archetype not be used to rationalize *magical regression,* but rather that she may guide to higher levels of human development.

CHAPTER 5

The Mythological or Imaginal Phase: Dionysus and Apollo

In olden lays and rhymings
Wondrous tales are told
Of suff'ring and of striving
Of heroes grim and bold.
        The Nibelungenlied

Battle-wont and famous, Odin war-glorious, sates Geri and Freki; the Father-of-armies himself lives always only on wine.

All the champions, every day contend in Odin's courtyard; they chose the slain and ride from the field, thenceforth sit reconciled.
        The Prose Edda

Dionysus, the lusty God of the year, incarnated in the sacred king of the year, presides in glory at the budding of his scarlet blossoms (and) . . . is doomed to death by the ripening of his crimson (pomegranate) fruit.

        Robert Graves, *King Jesus**

The mythological phase of consciousness is a bridge from magical to mental functioning. As the hot lava of the magical level is touched by the first, cold air of the discerning mind, it gels into forms. These are

* p. 75.

the mythological images. The current moves back and forth all the time between the earthly unitary field awareness and the airy abstractions of thought. It marks the transition from a gynolatric to an androlatric world and reaches back into the cult of the Goddess and her child consort who constantly dies and is reborn. Its height may have been marked by a splitting of the male Yang element into Twin Gods. Apollo and Dionysus are the Greek prototypes. We shall continue to use their names. Apollo represents light, life, immortality, harmonious balance, and permanence. Dionysus represents darkness, disruption, death, and transience. At first this *twoness* is still a polarity. Permanence and transience, life and death are still aspects of an unbroken Great Round. At the close of the mythological age the twoness becomes dualism. No longer polarities, the opposites exclude each other. The sexes are separated and oppose each other. Light opposes dark; inward opposes outward; life opposes death. Then the androlatric age has begun. Patriarchal forms of social organization and of religious experiencing take over. The Apollinic and Olympian male deities rule publicly. The feminine and dark Dionysian elements are encountered only in the mysteries. Eventually with the transition to the mental epoch and the full patriarchy, they are completely outlawed. Their followers are branded demon- and devil-worshippers.

The evolution into the mythological frame of reference is a step into a first sense of inwardness and personal separateness from what is now conceived as an outer, object world. Existence is split in two. The individual feels an identity separate from others and the world at large. (Gebser draws attention to the fact that in the words "I am Odysseus," *I am* occurs for the first time of which we have record.) A step toward a first awareness of the soul itself has taken place. Yet ambivalence and polarity still prevail in the soul's experience of the world as its own reflection.

As in the fairy tale, at this stage opposites are inclusive, not exclusive. *A* can be *A* and also not-*A*. Aristotelian logic does not yet apply. A figure can be both here and absent, past and present, self and not self, dead and yet alive simultaneously. Mice can turn into horses, a pumpkin into a coach. This resembles the dream state in which the soul becomes aware of itself and converses with itself, as it were, in terms of imaginal emotion-reasoning.

This step in the history of consciousness probably occurred for the first time in the Neolithic period. It reached a blossoming in the Bronze Age, and ended in the heroic, war-torn Iron Age. Most extant European mythological tales, with their heroic deeds, date from that latter period. The older myths which were transmitted orally, first by song and later by story, were probably edited with the advent of historical writing to suit the new androlatric trends. They were preserved in this altered form.

The Neolithic period saw a change from nomadic to sedentary life, from hunting to planting, hence also planning, cultures. The direction though not the control of natural life begins now. The inward experience of self and its boundaries is reflected in the enclosed bounded settlements of the time. These focus upon a center—a stone monument, a phallic pillar, or an open space which eventually becomes a sanctuary.

According to V. Scheltema, the corresponding phases in the development of the child are approximately from three to seven (Neolithic) and seven to twelve (Bronze Age). Puberty corresponds to the heroic Iron Age and the beginning of androlatry.

In the mythological world view, everything partakes of *mana* and soul. Everything is a manifestation of the sacred.[1] Work also is sacred. It is not a task to be finished in order that one may then retire or enjoy tranquility. Eating, drinking, hunting, fighting, playing, mating are all celebrated in a festive spirit. There is a story that when Christianity was brought to Norway in the eighth century A.D. the peasants took special offense at the injunction that forbade work on the Sabbath. To avoid work in order to sanctify a particular day felt like the height of absurdity to members of a culture in which the sacred was not separated from the body and physical activity. It has been a long way from there to the splitting apart of spirit and matter, to the ensuing secularization of matter and work. Inevitably, an unconscious compensation resulted. The modern mind is invaded by the repressed *mana* power of matter and material activity, as shown by our obsessive preoccupation with things and our Puritan work compulsion, paired with a grim pursuit of fun devoid of festivity or celebration.

In the mythological consciousness, space and time become categories, but are limited to the here and now. Space is what is concretely and immediately given. Either it is here, or it does not exist. Ancient paintings show no sense of perspective. Nor do children's early drawings. As late as the beginnings of recorded history the known world for European man ended at the Pillars of Hercules and the shores of Britain. Beyond that was infinity. The rim of the earth and ocean fell off into the dark abyss. Until the beginning of the second millennium A.D., there was no inclination to extend the search into the unknown. The ships in which Columbus crossed the Atlantic and the caravans which took Marco Polo to China were in no way superior to those available to Romans, Greeks, or Phoenicians who, prior to the discovery of the compass, were skillful in navigating by the stars. It is as though the idea, the concept of a space, other than that which is directly accessible, did not exist.

Time was likewise limited to the *now* and the directly remembered. To the "magical" young infant there is only the present, timelessly given. To the mythologically functioning child and mythological man, time is today and yesterday. Beyond that—eternity. Events of the *past* are the material for fantasy to enrich the *now*. Tradition was whatever was said and sung, regardless of historical fact. There was no sense of history as a continuity leading from past to present to future. Hence, there was no written recording of events. It was still prehistory.

In the mythopoetic fantasy, the soul experiences its own subjective reality. Myth is unashamed subjectivity. It depicts how the soul perceives existence. "Once upon a time" implies forever and "here" implies everywhere. This gives the fairy tale its moving impact. It evokes timeless truth. Another example is the formula given in the Book of Common Prayer of the Episcopal church, "As it was in the beginning, is now and ever shall be, world without end, Amen."

This inward centering entails a beginning sense of *I* and consequently also of *Thou* and brings about the formation of social groups beyond immediate family and tribal affiliation. The transition from herd to group is a transition toward social structuring. A first social consciousness arises and imposes order and ethos, expressed in common rites, dances, and magical and religious celebrations. These are not expressions of individual emotion or feeling. Rather, they are rituals of a group organism. Here is an example from a contemporary mythologically-minded people. Laurens van der Post describes the powerful effect of the ritual group dancing of the Bushmen of the Kalahari desert:

It was amazing that as he danced, usually only in the darkest hour of the night, the fact that he was dancing conveyed itself to all nature around him, not only compelling it to recognize the rhythm but also to become a party to it.

I remember, for instance, a night when they danced their great fire dance and how, as the dance approached its climax towards midnight, the lions began to roar as I've never heard them before, almost as if keeping time with the stamping, dancing feet which made the desert reverberate like a drum, and harmonizing like great bass accompanists, with the voices of the women singing to keep their men dancing, and the sound rising clear, bright and lofty as the highest of the stars. In the end all of desert nature was drawn in, ostriches with their booming, night plovers with their deep-sea piping, owls with their solemn hooting and the nightjar with its castanet voice. And in the gaps between the waves of the swelling tide of sound, the night cicada sopranos could be heard like rows of seraphim and cherubim piled on top of one another, their song soaring until it seemed to me it reached high enough to stir the stars themselves and make them succumb to the rhythm below and go tap dancing all over the shining black floor of that desert heaven. In the end the dancing produced such an atmosphere of oneness and belonging between all that when the climax came and the fire was found I felt that I, who had come so far from so remote a world, was no longer a stranger, standing alone and isolated, but someone who had found sanctuary in an ancient temple participating for the first time in an act of natural Communion with one of the greatest congregations of life ever gathered.[2]

The social structures are of limited size and number: villages or city states in which every member has a direct participatory share. For only that which can be directly seen, touched, and brought face-to-face is real in the mythological, preabstract phase: the visible person, the immediate group, the divinity in visible form as stone, tree, spring or idol. The idea of a state, nation, remote ruler, or god in nonvisible, abstract terms is incomprehensible.

Structured group life and social order mean ethics and morality, although a collective, not an individual, morality. Order rests upon peer approval and respect for taboo. What is to be shunned and what is required of each member are regulated. This curbs the most disruptive asocial impulses and imposes elementary social obligations. It is far from our sense of ethics or morality, though. *Good* is what is practical and collectively approved. *Bad* is what brings about visible harm or damage and is not in keeping with custom. Damaging group property and violating a taboo are bad because they invite retribution from a superior force, whether leader, god or demon. The violation of a custom is bad because it invites rejection and isolation. One is shamed, loses face. On the magical level, isolation from the group is felt as a threat to life. Shame is a mythological reaction to isolation; yet the feeling of a profound magical threat to life lingers on, reverberating in the depths. Until recent times loss of honor brought a shame greater and more threatening than loss of property or life. In Middle and Far Eastern cultures, even now, *bad* is anything that leads to loss of face, shame, and the derision of one's peers.

This early code of honor is relatively simplistic and comparable to early childhood morality. It can still be studied in the moral codes of myths and fairy tales. Lying, stealing, cheating, brutality, torture, cruelty, and killing are commonplace and seemingly acceptable if they suit one's own or the group's purpose. The practical effect is what counts, and whether one has successfully avoided retribution from superior powers. Only toward the end of the mythological phase, as patriarchy begins to dominate, does a new sense of a more encompassing ethic turn taboo into God-given law. A generally valid ethos was pioneered in the Decalogue and more fully in prophetic Judaism and then Christianity.

Similarly, religious and magical rites and sacrifices were originally intended to avert evil, which was not an abstract moral problem. Evil is seen as disaster, illness, ruined harvest, failure in the hunt, or defeat in battle. Averting evil requires "knowing" how the powers operate in order to appease them. This knowing, conveyed by the myth, works through invocation, *mantra,* magic formula, appropriate ceremony, and sacrifice. *Sacrum facere,* as Kerenyi points out, has the original meaning of devotion to the gods of the dead and of mother earth.[3] The one to be sacrificed is "called" and voluntarily fulfills the duty to enter the realm of the dead and become one with the gods in order to help the group. As an ethical patriarchy develops, sacrifice serves as purification from evil and then from guilt.

The early mythological phase is still dominated by the image and rites of the Great Goddess in her triple aspects as source of life, nourisher, and cruel destroyer. The ephemeralness of the existence to which she has given birth is represented by her consorts, who are her lovers, kingly partners, and sacrificial victims. The king and his court have to die periodically as offerings to the forces of death and renewal.

The deliberate sacrifice of human life was central to early religious ritual. Communal needs and impulses to violence were ritualized into ceremonial observances, ostensibly for the purpose of protecting the life and prosperity of the community. Thereby, violence was limited to these sacrificial rites and perhaps later to those war-like measures necessary to procure prisoners as victims when kings were no longer willing to satisfy the need for sacrificial blood in times of national emergencies. It would be easy to dismiss these ancient customs as just barbaric atrocities of a primitive past, were it not for the uncomfortable fact of their spontaneous reemergence in our own time. The murderous violence of the two World Wars, the Holocaust, Vietnam, Cambodia, and the seemingly endless torture, terrorism, and killing in the Middle East, South Africa, and Central America, show all too clearly their psychological relevance for modern man. Modern history also shows that the compulsion to shed blood invariably arises after periods of peace. This does not spring solely from economic distress; it arises just as often during periods of prosperity. The phenomenon is like the previously described dry run of animals. The sacrificial blood rite is compulsively acted out because sufficient awareness and psychological maturity to integrate the spontaneous eruption into a form of psychological experience commensurate with modern consciousness and ethics are lacking.

When that happens the "gods" are asking for blood again. The history before and at the onset of World War I, the war that "nobody wanted," is a perfect illustration. But especially in times of want and need, the favor of the gods is to be restored by a holocaust. In the past, in times of drought, starvation, or a poor harvest, the king was sacrificed before the end of his allotted term. The victim was either expelled (in the early Roman rite of spring a whole generation of young people were thus expelled) or completely incinerated: the Greek term for this rite was *holocaust*.

The reader needs no reminding that this grisly rite of exterminating a whole generation of victims in the name of a national need, real or imagined, has been repeatedly acted out in our own time.

Lorenz' thesis that "like the performance of any other independent, instinctual act, that of the ritual has become a need for the animal, in other words an end in itself"[4] seems as valid for humans, rationality and good will notwithstanding, as it is for animals. The ancient rites of sacrifice give expression to this need in terms of the magical and mythological dynamic. They embody past expressions of the archetype that might be expected to regulate the human equivalent of the aggression-containing (in the double sense of embodying and limiting) and need-satisfying rituals of animals. Their prototypes are the matriarchal sacrifice of the year-king, the *pharmakos*, and the scapegoat, among others.

Therefore, we shall investigate the psychological dynamic expressed in sacrifice. This rite symbolizes a quasi-voluntary self-offering of the transient to its source ground for the sake of transformation and renewal. It is saying yes to the life cycle, the Great Round. Sacrifice is man's renunciation of his claim to control, permanence, and superiority, and his admission of neediness.

During the gynolatric, magico-mythological phase of consciousness, external visible activity was perceived in the form of the Twin Gods or Powers who embodied the alternating, complementary cycles of existence: growth and breakdown, day and night, summer and winter. Birth and death were equivalent and mutually supportive aspects of existence. They were contained in the figure of the Goddess, perhaps originally worshipped as the sacred snake who kills and heals, renews and devours, and gives birth again. She later appears in the Minoan tradition holding two phallic snakes. Her temporal, ephemeral male manifestations were represented as lion and bull. They chased and destroyed each other; they revived as summer and winter. Likewise, her human twin companions slew each other, or else were slain in a sacrificial rite, to be reborn as her sons and lovers. Her joy and her playthings, they were her victims as well. Sexual union and violent death were the two manifestations of the Great Mystery. Variations of this myth are to be found in all cultures: Tammuz, Attis, and Adonis are examples.

This attitude has scant regard for individuality and individual life. Its cultural customs, which include human sacrifice, ritual cannibalism, and immolation of the whole retinue along with the sacrificed king, appear barbarous to us. Yet in their primitive fashion these customs took account of the sacrificial dynamics operating in nature and in the psyche. Our lack of awareness of these forces exposes us to the danger of unconsciously and involuntarily falling victim to them and to barbarism.

In the gynolatric view, for life to proceed and renew itself, it must also be destroyed; joyous living and painful destruction are mutually interdependent, and need each other. The experience of the fullness of life is ecstasy. So is the experience of death and destruction (even though the latter ecstasy may be buried beneath life-preserving anxiety).

By the magico-mythological view, nothing can come into existence unless something equivalent goes out of existence. Therefore all creation requires sacrifice. We may perhaps choose the *how* and *when* of sacrifice or loss, and sometimes even the *what,* but we cannot avoid sacrifice as such. We are motivated not only by an urge to live but also by an irresistible urge toward undoing and destroying—a death urge. Freud's intuition of an unconscious death drive (not *instinct* as it has been mistranslated into English) is consistent with mythological dynamics.

Sacrifice appears as the central theme of most mythological cosmogonies. The nonpersonal psyche perceives sacrifice as the core of the creative process and as a fundamental condition for every new step of life development. Every evolution corresponds to an involution, every crest requires a trough. For every particle of matter, there is one of antimatter. Every conscious effort calls forth a corresponding opposite unconscious force, every so-called good its compensating evil. The evil which has been suffered through may in turn bring forth a good. Sacrificial rites, then, are a sort of psychic technology, attempts to utilize these fundamental facts for the communal benefit. They satisfy the needs for nurturance and protection (by propitiating the "powers") and channeled aggression into a socially viable container. An understanding of their symbolic patterns may provide us with helpful insights of forces operating similarly behind the reasonableness of the modern mind. Just as we sacrifice fuel to gain heat, or money for a desired object, so may we psychologically sacrifice one activity to gain energy for another. Loss is inevitable for the sake of gain. Not to choose means nonparticipation in the life process. (This may in itself be a choice, a renunciation for the sake of another, perhaps spiritual, gain.) Consciously or unconsciously, loss and destruction are chosen in terms of a desired goal. To exert one's choice of sacrifice consciously means conflict and pain. The tides move according to their inherent rhythm, regardless of man's activity. Our conscious choice, however, offers us the chance of utilizing the limited freedom at our disposal. Choice constitutes growth and differentiation of consciousness. Hence an old Jewish saying: "Man was born for the sake of choice."

Ample evidence testifies that this dynamic is basic to life, even on the biological level. There is an endless circulation of coming and going that prevails through all of nature and existence. Life requires renewal through breakdown, casting off, and rebuilding. The result of this Great Round is the organization and differentiation of structure and of consciousness.

In its early magical phase, and today in infants, primitives, and animals, consciousness is interwoven with the biological procession. Outer and inner, group and individual awareness, are not markedly differentiated from each other and from organic dynamics. Gradually growing individual awareness functions in terms of anabolism: the structuring of tribal, clan, and blood bonds. But it also requires catabolism, the urge to break bonds, to destroy and cast out. Every group or clan needs sacrificial victims, black sheep, scapegoats. By killing or expelling the scapegoat as a means of venting its destructive, violent, sadomasochistic urges, the primitive magical community satisfies its welfare and survival needs; it heals itself. Primitive group life, like a biological organism, renews itself by literally casting off and destroying some of its members.

The endless cycles of the Great Round, the merging of the death of the old with the birth of new life were celebrated in sacrificial festivities in which the violence of destruction merged with sexual ecstasy and drunken intoxication. The alternating rule of the twin forces or Twin Gods was enacted by their human substitutes as a sacred play. They went through the ritual steps of being tended, nourished, feasted, and played with like the child of the Goddess Queen. They acted out the role of her beloved suitors and eventually were slaughtered and dismembered by their successors, who later passed through the same phases. The victim was supposed to reach transcendence through identity with the ever-dying and reborn Dark Twin God. The community, through partaking of the sacrament of the dying and reborn god, likewise renewed itself.

In Minoan and early Greek, the stress shifts to propitiation and purification. Dionysus is now the dark brother of Apollo. In order for life and light to prevail, the dark-twin force must be carefully propitiated. Otherwise one might fall victim to its revenge for being neglected. Euripides' *Bacchae* refers to this state of affairs, and the dilemma of the "downtrodden housewife" described in Chapter 2 is expressive of it. With the advent of the patriarchy, the propitiation and purification rites become guilt-riddance ceremonies. The prototype is now the scapegoat or *pharmakos*. Life becomes finite. The stress is no longer upon renewal, upon rejoining the light by passing through the darkness, but upon preserving light and life by ridding oneself of darkness, of what is held offensive to the gods as guardians of morality. Apollo, in the name of clarity, purity, order, and harmony, has prevailed over Dionysus; Jehovah has triumphed over Azazel (the Sumerian equivalent of Dionysus). The Dionysian figure that was alluded to in our patient's material, the central figure of the earlier, matriarchal and gynolatric mythical world, is made into the scapegoat and eventually into Satan by the patriarchy.

In the Greek myth Dionysus is a power of both life and death, an underworld god, lover, son of the Great Goddess in both her life and death aspects as Rhea and Persephone. He is a force of death, a Hades as much as the light of Zeus. Stag god, he is a lord of wild beasts and hunted stag, torn to pieces by maenadic women or wild dogs (Acteon). He is a hunter, a devourer of raw flesh, and himself devoured. Killed as a child and himself killer of children, he is also an awakener of life after death, the god who dies but does not die. He embodies the play, aimless joy, and neediness of life, as well as the aggressive murderous lust for destruction that lurks in all of humanity. Sadist and masochist, he represents the raving of sexual lust paired with the ecstasy of destruction, as expressed in the raving menads. As potent phallus he is a woman's sexual god and plaything. He embodies the phallic power of maleness, aggression and emotion, given and taken by the goddess. As nursling child he embodies the need for nurturance and protection, as old man the wisdom of the transrational. As goat and kid that was boiled in its mother's milk and as phallus in the *cista mystica* (the *liknon*, an archaic Grail), he is the male expression of visible manifest life which arises from and again returns to its maternal origin. Ever and again he dies the sacrificial death, ever to rise again. "The myth of Dionysus expressed the reality of 'Zoe' (life), its indestructibility and its peculiar dialectic bond with death."[5]

In Otto's words,

Dionysus is the monstrous creature which lives in the depths. From its mask it looks out at man and sends him reeling with the ambiguity of nearness and remoteness, of life and death in one. Its divine intelligence holds the contradictions together. For it is the spirit of excitation and wildness, and everything alive, which seethes and glows, resolves the schism between itself and its opposite and has already absorbed this spirit in its desire. Thus all earthly powers are united in the god; the generating, nourishing, intoxicating rapture, the life giving inexhaustibility and the tearing pain, the deathly pallor, the speechless night of having been. He is the mad ecstasy which hovers over every conception and birth and whose wildness is always ready to move on to destruction and death. This unfathomable world of Dionysus is called mad with good reason. It is the world of which

Schelling was thinking when he spoke of the "self-destroying madness" which still remains the heart of all things. Controlled only by the light of a higher intelligence and calmed by it, as it were, it is the true power of nature and everything she produces.[6]

Psychologically, the world of Dionysus is the world of embodied raw nature, of desire and of passion in its double aspect of rapture and suffering. It expresses the primacy of longing, lustfulness and joyous ecstasy which includes raging violence, destructiveness, and even the urge for self-annihilation. It shows the double aspect of sado-masochism as a primary inborn drive. This is the archetypal force which Freud called libido (the Latin word for desire) and split into the bipolarity of Eros and Thanatos, life and death drives. Yet Dionysus represents the identity as well as the opposition of sexuality, love, violence, and destruction. To the sense of order and meaning, Dionysus opposes the rapture of losing oneself in irrationality, in pure emotion, in the drunkenness of passion, the abandonment of the ego sense. A similar feeling is also expressed in the following song of a Hindu devotee (*bhakta*) of the Mother Goddess:

> *O Mother, make me mad with Thy love!*
> *What need have I of knowledge or reason?*
> *Make me drunk with Thy love's Wine;*
> *O Thou who stealest Thy bhakta's hearts,*
> *Drown me deep in the sea of Thy love!*[7]

In excess this dynamic can lead to madness, nihilism, and annihilation; yet its total absence means petrification, rigidity, and grim, joyless boredom.

With the loss of magical identity, as *I* and world are split apart, the sense of the continuity of life and death is lost. The emergent *I* refuses to surrender to death: "Do not go gentle into that good night. / Old age should burn and rage at close of day. / Rage, rage against the dying of the light."[8] The sacrifice now requires substitutes for the voluntary offering, victims whose destruction can be justified ethically, such as prisoners of war, outcasts, offenders against the group, or animals.

The discovery of *twoness* means the splitting of the original undifferentiated One not only into man and world, but also into female and male.

But as consciousness evolves further into the androlatric frame of reference, the one unitary reality is increasingly fragmented into a multiplicity of mutually exclusive opposites: good, evil; subject, object; etc. This tendency toward awareness by means of splitting is inherent in the masculine character, which gains increasing importance. The divisive and eventually analytic character of patriarchal consciousness is of male character. This particular way of experiencing is obviously only one among others. It is not a necessary or intrinsic quality of consciousness as such. Used as we are to the patriarchal ways, it has come to appear the only possible way to us. However, a more Yin-toned consciousness, which is beginning to emerge again in our own time, does not operate in divisive separation, but through intuitive perception of whole processes and inclusive patterns. This is the predominant function of the right half of the cerebral cortex.

We have jumped ahead. At the present point of our description, fragmentation is on the rise, and it affects not only perception but also feeling and judgment. The dichotomy of opposing experiences means also opposing feelings. We like and dislike; we desire and reject. In turn, feeling valuation sets standards of judgment and systems of order, and eventually even of ethics. At the early stages of magical and mythological consciousness, feeling and thinking are not yet differentiated from each other, nor are sensation and intuition. In Homeric word usage, people still "think-feel" in their diaphragm. They pronounce emotional judgments coming from the heart and breath, not from the rational cortex of the brain. Only in the later period of Socratic dialectics do we see how rational logic is quasi-discovered. It is systematized by Aristotle and his disciples and completely differentiated from feeling by the scientific attitude of Renaissance and post-Renaissance days. While thinking was refined by western culture, feeling was left behind at its archaic, undifferentiated level. Likewise, sense perception and precise observation of detail were developed while the intuitive, holistic, and extrasensory faculties were left behind. Both rational, deductive, abstract thinking (what Jung called *directed*, in contradistinction to associative or imaginal thinking) and analytical observation of detail are left cortical functions.

At the level of "think-feeling" identity, whatever is liked and desired is judged automatically to be good and right; whatever is feared is deemed evil and wrong. Even today, such judgments are the basis of our good-bad value system. The feeling opposites establish existential standards of judgment and ethics. We favor and emphasize the constructive pole of existence; life-preservation, light, order, absence of pain and difficulty. The opposites of these are bad. The fact that both good and bad are aspects of one cyclic reality is forgotten. The rejected, devalued opposites then right the balance by exacting an unconscious fascination; the more unconscious, the more dangerously compelling.

Mythologically this ethical polarization is depicted as an estrangement of the Twin Gods and the assumption of power by Apollo over

Dionysus. It culminates in ethical monotheism. The highest value is vested eventually in the one and only supreme God. He is king, judge, creator, preserver of world and existence, and originator of morality, ethics, law, order, and justice. He is light, love, and the embodiment of all that is good and desirable, at least that which should be desirable from the standpoint of established ethics.

His opposite, the dark twin, representing dissolution, transformation, the nonrational, and the destructively violent aspect of the Yang, is demonized, rejected, and repressed. The Dionysian night side of existence—ecstasy, passion, death and rebirth—is gradually relegated to the sinister (our word sinister is derived from the Latin meaning *left*, therefore left-handed and coming from the right cortex of the brain), earthly deities: to Seth in Egypt, who opposes Osiris; to Ahriman the enemy of Ahura Mazda, the light, in Persia; to Dionysus as the python snake subdued and slain by Apollo in Greece, to Azazel, a desert demon in ancient Israel, and to Satan, the evil antagonist of Jehovah in medieval Christianity. If the destructuring aspect of the Yang is unacceptable to the rational, patriarchal consciousness, the abysmal, chaotic mystery of the Yin darkness is even more so. The Goddess, the dark mother, shares her dark son's exile. Women must be good, nice, nurturing, and receptive in the orderly, wishfully-thinking, androlatric world.

Aggression, death, and destruction, then, are no longer accepted as inevitable aspects of life. Hence, as we have said, sacrifice as voluntary self-offering is no longer possible. If aggressive violence is to be channelled and prevented from inundating the community, the right sacrificial victims must be identified, their slaying justified, and taboos fixed against killing improperly chosen victims. Since the undeserved slaying of the royal victim no longer felt right, the necessary victimization for sacrificial purpose needed an ethical justification: the victim must be beyond communal bonds, either by virtue of having infringed upon its taboos, or of being an outsider, such as a prisoner of war.

Wars for the purpose of procuring sacrificial victims were either staged deliberately or arose spontaneously—that is, from the unconscious urge to violence. In the next step, animals were substituted, usually those which embodied the ruling divine symbol of the age: the goat for the ages of Cancer and Gemini, the bull and ram in the following epochs of Taurus and Aries. Eventually ethical rationalization became paramount; the victim was charged with the evil to be averted. No longer did he impersonate the divine deliverer and renewer; he was now the one who carried the stigma of wrongdoing. Under the rule of the just and benevolent god or gods, he was at times expelled instead of killed. Human sacrifice could now be rationalized only as punishment for breaking a taboo, or for personal wrongdoing; the unauthorized satisfaction of desire. The urge that still continued to be felt toward sacrifice could not be justified in the name of a righteous God. Thus the demand for the sacrifice of Isaac by Abraham is explained as a testing of loyalty. Once the test is met, the ram is substituted by divine intervention. Cain, in Buber's phrase a "Son of God"[9] and hence a royal victim, is charged with the crime of fratricide as a justification of his ritual banishment. Oedipus, the swollen-foot (laming was also inflicted upon the elected victim, the elected one of the god), was charged with incest. In these stories we recognize readily such ancient sacrificial motifs as the ritual slaying of the "twin brother" or father by his successor and the sacred incest with the Mother Goddess or priestess by her son-lover-victim. At-onement, becoming one with the God through sharing his sacrificial destiny, takes on the meaning of penitence. In animal substitution, as for instance the scapegoat, the sacrifice is a sin offering. When the sacrificial victim is human, he is now an outcast. A slave or criminal is chosen for the role of human scapegoat. As violence is contained by the rule of secular law and justice, the nonconformist (in addition to the ordinary taboo breaker such as thief and murderer or tribal enemy) is forced increasingly to serve as sacrificial victim or human scapegoat.

These changes of custom and behavior reflect a most important psychological development: the beginnings of a personal sense of accountability and responsibility brought about by feelings of shame and guilt. This is fundamental for individuality and self-control. Only through feeling responsible for the effects of one's actions, and learning to control them by reasoned planning, regardless of spontaneous impulses and shifting feelings, can a sense of solidity of the *I am* be gained. The achievement of a firm and responsible *I* is seemingly necessary before the next step in the evolution of consciousness can be achieved. Paradoxically, the differentiation of individuality from the group is brought about by virtue of the disciplining effects of the group consciousness, the superego, upon the developing ego. Individual responsibility is groomed, as it were, by group discipline and group solidarity. The Golden Rule in its original form enjoins, "You shall not take vengeance or bear grudges against the sons of your own people" (Lev. 19:18). And while the Decalogue commands you not to kill, wars of extermination are still sanctioned, in fact even enjoined; not only against enemies and breakers of the law, but also against nonconformists (Deut. 13:5).

The psychological significance of taboo and ritual needs to be understood in order to appreciate their role at the point in history under discussion, and also if we hope to discover their role for our own present need to integrate the reemerging feminine and Dionysian forces.

Taboo is a pattern of interdiction by communal consensus. On the primitive level, the breaking of a taboo is felt to arouse a power, an energy process, which the group as a whole is not prepared to deal with. This power is awesome, sacred, belonging to the *other* world. The offender is rendered over to that power, for better or worse, without group support. Indeed he is excluded from the community in proportion to the severity of the nonconformism. A *cordon sanitaire* is erected against him in order to protect the group from infection, from the evil or danger he has stirred up. For on the still concretistic level, evil is simply the threat of disturbance by the unusual, the threat of change, breakdown of the familiar order of life protection. Only later does it become a moral and eventually a psychological category.

What on the level of mythical identification was literal physical expulsion and banishment becomes at the later stages of moralistic and ethical justification, social ostracism and shaming. Then evil is no longer a concrete demonic power, but a dishonor and eventually a moral wrong. Eventually the *pharmakos* carries the moral evil of the community; he is expelled as a scapegoat.

Taboo, "thou shalt not," ostracism, shame and riddance, psychological splitting and repression of an unacceptable content from the conscious self image, are all variants of dealing with the threat of evil by avoidance. They are escapes, unconscious admissions of subjective inadequacy in the face of the threatening temptation of the outlawed urge. Yet the fundamental law of preservation of energy applies to psychological functioning as well as to physics. What is expelled, repressed from individual consciousness, reappears in projection upon another person, group or figure. The unacceptable sadomasochistic urge, the ecstasy of destructuring, the neediness are ascribed to the *other* who now is felt to be evil, criminal, greedy and covetous, an enemy. The tremendous energy of these impulses is no longer felt as divine, but satanic, inimical to the good and just God.

The Great Pan dies. Dionysus goes into exile. In the fully developed mental and rational world, he becomes a *deus absconditus* ("hidden God"). As the biblical Azazel (Lev. 16:7), he is a remote desert demon to whom the scapegoat ("escape" goat) is dedicated. As Lucifer, Satan, Devil, and the Great Beast of the Book of Revelation, he leads an underground existence in the Christian age, which is ruled over by his Apollonic opposite, the good, all-knowing and just Father King, preserver of law and order unto eternity.

But in our present time, Dionysus seems unwilling to remain in the exile of unconsciousness. As our own unadmitted evil, he may destroy us if we do not find space for him in an ethically acceptable fashion. In the following perceptive verses, Yeats prophetically saw this danger of the present hour. Interestingly, the first three stanzas correspond to the magical, mythological and mental phases respectively.

THE FOUR AGES OF MAN

He with body waged a fight,
But body won; it walks upright.

Then he struggled with the heart;
Innocence and peace depart.

Then he struggled with the mind;
His proud heart he left behind.

Now his wars on God begin;
At stroke of midnight God shall win.[10]

A next step in the evolution of consciousness is upon us, heralded as always by a breakdown of the old and outdated adaptation. The dragon chained for a thousand years (Rev. 20:2) rears up and demands to be seen, received and integrated.

Turning now to the relationship between the sexes in the mythological era, the Dionysian force as Eros represented primarily the physical aspect of the desire for union. It served the practical needs of partnership, home, and family. Love as romantic, personal, or spiritual yearning is as yet unknown. Genuine love poetry does not occur before the tenth century A.D. Earlier erotic poetry concerns itself with physical desire and seduction. Ovid's *ars amatoria* is an impersonal manual on how to get and seduce a woman. Boccaccio's *Decameron* of the fifteenth century is also still largely devoid of personal feeling, despite the sexual acrobatics. Paris is infatuated by the beauty of Helen, he is not in love with her as a person. Even the Song of Songs describes only the physical attributes of the beloved. Where a passionate personal involvement does occur, it is dealt with as a calamity akin to an illness (Dido and Aeneas, Heloise and Abelard; Tristan's love for Isolde is explained as the effect of a poisoned draught).

This helps us to appreciate the cultural progress represented by the later Christian position, which opposed Eros with *agape* or *caritas*, with a dispassionate, caring concern for the person. This spiritual ideal of a new human relationship required as a first step respect for another embodied soul regardless of desire or personal feeling. Individuality, in the sense in which we are beginning to see it, was still remote. This dispassionate caring, regardless of personal feeling, necessitated a discipline of good will to subdue spontaneous emotions. The hero, in the sense of the responsible *I*, had to slay the dragon of desire and hate. If today we feel these expressions of charity to be cold and sterile, we need only look back at the gross brutality of antiquity and the disregard for those human values which we now take for granted. Certainly brutality occurs in our time, but in late Roman and early Frankish periods it was not only taken for granted; it was universally gloried in and applauded. To introduce the idea of *agape* at this time was a heroic feat. Without it the humanistic concerns of our time would be impossible. And we could not have approached the next step of finding a new expression of love in which feeling and desire are joined with concern and respect for the other, who is given the freedom to grow into what he or she intrinsically is in the I-Thou relationship. This occurred first in the form of the law "Thou shalt love." We find it incongruous with our concept of love, but it was necessitated by the time.

Subduing one's spontaneous emotions and desires means subduing the realm of the feminine for the sake of the masculine ideal of self-control. This is symbolized by giving dominance to that aspect of the masculine which is concerned with light, order, and constructiveness at the expense of the dark, chaotic, destructive opposite. The Judaic command to "love thy neighbor as thyself" (Lev. 19:18), and even more the Christian commands to "love one another" (John 13:34) and to "love your enemies" (Matt. 5:44) mean turning away from the dark twin within and forcing him to submit to an intentionality that for most people is outer imposed. The postmythological next step in ethical awareness is of necessity toward an androlatric ordering. The consequence of that step is that the boundlessness of the life of the Goddess is viewed as chaos. She represents the threat of being sucked back into primordial darkness and becomes thereby the embodiment of evil. Her twin companions become a pair of adversaries. In both sexes, the male-oriented consciousness, the *I*, identifies with the light god, with heaven and the sun. It sees itself championed by the sun hero. Eventually the ego looks up to the one God who is in heaven, from whose imitation it derives its own claim of supremacy. The serpent's *gnosis*, the divinity within, is forbidden. (The perception of the biblical kinglike God as "knowing good and evil" contains a terrible ambivalence in view of the ancient significance of "knowing" in the sense of being united with or existentially experiencing. It hints at the awareness of good and evil as divine principles inherent in creation itself. This secret is forbidden to the now awakening ego consciousness which is pressured to shun the evil and follow the good in obedience to the taboo that is to evolve into God's and man's law in the further course of evolution.) The heroic, self-disciplined will that shall rule henceforth is embodied in the hero figures: Marduk, the slayer of Tiamat; Apollo, slayer of the Python; Beowulf, Siegfried, and later St. George, all slayers of dragons, serpents or swamp monsters, representing the now repressed swamp unconscious of the Feminine. The onset of the heroic period coincides with the beginning of iron technology. It is dominated by the mind, the ego, the spirit. Abstraction leads to an eventual loss of the gods, and of the soul. Yet it facilitates conquering the world through technology.

Toward the end of the mythological era, the ego endeavors to set its strength against nature within as well as without. The turn inward has produced that ego center which now, like the God in heaven, sets out to make itself the absolute and exclusive ruler. The "I am that I am" (Exod. 3:14) condemns graven images, issues commandments, and sets up tribal laws of communal taboo. Eventually the laws expand into an ethic which claims universal validity. This rule by an *idea* instead of by an image concretely seen was previously unheard-of and inconceivable. The newly discovered personal *I* may now obey or disobey divine commandments under the risk of penalty for disobedience. Evil is no longer an external misfortune, but a human act of disobedience. Misfortune is the retribution for this disobedience. Personal responsibility for one's actions arises now, and guilt for disobeying God is added to the shame before one's peers.

The training of the will through heroic endurance became the ideal of this era, which concludes the mythological epoch and ushers in the rational phase of ego-centeredness. The beginning of this Iron Age (Ovid's period of evil and decadence) dates probably from about 1200 B.C., considered the approximate time when Abram received the call to leave family and kindred and move "into a new land that I will show you" (Gen. 12:1). This rebellion against home and family, this restless seeking of new horizons and rebelling against the old ones, is familiar to us in the prepuberty stage. It is a time historically of nomadic wandering, of severing tribal and soil connections. In this phase, young people start diaries, and mankind began its diary with the first written histories.

Toward the ending of the mythological period reasoning acquires increasing preponderance over empathic and intuitive mythological fantasy thinking. Yet this reasoning was at first still based upon affect and not yet upon dispassionate evaluation of fact and meaning. It began as a reasoning that is preverbal and predominantly a function of the right brain hemisphere. Toward the latter part of the mythological phase, perhaps, the separation between right and left brain thinking may have developed.

This dichotomy between words, what they can convey, and the wordlessness of the affective and instinctive experience, constitutes a paradox of the mythological level and a basic split in man. The mythological cleavage is between an inwardly felt reality of emotion, fantasy, and imagination and an outer reality which requires the development of practical thinking. The root word of *myth* means "disguising in silence" as well as "telling." This expresses the fact that what can be said does not really reveal what it means to say—"The Tao that can be told is not the Tao."[11] With the development of verbal thought, the mythological and magical reality accessible to and expressible by images and body response is increasingly lost.

This reality can perhaps be reached again through modern man's newly developing capacity for symbolic experiencing. Jung defines it as an approach to a dimension not directly knowable to the reasoning mind. Symbolic experience is conveyed not only through words but through image, sound, touch, and movement. These sensory means point beyond themselves and make possible non- and extrasensory experiences.

For the child, the focus of consciousness shifts to the mythological level at the age of three or four and lasts until puberty. At the age of three or four, an inner person begins to emerge who starts to say *I* and connects inner experience with outer perception. Becoming a separate person brings first a social consciousness, an awareness of ceremony and social right and wrong as regulated by family and group mores. It appeals to the sense of shame. There is a first discrimination of time and space, centered upon the here and now. The *I* begins to feel itself increasingly separate from the body and the outer world and initiates control of desire and aggression. Magical identity and containedness yield to animism and gradually expanding reflective thinking. Things have souls with human as well as fantastic qualities. A witch may be argued with and offer good advice, and then take off her head and fly away on a broomstick. The world of singing and saying, the world of the fairy tales, begins.

In summary, the mythological consciousness is a consciousness of soul, a reflectiveness in terms of emotion and affect, of images and fantasy. As an inner experience, individual soul reflects in its resonances the soul of the cosmos. Therewith the achievements of the preceding magical level receive a new direction and a change in quality. The magical interaction with the containing field was relatively subjectless. Impersonal field intention now becomes personalized into soul intentions. Motivations are of one's own will as opposed to the will of the cosmos. As people with a feeling and will of their own look up from the ground, from the mere animallike containment in nature to the opening sense of freedom of the heavens, they call themselves *anthropos,* Greek for "who looks up." The cosmos is anthropomorphized in the reflection of the soul. The inner "knowing" of the soul is *gnosis.* Yet with the development of self-will the instinctual immediacy of cosmic will is lost. The result is the "fall" of man. The fulfillment of the mythological phase comes through a centering of soul in *I,* a sense of unification of the personality. This occurs simultaneously with a unification of the cosmic pantheon under the monotheistic rule of the superego, perceived as God, king, or Father in heaven. The reasoning power that hitherto had been a *field* reasoning, a function of quasi-autonomous images and emotions, now becomes available to the *I*. The individual begins to reason, first about self and then, increasingly, about the outer world.

As the reasoning light of the mind grasps the world in its outer, concrete manifestation, the inner *gnosis*, with its magical, instinctual attunement to fundamental survival needs and collective dynamics is lost to consciousness. The world of the Feminine, of the Goddess and her consort Dionysus or Pan, yields to the God whose name is "I am that I am." Toward the end of the mythological age the cry is heard that the Great Pan is dead. He is replaced by the Father in heaven, whose place eventually is usurped by the now deified reasoning *I*. At the end of the mental epoch we shall hear again the cry: "God is dead."

CHAPTER 6

The Mental Phase

Cogito ergo sum ("I think therefore I am")
DESCARTES

God guard me from those thoughts I think
In the mind alone;
He that sings a lasting song
Thinks in a marrow-bone. . . .
W.B. YEATS, *"A Prayer for Old Age"**

In the mental or patriarchal ego phase, control of aggression and desire is a matter of law and ethics. The rational mind becomes the supreme arbiter. Even the medieval church held that God's creation must be consistent with natural reason. The uncontrolled expression of spontaneous, passionate urges—whether erotic, or aggressive—is frowned upon and eventually repressed. "Selfishness," concern with one's own, rather than the community's or other person's needs, is considered a vice. Violence and sexuality are held to be evil. They are outlawed except under special conditions regulated by law. Aggressive violence is permissible only by males in the group's service and at its command against scapegoats—dissenters, law breakers, and members of communities other than one's own; in a word, enemies.

Control of nature, inner and outer (now separate), marks the patri-

* *The Collected Poems of W. B. Yeats* (New York: Macmillan, 1979), p. 281.

archal, mental phase. It is the first superego- or persona-dominated phase of ego control. Basic to the patriarchy and its androlatric frame of reference are rejection and devaluation of (*a*) the feminine deity (and, correspondingly, of feminine values); (*b*) natural drives; and (*c*) spontaneous emotions and desires. The first vestiges of a conscious ego are developed by controlling and repressing subjective urges and needs, that is, by self denial. Before investigating separately how these three aspects affect our present day functioning, we shall give some general characterizations of the mental phase of consciousness.

The Mental Level

The transition from the mythological to the mental stage of consciousness involves a transition from animism and soul to the three-dimensionality of the outer spatial world, of things perceived by the five senses. The word reality derives from the Latin *res,* a thing, and means "thingness." What is perceivable in three-dimensional space terms has existence. Whatever is nonmaterial and cannot be spatially perceived or demonstrated is denied reality. It cannot exist. Virchov, the great nineteenth century anatomist, is quoted as saying that never in his thousands of dissections of cadavers did a vestige of anything resembling a soul come under his knife; *ergo,* there is no such thing. This viewpoint has been shared by modern behaviorism. In the same vein, Khrushchev observed that Russian astronauts had not seen any evidence of God up there. This extroversion, following the introverted mythological phase, led to the conquest of spatial, material "reality," culminating in our twentieth century explorations of the atom, the moon and outer space.

What is not observable in physical space now becomes increasingly unimaginable. The perceptions of the mythological world focussed on two-dimensional images. These images were not yet space-bound nor where they space-filling. We may presume that, like dream and fantasy images, they were mutual reflections of what was not yet fully separated into inner and outer space, each reality merging into the other or representing the other. Paintings, for example, do not show a grasp of three-dimensional perspective until the early Renaissance. The facial expressions in the sculptures of ancient Greece, which herald the beginning of the mental age, strike one as though the sculptors had discovered a new clarity, a new dimension akin to the discoveries of Socrates and Aristotle in deductive thinking, reasoning, and logic. Roman faces already look hard, even cynical, like modern businessmen or politicians.

The mental epoch's notion of reality is limited to what is visible. It no

longer refers to perceptions of the psyche. For the Greek mind, an idea
was still something to be seen. For the modern mind, an idea is abstracted—pulled away from the visible. It is therefore not as *real* as an
object. Spatiality and phenomenology rest upon separation; inherent in
them are division and organization of that division. The infinite is
cross-sectioned and organized according to the cardinal points of the
compass. The cross becomes the dominant symbol.

A *thing* is now a unit of space division, a part of what constitutes
space. The smallest unit of matter during the mental age is called atom
because it was considered *a-tomos,* "indivisible." In dividing, organiz-
ing, and manipulating the disjunct entities of space, which it now considers the only reality, the inner identity established in the mythological period finds a new level of reality by perceiving itself as the
directing agent. The ego becomes aware of itself as a spatial body. Self-
experience in the young child begins as and rests upon *body* experience,
which can affect and direct other bodies to varying degrees. Ego
strength is the capacity to affect other bodies, living or dead, by the use
of will. *Ego* is a Roman word. Divide and rule was the motto of ancient
Rome, the first fully ego-conscious society. It is also the motto of the ego.
The orientation of the ego, of space-thing consciousness, is toward aggressive competitiveness, the use of manipulative power, and willful
rule. Ego strength is measured by the capacity to assert one's will over
nature, forcing it to serve ego's striving for permanence, comfort, and
avoidance of pain, and by the capacity to control one's urges, needs
and desires. Existence is perceived as limited to the world of space;
hence it is irrevocably terminated by death and decay of the space-
visible body.

In large part, our present-day conceptual categories and the language that expresses them are based on spatial references: *structure,
form, taking a stand, building on a premise, I see.* Time is measured
and demonstrated in terms of space: the movement of the earth, or of
the hands of the clock. Time is an epiphenomenon of space: *epi* means
"on top of"; a *phenomenon* is "that which appears in space." Even the
recently rediscovered soul is called *inner space.*

The sense of soul as a nonspatial essence is lost. In theology, the soul
is a thing. Only in the form of poetic imagination does the mythological
fantasy continue, where it compensates for the more and more abstract
world of thought. While being accorded no more than poetic value at
best, the soul is more often relegated to the categories of superstition
and sentimentality.

We no longer see with the inner eye but entertain abstract ideas
about things, which replace the living spirit behind or within things.
Cartesian dualism sees no connection between the subjective world of

thought and the objective outer world. Animals, trees, and flowers
speak only to poets and children. For the rest of the world, they are
dumb and soulless, mere objects conceived of as the work of an anthropomorphic god. By the end of the mental epoch, they are perceived as
being there as though by accident. No plausible explanation is available. The ideas about them are no longer conceivable as *inherent* in
them. Thoughts are held to be products of the human mind or brain,
separate from the things to which they refer. Thought is a play of mind.
It is presumed to have no effect without direct physical action. God also
becomes abstract, requiring that no graven images be constructed to
belie that abstraction. The divine, originally seen as present in the object, becomes in turn thought, idea. The primal shudder of the experience of the transcendental is "corralled" into theological speculation
and dogma. Finally, God is held to be a primitive explanation of the
world, a means of assuaging anxiety or of exerting political control.

Ironically, this separation of the divine from the physical inherent in
the injunction against graven images which leads to the conception of
God as abstraction—and eventually to God as less than real in any
sense—is perceived as obeying a commandment from God (Exod. 20:4).
It is willed by those very powers of evolution which the "enlightened"
reason lost sight of thereafter.

Two qualities are still held as intrinsic to the world of things: causation and randomness. The world is perceived as clusters of inert, lifeless
particles pushed around randomly by something called energy. The
latter is defined as the ability to perform work or, more abstractly, to
have effects. This is a circular definition. Work in turn is defined as the
effect of applied energy. The unconscious premise behind the definition
is the concept of work, the bringing about of changes in the spatial
world by deliberate application of ego-will. This culminates in the Puritan morality and work ethic. The intent and capacity to control and ar-
range nature to suit one's purpose, the prime motif of modern man, is
anthropomorphically projected into his concept of "energy" as the *pri-
mum movens* that has temporarily taken the place of the god-image.
Doing rather than *being* establishes identity. The work concept underlies mechanics, which is the basis of nineteenth century physics.
Through his work, man will bring the order envisaged by his rational
mind into a world of blind, meaningless, mechanistic causation and
randomness which, left to itself, would dissolve into chaos.

Throughout this development of thought the concept of causation as
formulated by Aristotle at the beginning of the mental epoch still included formal and final causation. With formal causation, effects result
from a formal immanency. With final causation they come from an inherent orientation toward a goal, meaning, or purpose. An example of

formal causation is a bird's flying, as an expression of birdness. Final causation is seen in the development of the hawk's eyes for the purpose of catching small animals. On the human level, the idea of such formal and final causation might help one to assimilate and accept painful or difficult life events. They can be seen then as expressions of one's deepest nature; necessitated, indeed destined by one's unconscious being for the sake of experiencing and fulfilling one's authentic individuality. This form of formal and final causation, which medieval thinkers called "immanent causation," became increasingly foreign to the modern mind.

In our time, the concept of causation has come to be limited to what can be demonstrated by a sequence directly observable by the senses and mechanically, statistically reproduceable in an experimental setup. (Aristotle called this efficient or occasional causation.) It is an expression of linear reasoning which moves from arbitrarily isolated part to isolated part. It has lost sight of the encompassing form, function, and purpose of the whole gestalt.

The feeling-reasoning mode of the preceding phase, the emotional ordering of experience, gives way to a coldly objective weighing of fact and detail as perceived by the senses. Objective facts are the units of a three-dimensional, extroverted consciousness. Objective facts, however, are just another form of experiential subjectivity. Fact is derived from *facere*—"making" or "doing," like the German word *Tatsache*. Literally, a *matter of fact* refers to something made, a visible effect brought about. This is a new way of interpreting the world of images. It excludes their emotional and trans-spatial implications. Thinking is now separated from feeling; sense perception from intuition and imagination. Thinking and sense perception are stressed and increasingly developed. Feeling, imagination, and intuition are devalued and eventually repressed. So is any awareness beyond deliberate thinking and willing of the reality of the soul. Identity is vested in the thinking and sensing ego—"I think therefore I am"—which seems to be the sole originator of will. The will, for its part, focuses upon exploring and changing the world of things in order to increase our physical comforts. But while the focus of consciousness has shifted to the new mental quality, the older dynamics do not cease to operate. They are merely split off or repressed from our new awareness.

Independently of our rational consciousness, the repressed, split-off psychic organism continues to function in the form of what we now call the magical and mythological dimensions of the unconscious. Our unconscious fantasies, imaginings, emotions, drives, instinctual awareness, ESP capacities, and "participation mystique" are all parts of this. Unbeknownst to us, these unconscious strata modify and comple-

ment—but also thwart—our reasoning. Our scientific world view, the
moral standards held by collective consciousness, and our personal
goals based on those values, come from rationalizations and codifica-
tions of the preceding periods. Yesterday's myth, poetical aspiration,
fable, or fantasy becomes rationalized into today's space-visible, historical fact. God is said to have literally "given" the Decalogue to Israel.
Jesus' sacrificial death and resurrection are believed as historical facts.
Meanwhile, unconscious psychic activity never stops. All established
value standards eventually evoke extensions and amplifications as well
as complementary or antithetical counterpositions in the unconscious
psyche. These are again modified, extended, or opposed once they become entrenched in collective standards. New motifs and variants then
arise with a still later cycle. These back-and-forth rhythms in their larg-
est spacings occur also in smaller cycles, down to the ten- and twenty-
year cycles that make for the proverbial generation gaps. Thus, one
mythopoetic wave follows the other, little waves within larger ones,
within centuries, within millennia-spanning epochs. The Renaissance,
Enlightenment, Industrial Age are all subcycles of the epoch of the rational mind. Each has its own submythology, its variation of the
Judeo-Christian myth, varying and counterpointing the preceding
rhythms of outward and inward turning. Within the larger outward-
directed mental cycle the Renaissance and Industrial Revolution
turned even further outward. Medieval mysticism and the romantic era
looked inward. Hence the precipitate of yesterday's myth in the collective consciousness is at variance with its contemporary, unconscious
mythopoetic activity. Likewise, in the psychology of the individual,
dreams extend, complement, amplify, and compensate the dreamer's
current conscious position. Today's mythical fantasy, unconscious and
rationalized by the mental attitude, points toward tomorrow's development of consciousness. In a later chapter we will deal with the modern
fantasies of the Grail theme as they have been rationalized into political
and social creeds. Hence today's publicly professed standards and beliefs reflect what has been accomplished and codified as the result of
past mythologizing. Much of the conventional accepted wisdom and morality may be marked for change in the future. Indeed it may already
be at variance with the actual facts and beliefs of contemporary life.
The publicly accepted belief in order, obedience to law, the Christian
ethic of love, are turned, twisted, flaunted, and disregarded whenever it
suits our purpose. In turn the experiential fulfillment of the authentic
Christian myth and ethic may still be waiting to be accomplished in the
period ahead of us.

The extroverted, rational, and materialistic orientation of the mental
epoch of contemporary modern man corresponds to postpuberty from

the ages of twenty to the age of the midlife crisis. This heralds the transition into a realm culturally and collectively uncharted as yet, *terra incognita,* a level of consciousness to be explored as the next step for mankind. This new level is being pioneered by the few, now turning inward toward the unconscius psyche and away from the conscious sphere exclusively defined and dominated during the mental period by will, rationality and the power urge. The inner realm is the domain of the Goddess.

The power drive is indispensable for initial patriarchal ego development. At the same time, it is the root of alienation. Fed and unconsciously motivated by the archaic emotions and instinctual habit patterns of the deeper mythological and magical strata of which it knows nothing, the patriarchal ego operates in increasing maladaptation to the natural and communal world. The critical impasse resulting from this maladaptation manifests the transition crisis which heralds the end of a past and the beginning of a new period. We must take the next step in the metamorphosis of consciousness whether we like it or not. From individual clinical experience we have learned that a next step in evolution, while often painful, is inevitable. It can be greatly facilitated when its necessity is accepted and a sense of its general direction understood. However, only a sense of its general direction can be apprehended by us. Any attempt to plot or forecast future development inevitably rests upon projections of elements of the past or present into the future. Such projections are based upon a tacit assumption that the steps ahead are repetitions of phases already in existence. This errs in leaving out the very nature and unpredictability of creativity.

Dionysus male-female. Mus. Nazionale, Rome.

Part 3

THE PATRIARCHAL MYTHS

Be ye perfect
even as your Father
in heaven is perfect.
MATT. 5:48

If God is God He is not good
If God is good He is not God.
Take the even, take the odd.
I would not sleep here if I could
Except for the little green leaves in the wood
And the wind on the water.
ARCHIBALD MACLEISH, *J.B.**

* (Boston: Houghton Mifflin, 1956) p. 11.

The increasing alienation from the maternally containing cosmic organism, from the later part of the mythological phase onward, finds its expression in four grand myths: the divine kingship; the human exile or loss of paradise; the propitiatory sacrifice of the scapegoat; and the inferiority of the Feminine. Unbeknownst to us, these myths still underlie to a large extent our modern world view. Since we no longer think-feel mythologically in a conscious way, however, we have now rationalized them. They have become unconscious fantasy premises. They determine our conscious ethos, our social values, and our modern religion, which now goes under the name of science.

They also determine the ways in which we still try to control our instinctual needs and to channel aggression: by command of law and willed discipline, by assigning guilt to ourselves and to others, and by expulsion of the guilty outcast from the community.

Since they constitute the unconscious premises of a world system that is about to evolve into a new phase, these four myths need to be understood psychologically. Only then may we properly comprehend their metamorphoses into new forms and what the *new* mythologies may require of us.

CHAPTER 7

The Divine Kingship: Superego and Ego

I am that I am.

EXODUS 3:14

Blessed art Thou, Lord our God, King of the Universe, who has sanctified us with His commandments ...

The Evening Kiddush

Our Father our King, we have sinned in your face ...

Yom Kippur Prayer

The myth of patriarchal kingship engendered that particular form of ego consciousness we have come in our time to consider consciousness *tout court*. It is centered in a rationalizing, abstracting, and controlling *I*, ego. In terms of this myth, the directive force of the universe is personified as a male ruler who operates through personal will and a quasi-rational intentionality. He is Lord of Hosts who slays his enemies and expects heroic allegiance from his subjects. He purportedly fashioned and rules the world as his domain. Social order is a reflection of his mythical order. The *civitas dei* is a community ruled by God as King: Jehovah in Israel, Allah in the Islamic world, Zeus in Greece, Jupiter Capitolinus in Rome. In the Christian States, a king ruled by

God's grace. In the modern totalitarian state, the ruler is a divinely inspired or graced dictator. Each regime is monolithic, ruled by an absolute quasi monarch, whatever the name. In each, the laws of the community were conceived as identical with the will of a deity, and administered either by a son of that deity, or by a human ruler who was held nevertheless to be his incarnate representative. In the same way, the human personality is conceived as properly to be ruled over by the will, which proceeds from the *I,* and is ready to battle against resistance, whether outer or inner.

Psychologically, the motif of patriarchal kingship resulted in a first sense of individual centeredness and a capacity for rational intentionality and personal will.

The godlike qualities of personal autonomy and conscious will were first ascribed only to God, then to king or pharaoh and a few initiates who were God's children or God embodied. Eventually however, in the history of consciousness, these divine (ego) qualities were extended to leaders, to nobility, and to the educated. Only in later Judaism and Christianity were the multitude credited with at least the potentiality of being individual persons with an individual soul, provided of course that they were male.

The focusing of consciousness around a centering heroic ego fostered the emergence of an almost totally masculine system of values, with a corresponding emphasis on separateness and individual will. Perceiving the self-conscious *I* as a masculine hero-warrior and enforcer of order, it became the task of ego in obedience to the laws of its liege lord the Divine King to conquer and suppress its feminine qualities, as well as its wayward urges, and relegate them to the unconscious.

Eventually the patriarchal ego-kingship myth resulted in an accelerating monotheism, and in a rigidity of the centering and focusing function of awareness. The earlier magical and mythological world views had allowed for the experience of a plurality of forces, powers, and personalities. This was expunged by the centralized, monotheistic world view. Theologically the myth appears in the concept of the one God, psychologically in the concept of a unified self, an *I* personality. This *I* personality deified the conscious aspects of experience while denying the multiplicity of pre-ego-conscious aspects and complexes from which it had emerged.

This development sets the pattern for the ego's dictatorial use of will to enforce the fiction of being the supreme ruler of the total psyche. The Greek mind still considered it a dangerous hubris to serve one god to the exclusion of others. From the time of the Middle Ages, the modern mind has demanded exclusive loyalty to one god, one way of seeing things, whether in the name of religion, politics, or psychology. Parochialism, intolerance, and fanaticism are the shadow aspects of mental and ego brilliance.

This general trend achieved maximum expression in the three great Western religions, Judaism, Christianity and Islam. The first two, particularly, were instrumental in shaping the culture and ethics of the Western world, and are therefore of particular interest to this investigation. As for Islam, we are witnessing a resurgence of fundamentalism in such countries as Iran and Libya and do not yet know its ultimate import.

The fundamental formulations of this Western doctrine may be seen in the first two commandments of the Decalogue.

I am the Lord thy God which has brought thee out of the land of Egypt, out of the house of bondage. Thou shalt have no other gods before me. Thou shalt not make unto thee any graven image, or any likeness of anything that is in heaven above, or that is in the earth beneath or that is in the water under the earth. Thou shalt not bow down thyself to them, nor serve them, for I thy God am a jealous God . . .

EXOD. 20:2–5

Note that the opening statement of the Decalogue is "I am." This needs to be seen as more than a mere grammatical phrase. It expresses from the very outset the nature and quality of the entity that addresses itself to Israel. The god who speaks identifies himself as "I am." This fact becomes clear in Exodus 3:14 when, in reply to Moses' request for his name, he responds: *"Eyeh asher eyeh,"* literally, "I am that which I am"; in other words, existence which is conscious of itself as an *I*. Here the root experience of selfness erupts into consciousness, bringing with it, as well, the decrees "Thou shalt" and "Thou shalt not." What speaks here is a quality which, at the end of the mental ego period, will be experienced as individual conscience rather than as an external and projected command. At the beginning of this period, however, the commandments are addressed to a collective body, not to an individual. They set collective standards of belief and behavior that claim divine authority. At this point, the developing ego may seem more like a superego in the Freudian sense, or animus or persona in Jungian terms. But the trend (we might even be tempted to say, the intent) is clearly towards self-control and self-responsibility.

Significantly, this self-responsibility rests upon the self-enforcement of collective standards of value and behavior. The rules and taboos are as yet extrinsic to the individual person. For the most part they are forcibly impressed upon frequently recalcitrant individual feelings and instinctual drives. The standards of right and wrong are expressions of a group soul and a group consciousness. They are enforced by a system of ostracism, penalizing, shaming, and scapegoating. Eventually this superego system is internalized as individual guilt feeling which, however, continues to be based upon externally derived collective standards. This world view stresses objects and distinctions in space, hierarchical order, law and proportion. The Greco-Roman Apollo judges primarily in aesthetic terms. To the Greek mind, beauty and goodness were largely synonymous. The Hebrew Jehovah judges ethically. Whatever offends against their measures, proportions, and set limits is judged ugly, bad, impure, and evil.

For a while, Apollo and Jehovah managed to maintain an uneasy coexistence in the Christian system. Eventually Jehovah assimilated Apollo and prevailed. For the Christian West, good and evil have become primarily ethical. Indeed, the enjoyment of beauty for its own sake has often been suspected of frivolity, a temptation of the Devil detracting from service to God. Purity came to mean strict, even harsh control of individual spontaneity, of instinctual and emotional urges, of "selfish" needs and desires, in favor of superego standards. In his poem ironically entitled "The Voice of the Devil," William Blake commented on this suppression of spontaneous instinct:

All Bibles or sacred codes have been the causes of the following Errors: . . . That God will torment Man in Eternity for following his Energies . . .

To this "Error" Blake's answer was "Energy is Eternal Delight." Thus he was a prophetic forerunner of the age of the return of the Goddess. However, still under the Divine King's rule, whatever does not accord with the collectively approved ego ideal is to be repressed. As an unconscious personality pattern it lives on and is projected upon the other person who then appears tainted with the vice which one has purportedly conquered. The suppression of spontaneous body and instinctual urges, the processes of self-control and self-denial, are comparable to the very process a child undergoes in toilet training. So far they have been more prevalent in our ego training than self-expression, which is the ultimate goal of ego discipline. Favoring the needs of self, even when it does not conflict with the needs of the other or of the community, is branded selfish and evil.

Even love—which we now consider an expression of spontaneous feeling—has been made an object of commanded volition and self-denial. Under the reign of the God-king, Eros was superseded by *agape.*[1] Spontaneous attraction was replaced by willed good feeling as an ethical goal. "You shall love the Lord your God with all your heart and all your soul . . ." (Deut. 6:5) and "love your neighbor as yourself" (Lev. 19:18).

The assimilation of Apollo by Jehovah concretizes law, order and proportion. From relatively abstract, or at least impersonal concepts, they become interpersonally relevant. This development constitutes a forward step in the evolution of consciousness and civilization. Balance and proportion now apply to the space and body of the human community and the mutual relationship of its members. The Hebrew command to love God and one's neighbor—rather than the Greek ideal of the beautiful—defines the highest communal good.[2]

The mythological allegories of the superego-dominated ego are the creation of heaven, earth, and light by God who "found nothing around Him but Tohu and Bohu, namely chaos and emptiness. The Face of the Deep over which His Spirit hovered was clothed in darkness."[3] Tohu and Bohu were possibly ancient feminine deities, later bestialized into monsters.[4] We find analogous motifs in the legends of the Hebrew Tehom, a sea monster slain by god's fiery chariot, in the Chaldean Tiamat slain by Marduk's sword, in Apollo's slaying of the Dionysian Python and the Teutonic Siegfried's and medieval St. George's slaying of the dragon. The patriarchal ego is heroic. Its idealized achievement is conquest of self and world by sheer will and bravery. Personal feeling, desire, pain and pleasure are disregarded. Failure to do so is accounted weakness. The resulting psychological achievement is a sense of personal identity vested in a body-limited, separate self, answerable to the law of group and God-king. Consciously, now it no longer feels organically contained in, or one with, group, world, or the divine. Unconsciously, however, it is still dominated by group values.

We have come to take for granted this rationally isolated sense of selfness. Yet it is only one particular form of self-awareness. The heroic ego is not the only possibility. The failure to realize these developmental dynamics can all too easily lead the modern psychologist to suspect psychopathology, ego weakness, or even fragmentation where it is simply a case of a different way of self-experiencing at variance with the narrow, traditional, object-limited rationality and body- and sense-limited consciousness. People who happen to relate to the unseen, who are open to what to others is still unconscious, or who see visions or hear voices, are not necessarily schizophrenic. Only when the transpersonal dimension displaces rather than widens personal awareness and rationality may we speak of ego-weakening or fragmentation.

It is also erroneous to equate consciousness and ego with masculinity and the unconscious with femininity. This has been a tendency among Jungians based upon an uncritical acceptance and superficial reading of E. Neumann's original cautious statements.[5]

Women have an ego which is indeed feminine and not necessarily masculine. Nor is it represented by male figures as the above theory would have it. Women do not dream of themselves as men when the dream ego is evoked. It is only the persona, animus or superego-determined patriarchal sense of identity, that is represented by male authority figures. This applies equally to both sexes. In the same way, wisdom and authority figures may appear in female form to either sex when the Yin dimension is to be emphasized.

Consequently, when the *I* or ego-consciousness appears in male images in myths, dreams, and fantasies, it refers to a patriarchal attitude which is assertive, focused, divisive, abstractive, and possibly, one-sidedly rational. In its world, a spade is a spade is a spade. White is white and black is unequivocally black. The patriarchal "I am" stresses existence to the exclusion of nonexistence. The archetypally feminine, in contrast, is ambivalent, receptive, connective, and unfocused. In its realm, existence and nonexistence, life and death, are one. Consequently, from the standpoint of rational logic, the feminine seems blurred, irrational, or at least nonrational. And it is unconscious, since its frame of reference has been largely repressed. To accept the world of the feminine is to regress into unconsciousness from the masculine ego point of view. Consequently "I am" opposes the worship of the feminine and the cults of the mother and of the triple Goddess and her consort.

The Hebrew word *Elohim*, commonly translated as God, etymologically refers to a plurality of beings. Originally it most likely included a female aspect. Yet it has become conceptualized as an exclusively male deity without female consort, mother, sister, or daughter, representing unity rather than plurality.

"Hear, O Israel, God, our God is One"[6] is repeatedly stressed in Jewish prayer. It is an assertion destined to overcome a deep-rooted experience of the plural. "I am" is a singular god. He encompasses and rules over everything. He demands adherence to himself alone, and commitment to his rules and taboos.

Graven images are forbidden. These symbolic representations of the divine numinosity might fragment the conceptual identity of "I am" into iconic multiplicity. After the injunction against the images comes the statement, "For I the Lord, thy God, am a jealous (*zealous* according to a different translation) God." The jealousy or zeal which is projected upon the godhead is an ego reaction which compensates both for a fear of separation and a fear of loss of control. Jealousy no less than zealousness is a primitive form of ego protection.

The idea of law and the myth of the law giver are fundamental premises upon which the new age of the mind develops. Ethics, morality, and human relations are to be based on rules. Initially human law is seen as the reflection of God's law. With enlightenment, the god figure is depotentiated, and natural law is held as governing the nonhuman and human realms alike. Law is to be obeyed by the use of man's free will: disregard of law brings about punishment and calls forth guilt. Discovering the laws underlying things (mechanical cause-and-effect relationships of energy) is expected to answer all problems. Emphasis shifts from the death-rebirth myth of the son of the virgin mother goddess to a legalistic point of view: atonement for Adam's breaking the law. God is proclaimed to be love, but is known primarily as the avenger of disobedience. He is the source of "Thou shalt." Love itself becomes a command to be enforced by the will.

Discipline and obedience to rules require the repression of spontaneous needs and urges: especially of aggression need and of the sexual urge. These are intrinsic to the worship of the Goddess and her instinctual, orgiastic (*orgia* meant "secret worship") ecstatic renewal. Natural spontaneity, sexuality, the desires of the flesh, woman and the Feminine, dance and play, all become the powers of the adversary, Dionysus made into the Devil. They are dreaded and repressed. The discovery of such desires in one's heart taints one with guilt. A rebellious, romantic, poetic genius like William Blake was able to see the unnaturalness of such a repressive conditioning and to sing out against it. Take, for example, his poem "The Garden of Love":

> *I went to the Garden of Love*
> *And saw what I never had seen:*
> *A Chapel was built in the midst*
> *Where I used to play in the green.*
>
> *And the gates of this Chapel were shut,*
> *And Thou shalt not writ over the door;*
> *So I turned to the Garden of Love*
> *That so many sweet flowers bore.*
>
> *And I saw it was filled with graves*
> *And tomb-stones where flowers should be;*
> *And priests in black gowns were walking their rounds*
> *And binding with briars my joys and desires.*

Ego development takes place in terms of rules that say "Thou shalt" or "Thou shalt not." By means of restrictions and artificial demands and prohibitions, the free flow of uncontrolled spontaneous psychic energy becomes subject to the control of a conscious center. To illustrate: by hitting my head against a wall I become conscious not only of the wall, but of my head as well, hence of the *I* who has a head and can learn to control its movements. In a similar way, every obstacle to the automatic spontaneous flow creates self-awareness. Obeying rules and taboos constitutes a form of mental exercise that trains will and self-discipline. The taboos do not have to make sense. In fact, for the purpose of will power training, the more arbitrary they are, the better they serve as pure disciplinary spurs. This phenomenon, long recognized as an essential component of military training, is equally critical to the development of psychic discipline. The generating of taboos fills a psychological need. It is a function of the psyche. However, taboos appear not only in the developmental phases of a cultural or ego structure, but in the degenerative stages as well. In the latter, they represent panicked attempts to shore up structural forms threatened with disintegration.

Phylogenetically as well as ontogenetically, consciousness and conscience in the early superego phases of ego development first arise through shame and guilt. When one fails to live up to the expectations of family, clan, or nation, one experiences shame, a sense of self as not acceptable. One feels diminished in status.[7] Shame enforces collective compliance and discipline. Guilt internalizes the taboo, making the nascent ego the executor of the collective standard.

The effects of shame and guilt, of "Thou shalt" and "Thou shalt not" are a training of judgment and self control. The law states what is right and wrong, good and bad. The will carries out the dictates of law and judgment. It enforces their demands upon the resisting natural and instinctual urges. Spirit is set against nature in a heroic effort to subdue man's animal nature. Symbolic representations of this struggle are such monster-slaying heroes as Perseus, Heracles, and St. George. Even Christ, who offers himself as a sacrifice and enjoins us to "judge not lest you be judged," "shall return to judge the living and the dead." He is made into a heroic conqueror of the Devil. The patriarchal superego-conditioned ego is, as a result, conquest oriented. Its sense of identity rests upon its power to enforce order and upon its capacity to conquer, possess, and assimilate resisting objects and opponents. Failure of any of these capacities engenders a sense of inadequacy and inferiority. Inferiority feelings, the power drive, anxiety, possessiveness, envy, jealousy, and the compulsion to subdue and conquer are the mainsprings of the patriarchal ego.

Only when ego-discipline and ego-firmness have been reached (toward the conclusion of the patriarchal phase) can the ego begin to relate to a deeper center that is both personal and transpersonal, one which speaks to the individual aspect of the collective myth. This center, the individual conscience, is none other than the Self in the Jungian sense. It calls to ego, as Pindar said, to "become what you are." The making possible of such a step could be seen as the psychological goal of patriarchal development, especially its Christian aspect. During the patriarchal phase, only a few individuals could manage to live by their individual consciences—at the risk of being burned to death at the stake. It is only in our time that the achievement of a Self rather than a persona or superego-directed ego is becoming a possible and culturally approved step.

External collective authority and internalized superego shame and guilt are, then, inescapable and necessary phases of patriarchal ego development. They cannot be avoided in child rearing. They have placed their mark on cultural standards. It is through the theophany of Israel, the Decalogue, and its subsequent Christian legalism that this decisive internalization of ethical standards has occurred.

The next development, falling due in our own epoch, is towards freedom of ethical and moral choice. This step has been prepared for by those religious and social disciplines which have made restraint of purely animal desires a matter of personal responsibility. In the theophany of Israel, the well-spring of existence and conscience was made manifest as "I am" and "Thou shalt." He generated individuality by setting limits for the individual, and then made the individual responsible for those limits. Toward this end, the Decalogue and the Golden Rule represented an initial step. Their effect upon personal responsibility was sharpened by the later Christian doctrine of the *privatio boni*,[8] that is, of evil as a deficiency of good. Thus, the elaboration of Judeo-Christian ethics was the indispensable guardian of a psychological development urged upon man by a mysterious need of unknown and unconscious psychic depths. This particular phase of evolution was to lead to rational consciousness, self-control, and a sense of freedom of will and of ethical responsibility. Even though these manifestations first occurred as collective rules, they correspond to archetypal motifs. They are developmental factors. Like the senses of beauty or love, or religiosity or awe, and the experience of moral conflict and guilt, they put us at the portal of becoming human.

The archetypal force behind the kingship myth manifests in a striving toward the "I am." Its goal is individuality and self responsibility. Yet that goal is still in a preparatory stage and unconscious. The kingship myth represents a guidance system for a kind of individuality which is still extraneous to the individual. The "I am"-ness is at first still only in the object, in the God-king and his community without, not yet in the subject. Thus, the commandments are to be literally obeyed and not just related to symbolically. The *chronique scandaleuse* of the philandering Greek gods gives way to the grim dictatorship of Jehovah.

Revelation is to be unconditionally accepted and obeyed in every detail, as though it were promulgated by a human magistrate or law giver. In time, the seat of authority comes to be occupied by the Church, the Inquisition, and their secular arm. Thus it became heresy punishable by the stake to doubt that in receiving the Host the believer literally ate the body of Christ. Galileo had to recant his heretical notion that, contrary to biblical description, the earth, not the sun, is moving. To engage in any even pleasurable activity on the sabbath was sinful. An Orthodox Jew would not even use the streetcar or telephone, even though these are labor-saving devices. But as the rational mind develops further, it can no longer find sense or meaning in this orthodox teaching. The myth is rejected by the conscious mind and discarded in its entirety as senseless. Yet it continues to operate unconsciously. It forms the premises upon which rationality builds its concepts and convictions. The anthropomorphic figure of the "I am" god is discarded. But a superego, a collective standard that speaks to all persons in the name of a collective code, takes his place. As the superego, the King-God remains present, albeit unconsciously, as a communal standard. This standard is pre-egoic and prepsychological in its origin. It is "given" as tradition and community conditioned. It is not a result of individual feeling or reasoning. Yet it *results* in the structuring of an ego and eventually of individual reasoning. It safeguards and engenders the development of individual consciousness, individual judgment and responsibility. Yet, like the protective shell of an egg, the superego becomes an encumbrance once the development which it purports to protect has achieved the egoic expression and needs to reach out towards the psychological experience of genuine, individual conscience. For many individuals this phase is being reached in our generation. For them, the superego God-King no longer carries the vital significance it had during the epoch of the Decalogue and the centuries of the Christian Middle Ages. Then the center of being was still exterior to man's psyche, residing in the state, the community, the Holy Roman Empire, or the all-embracing Catholic church.

No further step in development can be taken until its preceding phase has been adequately achieved. Psychologically, people are not all equal. Where self-discipline and ego-awareness and control have not yet been achieved by an individual, the medieval phase has still to be lived through in its own terms, whether the person in question happens to be five or sixty-five years of age. We must first learn to operate and live as conforming members of state and community before we can move toward guidance by a Self as a center that directly addresses the individual psyche.

It is true that without adequate ego discipline a visionary experience

of the Self as God-immanent may be possible in dreams or as a mystical
or drug-induced experience. The actual realization or living incarnation of the Self, however, requires the presence of a disciplined ego to
function as a responsible and conscious executor, in the limited world of
the here and now, of the Self's intentions and visions.

The ego's task in this respect is like that of the creative artist. Imagi-
native perception is called for, but is not enough. Work discipline, skill
in handling the materials available, and doing without those that are
not, are also needed. In addition, it requires a sense of what is possible
in a given situation and still assimilable by at least some of one's contemporaries.

The Decalogue was given to the community for the sake of the community. Individuality was as yet unknown, except in the king, the god
incarnate, or ruler by God's grace, and those members of the ruling
class who were so designated by initiation or by divine election of birth.
To these chosen ones fell the privilege and responsibility of protecting
the many who had, as yet, no individual personalities. Women especially were considered needful of this protection: "For I would have
you know that the head of every man is Christ, and the head of every
woman is man" (I Cor. 11:3), and *"mulier non facta est ad imaginem
dei."* [9] ("Woman is not made in the image of God.") Only membership
in the right (God-approved) community confers protection. The person
on the other side of the tracks is, at best, a nobody; at worst, an infidel,
heathen, son of Belial, or simply subhuman. This attitude, which lingers on in our unconscious—or not-so-unconscious parochialism, was
fundamentally codified by the original wording of the Golden Rule. It
is lightly and mistakenly quoted as a paradigm of universal brotherly
love and acceptance. It states: "Thou shalt not take vengeance or bear
grudges against the sons of *your own people* but shall love your neighbor as yourself. *I am* the Lord" (Lev. 19:18; italics mine). Note that potential individuality is credited here to the sons, not the daughters, of
one's own people only.

The dissolving of one's conscious, and even more so of one's unconscious, identification with one's group is a slow and painful process, but
it is a necessary part of ego development. The continuance of a fixation
in what at first is an unavoidable root connection results in national,
communal and racial intolerance, the bias of self-appointed chosenness
and a holier than thou attitude toward all outsiders.

In the early patriarchal myth, the Divine King rules through a special covenant with a chosen people.[10] Therefore, they are the only bear-
ers of God's truth. It is revealed to and known only by them. It is codified in their sacred books and deviated from only at the gravest possible
risk. Thus Deuteronomy 13:1–5:

If there arise among you a prophet or a dreamer of dreams, and giveth thee a sign or a wonder, and the sign or the wonder come to pass, whereof he spake unto thee, saying, "let us go after other gods, which thou hast not known, and let us serve them," thou shalt not harken unto the words of that prophet, or that dreamer of dreams; for the Lord your God proveth you to know whether you love the Lord your God with all your heart and with all your soul. Ye shall walk after the Lord your God and fear Him, and keep His commandments, and obey His voice, and ye shall serve Him, and cleave unto Him, and that prophet, or that dreamer of dreams, shall be put to death; because he hath spoken to turn you away from the Lord your God, which brought you out of the land of Egypt . . .

And in verses 12–16:

If thou shalt heresay in one of the cities which the Lord thy God has given thee to dwell there, saying certain men are gone out from among you, and have withdrawn the inhabitants of their city, saying "let us go and serve other gods, which ye have not known," then shalt thou inquire and make search, and ask diligently; and behold, if it be true, and the thing certain, that such abomination is wrought among you; thou shalt surely smite the inhabitants of that city with the edge of the sword, destroying it utterly, and all that is therein, and the cattle thereof, with the edge of the sword. And thou shalt *gather* all the spoil of it into the midst of the street thereof, and shalt burn with fire the city and all the spoil thereof *every whit,* for the Lord thy God; and it shall be a heap forever; it shall not be built again.

On the external stage of history, the establishment of God's kingdom on a global scale is to be accomplished through the efforts of the chosen ones. The infidels are to be converted to the only true belief through political and/or military conquest. If the standards, beliefs, and laws of the chosen people or nation are the only true ones, arrived at through religious revelation, then those of other peoples must be mere superstition or morally wrong. This attitude continued today in a secularized form, primarily in our national social and religious parochialism, but also in the dogmatism of much of current scientific thinking.

The God-King and supreme law giver is good and just by definition. Any doubt of his goodness and justness or any infraction of his laws evokes a most catastrophical outbreak of his jealous rage. Whatever customs happen to be at variance with his law are heretical and deserve the severest punishment. The result is a rigid legalistic system, a codification of acts, actions, and attitudes purporting to represent standards of goodness in absolute terms. Thereby culture-bound customs become identified with absolute and eternal ethical values. Morality becomes petrified in legalism. Variant opinions, in respect to what in any case is humanly unknowable, are heresies punishable by death or exclusion from the community. "Sin is the transgression of the law."[11] To work on the sabbath, a day selected by communal consensus, is a punishable sin. Homosexuality is a punishable sin, no less than murder. As the communal code is identified with absolute goodness, the individual dissenter is, by definition, evil and a public enemy. Hence goodness, which is synonymous to obedience to the communal law, must be accomplished by an act of will and self-denial; by compliance and social adaptation. Since whatever has been established by the God-King, can only be' good and just, whatever evil exists cannot be part of his plan or being. Said Ireneaeus: "Nothing evil was created by God. We ourselves have produced all wickedness." Evil, then, is disobedience and nonconformity, freely willed, preventable and punishable. "Sin in man and angels is a free act. Why some fail and others do not is a mystery."[12]

On the positive side, this assumption introduces responsibility on a personal level. But a split is forced between the desired self-image and the unacceptable aspects of one's individuality. While unavoidable as a first step in individuation, this split needs bridging-over once an ego is established. Only through perceiving one's transgression as "missing the point" (the original meaning of the Hebrew *chatο* and the Greek *hamartia* which came to mean "sin") rather than as reprehensible sin, can the individual personality liberate itself from rigidity and continue the course of its evolution.

As long as the God image of universality is conceptually limited to communal and collective legalism, the ego-shadow split cannot be healed. Man must be burdened with the monster of his own creation, the concept of absolute evil, and remain alienated from his own nature.

The consequences of this dilemma are summed up in the Christian doctrine of the *privatio boni*. Evil has no objective existence. God is good. He created the world and saw that it was good. God cannot have created evil, and even less can it be considered inherent in the very deity itself. Hence evil is seen merely as a lessening, a negation or an absence of the good. Evil then is diminished existence or nonexistence. Essentially this is an attempt to preserve a strict monotheism and yet maintain God as *summum bonum*—without any inherent ambivalence—as befits the supreme lawgiver and king. It follows logically from the myth of the lawgiver that he cannot have created what he forbids. Since the creation of evil by a different power would postulate the existence of an antigod of equal stature, evil cannot exist. Evil must represent merely a diminution of the universal good, brought about by human frailty and disobedience.

Much more than theological hairsplitting is involved here. The psychological significance of this doctrine lies in its denial of polarity. If there is only more or less *good,* it is our personal duty to increase the supply in order to please God. It is also possible, in principle at least, to eliminate the appearance of evil completely. Our progress mania, our social utopianism and our lack of realism in dealing with the human existential situation may be traced to the secularization and trivialization of the *privatio boni* concept. Since only good is acknowledged, we are unable to accept and deal with violence, aggression and suffering other than by trying, impotently, to legislate it away. Moreover, when existence and life are held to be synonymous with goodness and virtue, their opposites, death and destruction, must be seen as punishment ("The wages of sin is death" . . . Rom. 6:23) or, at any rate, a state of diminished goodness. Since they have no meaningful place in our universe, death and destruction elicit dread and moral condemnation.

This rejection of suffering and death accords well with the developing ego's identification with physical existence in the body. In ego terms, that is the only existence possible. Nonbody states of awareness, with their prenatal and postmortem possibilities of psychic continuity, are considered impossible. The earlier religious vision of the continuity of life after death is rationalized into a quasi-physical existence analogous to what life would mean to ego consciousness: namely, a resurrection in the body. When the literal conception of physical continuity loses credibility, death means total extinction. It is the unavoidable supreme evil. I remember a patient's once saying to me, "How can you enjoy living and find any permanent value or meaning in life when you know that someday all this comes to an end?" Paradoxically, however, it is precisely our awareness of the inevitability of the end of the ego's domain that makes life human and gives it poignancy. Consequently, the sense that death is evil prevents us from experiencing time and suffering as living creative dimensions. Time becomes an enemy. We have to fight it, to race with time, beat time, play for time, or kill time. We do not recognize time—and its limitation—as creative and necessary preconditions for unfoldment, for actualization.

Yet, since existence—goodness—has been rendered evil by man's sin, a fundamental ethical responsibility now rests upon the human psyche. The conflict of opposing values becomes a personal, internalized ethical conflict. This internalization, in the form of superego, of what was formerly god-given law or taboo, is an important step forward in psychological development. Shame and fear of communal or divine punishment are now differentiated into a sense of guilt and personal responsibility.

Compared to the earlier phases, man now gains a new sense of freedom. No longer does he feel himself a merely passive sufferer of calamity and pain, helpless in the face of fate and necessity; a plaything of powers beyond his control. Instead, he is a conscious participant in a social, ethical, and even cosmic struggle, personally responsible for the outcome of the drama of existence. "Your eyes will be opened and you will be like God, knowing good and evil" (Gen. 3:5,22). Forgotten, however, is the awareness that this knowledge is the gift of the serpent, of the very aboriginal, abysmal, instinctual wisdom which he is now to tread underfoot in order to realize freedom of will.

No matter what their culturally changing contents, or whether they are derived from collective standards or from individual conscience, good and bad and right and wrong are archetypal categories. They are indispensable ordering principles for the ethical, intellectual, and aesthetic development of mankind.

Therefore respect for taboo and law is psychologically important. It is an indispensable phase of development. It erects a barrier of will against the boundlessness of forces within the unconscious psyche. These forces are often so compulsive as to be experienced as demonic, or in more modern terminology, as obsessive complexes.

A person who would be self-motivated needs a prior initiation. This involves ego discipline, awareness of one's destruction and power urges, and consciously getting in touch with transpersonal guidance and ethical responsibility. Otherwise in transgressing a taboo, he risks being overpowered by the force of the affect that was prematurely touched. In the past, as also now for the child, such psychological awareness was not sufficiently developed to make possible the distinction between a hostile act and a hostile feeling. Feelings tended and still tend to compel acting out. Conformity on both levels was therefore necessary. "You shall not take vengeance" and "You shall love your neighbor as yourself." Self-control can accomplish the first of these commandments. The second, however, implies psychological repression.

Yet even such self-control by repression of feeling and impulses is no small developmental feat. For instance, not merely to restrain my impulse to hit somebody who has made me angry, but to put my anger aside and convince myself that this is a person who deserves respect and even affection, no less than myself, is a moral victory of a high order. It enables me to open myself to feelings and opinions hitherto at variance with my own. Hence I may grow beyond my former limitations. The untrained ego can purchase such a step only at the price of pushing the anger out of consciousness, declaring it wrong and even evil. This price must be paid until enough self-control is achieved to allow one to feel anger without repressing or acting it out and without losing touch with objective judgment and empathy. This capacity is barely beginning to be achieved in our time by a psychological avant garde.

Therefore, even the Christian control of affect by repression is an extension of a discipline to everyone of what in ancient times was still only an ideal condition of the elect. Medieval culture decreed it to be the realizable ideal for the many. This was a truly heroic development, appropriately symbolized in such images as St. George slaying the dragon.

Ego-controlled will power poses its force against the nonego, as well as against others, against objects, or against one's own self. Ego psychology is therefore a psychology of power motivation, as Alfred Adler described it. It is founded inevitably on competitiveness and the deliberate and controlled use of aggression to subdue one's own opposing nature and opposing others.

During the pre-Christian epoch, the channeling of the power drive against others was culturally sanctioned, indeed glorified, in the name of honor and valor. The heroic warrior ideal was supreme. The signature of that age was the combative ram, still found in representations of Abraham's sacrifice or in the Judaic ram's horn. In Christian culture, the ideal of the combative ram changed to that of the Lamb of God, whose humility and nonassertiveness were the results of having conquered himself rather than his fellow human beings. Power-control was to be exerted over one's own urges, drives and desires and needs: turn the other cheek, love your enemies, pray for those who hate you. Yet the merely displaced aggression, resentment, hate, envy, and ill will continue to exert pressure from the unconscious level. They demand outlets. While repression is unavoidable, as a first step of affect control it leads nevertheless to an unconscious continuation of hostility and to self-hate.

Since conforming group members *must* be loved, aggressive feelings are transferred to imaginary enemies, heretics and devils who can be fought and destroyed in the name of goodness and love. In our time this dynamic threatens us collectively and personally. Repression no longer suffices. On the contrary, it is dangerous. Now action and feeling motivations need to be distinguished and separately dealt with. Our sanity and survival depend upon this. By will we need to control our actions. Feelings need to be freed from repression, consciously accepted, experienced and, under certain circumstances, experimented with. Feelings can no longer be dealt with in "thou shalt" or superego terms only. They can not be forcibly controlled by ego power only. However a strongly established ego is essential to sustain full emotional awareness, yet resist its pull to action. We need discernment to choose appropriate times and circumstances in which a hostile or other forbidden impulse can be expressed without violating our own integrity nor the rights of our fellow beings.

We have reached a new stretch of the road. It leads us beyond what the superego-kingship myth can provide. A different orientation for ego consciousness may be required. Until now, superego guidance made the ego its steward. Today the ego feels itself supreme. To attempt to continue further upon the old course does not lead to further ego strengthening. It would rather mean ego atrophy, sterility, alienation, and even breakdown.

Under superego rule it was assumed that we can be *taught,* that we can *know* what is right, and that we are *free* to comply with the law or break it. Sin and guilt are the foundations of this way.[13] Consequently, superego values and personal ones conflict. As we have seen, the superego was and is needed to establish standards for conscience. But a continuing identification with these standards limits morality to mere group conformity. It allows no compassion for individual ethical conflicts. Self-righteous hypocrisy flourishes within this matrix. So does doctrinaire rigidity.

Moreover, since the collective will purports to represent nothing less than the *will of God,* it is presumed to be without flaw. Therefore, if in spite of one's righteous standards, something goes wrong, then someone must be responsible. Perhaps one's own weakness is at fault, but preferably it is the fault of someone else. Thus inevitably the scapegoat myth and a scapegoat psychology are a part of this cycle. Religiousness became confused with chronic guilt and the projection of that guilt onto the nonconformist. "A guilty conscience is the seasoning of our daily life. All upbringing is a cultivation of a sense of guilt on an intensive scale."[14] Our outlook became increasingly based upon a scapegoat and martyr psychology. It is spiced with vindictiveness and self-justification, with an attitude of "see what you are doing to me." Our own values and those of our fellows are judged solely in terms of performance and success. We overlook the ambivalence of every feeling and act. We forget that every motivation and impulse has a potentially constructive as well as destructive side. We identify with and see only what we consider good or bad, the light or the dark side. We lose sight of the fact that each comes with its opposite. A good motivation can after all, result in a destructive act. A bad act can have constructive consequences. "Do-gooding" can cover a lot of repressed hostility and ill will.

Discipline originally meant discipleship and learning. *Askesis* meant practice. They came to mean only external obedience, duty, a stiff upper lip, and self-denial. Personal satisfaction became suspect in later Christian ethics, particularly in Puritanism. It had to be sacrificed for success, progress and duty. We have learned harsh emotional attitudes. As we treat ourselves, so we treat our neighbors.

Faith came to mean blind conformity to collective doctrine. It lost the sense of trust in what must be intuitively experienced, because it cannot be seen or felt with the senses. Doctrine became increasingly rationalized until it was completely divorced from every depth experience.[15]

"Our faith rests upon the revelation to the apostles and prophets, but not any revelation that might have occurred to any other teacher."[16] "The sacred theology uses the warranty of the canonical sacred scripture as *apposite* to it by virtue of which its teaching is irrefutably grounded."[17]

This blind faith previously accorded to "thus saith the Lord" has now been transferred to "science teaches" with all its former inviolability intact.

Since God is just, our suffering, difficulties and trouble must be punishment for wrongdoing. Success and affluence, in turn, are to be taken as signs of grace, rewards for goodness. From this context springs the Protestant work ethic, in which the ability to produce wordly success has been considered a sign and expression of religious life. Failure and defeat have no positive significance within this system. Humanness itself is without intrinsic value except in terms of its social usefulness. Suffering and failure are shameful and expressions of wrongdoing or sinfulness. Since mistakes must be avoided under all circumstances, the possibility of experimenting and learning from one's past errors is excluded. One *has* to be right. A prerequisite for such infallibility is obedience to custom. Such was the psychology of Adolf Eichmann, and his defense against any accusation of moral turpitude ("I only obeyed orders").

As a counterreaction there appears the spontaneous urge to nonconformity at any price. Yet the nonconformist fails to see that conformity is so deeply engrained that even in his rebellion he conforms to projected nonconformist standards, rather than to any standard of his own.

John Wesley is reported to have said: "If there be no unquenchable fire, no everlasting burnings, there is no dependence upon scripture. No hell, no heaven, no revelation."[18] Thus goodness, justice, reward, and punishment, the basis of religious conviction and the root of life's meaning, become no more than the parameters of a vast penal system.

The myth of the Divine King has reigned supreme for thousands of years. In today's personal and social conflicts, we experience a revolution of primal powers of feeling, consciousness and emotion. Life is endangered. The foundations of the patriarchal kingdom are shaking. The heavenly king has dropped his scepter to earth. He has vacated the throne of his commandments. Where the scepter has landed, the stream of the waters of life is erupting. The Goddess returns with her Dionysian consort. Her masculine predecessor had ruled by means of "Thou shalt" and "Thou shalt not." The Goddess enigmatically smiles as she utters the new watchword, "You may." We may indeed, but as we sow, we shall reap. In the Goddess's unfathomable eyes we read the cautionary afterword, "But be careful."

CHAPTER 8

The Human Exile;
Paradise Lost;
The Death of God

"Cursed is the ground because of you. . . ." Then the Lord God said, "Behold the man has become like one of us, knowing good and evil . . ." therefore the Lord God sent him forth from the garden of Eden to till the ground from which he was taken.

GEN. 3:17, 22, 23

Pan is dead.

PLUTARCH

Modern nonreligious man assumes a new existential situation; he regards himself solely as the subject and agent of history, and he refuses all appeal to Transcendence . . . Man makes himself, and he only makes himself completely in proportion as he desacralizes himself with the whole. The sacred is the prime obstacle to his freedom.

MIRCEA ELIADE, *The Sacred and the Profane**

For centuries, traditional Christian theology forged an absolute gulf between humanity and nature. Pagan worship of the divinity within nature was rejected. Humanity was seen as the center of creation. All

* Trans. Willard Trask (New York: Harcourt, Brace, Jovanovich, 1968), pp. 202f.

nature was to be subservient. Exploitation of the environment was sanctioned. Nature was valued only for its contributions to human welfare, not for its own grandeur, beauty or mystery. These attitudes have directly contributed to our current ecological crisis. At a recent symposium on "The Theology of Survival,"[1] general agreement was reached on this point.

It may seem surprising that religious standards are basic factors in the origins of the environmental crisis. For traditional worship and symbolism have lost their power to give meaning and a transcendent dimension to the lives of many today. Yet the underlying premises of our culture are still rooted in religion. Like Moliere's *bourgeois gentilhomme,* who was surprised to find that all his life "he had spoken prose," modern rationally-minded nonreligious man may be shocked to realize that his own attitudes toward nature and survival are after all the expression of religious values.

We have, in a sense, secularized our religion. Having voided the sacred from nature, we have turned to new gods: technology, production of goods, greater physical wellbeing. Consequently, our environment is poisoned; resources become exhausted; ecological cycles are disrupted; demonic powers of the machine threaten us. Truly, however, our insensitivity to the living pulse of nature is the greatest menace. We feel like homeless aliens in a senseless, soulless universe. We would like to knock at the doors of authentic existence but find them barred. We would like to enter the country of being but do not know what authority to petition for valid passports and visas to that realm. Individually and collectively, our alienation leads us to the verge of neurosis or psychosis. What on earth are we ourselves if our world is nothing but a collection of soulless, mindless things to be exploited?

The anthropologist Colin Turnbull was living among the pygmies of the Ituri rainforest in Central Africa. He writes:

One night in particular will always live for me, because that night I think I learned just how far we civilized human beings have drifted from reality. The moon was full, so that the dancing had gone on for longer than usual. Just before going to sleep I was standing outside my hut when I heard a curious noise from the nearby children's *bopi* (playground). This surprised me, because at nighttime the Pygmies generally never set foot outside the main camp. I wandered over to see what it was.

There, in the tiny clearing, splashed with silver, was the sophisticated Kenge, clad in bark cloth, adorned with leaves, with a flower stuck in his hair. He was all alone, dancing around and singing softly to himself as he gazed up at the treetops.

Now Kenge was the biggest flirt for miles, so, after watching for a while, I came into the clearing and asked, jokingly, why he was dancing alone. He stopped, turned slowly around and looked at me as though I was the biggest fool he had ever seen; and he was plainly surprised by my stupidity.

"But I'm not dancing alone," he said. "I am dancing with the forest, dancing with the moon." Then with the utmost unconcern, he ignored me and continued his dance of love and life.[2]

By contrast, consider this testimony of the elderly William Butler Yeats:

> *Seventy years have I lived*
> *No ragged beggar-man*
> *Seventy years have I lived*
> *Seventy years man and boy*
> *And never have I danced for joy.*[3]

Let us look more closely at the religious background of our exile on this planet. The Decalogue's first three commandments present a deity separate from man. This God fashioned man for an exclusive covenant with Himself. No graven images are to be made of this patriarchal, kinglike leader. He exclusively is to be worshipped. The sacred is severely limited to abstract spirit. Experiencing the sacred in groves, animals, or objects of imagination is declared evil. Symbolic imagination is banished.

As the hidden God became identified with spirit and absolute good, nature and natural life, the realm of the now displaced Goddess had to bear the projection of evil. As nature became the realm of the Devil it had to be subdued and mortified by the godly part of man.

Although we now condemn this separation of Western humanity from its instinctive side, we have seen the psychological need to tear loose from the Great Mother Goddess of Nature. For the sake of an independent sense of personality one had to heed the command of the one and only patriarchal "I am that I am," and forget the powers of the encompassing unitary reality. These powers were the gods who are also *animals, plants, stones, places,* and *times.* These were henceforth to be considered reasonless dumb creatures and inanimate, even dead matter. Humanity had to subdue the earth and make it serve the *I.*

In the light of this urge toward rationality, will, and responsibility, we have to understand the various myths of the Golden Age or Paradise Lost. It is also the basis of the Christian doctrine of Original Sin. No human life can mature without moral conflict and the sense of guilt. To grow up into modern adulthood, magical participation and mythical identification must be overcome. The world and its events must at least hypothetically be seen in terms of impersonal cause-and-effect relationships. Thereby one's own actions have rationally explicable and controllable effects for which one is accountable.

By closing off the psyche from the direct experiencing of the living cosmos, modern rationalism has deprived humanity of conscious contact with the divine. The lean diet of ascetic rationality that promoted ego growth threatens to starve our souls and destroy our world. We have lost the visibility of the living God. God is dead for us. We have been taught all too well to look for the divine only in the imperative world of "Thou shalt." For lack of imagination we cannot see any spark of divine reality, except perhaps as a poetic metaphor, not to be taken really seriously.

The images whose worship has been outlawed by the second commandment are referred to as idols. That word derives from the Greek, *eidolon,* the root also of the word "idea." It signified to the Greek mind a visible experience of form, whether object or concept. A similar meaning underlies the Greek words *theoria* and *theatron* ("theatre") which to the Greek mind pointed up the visibilities of the divine.

This possibility of a direct experience of the divine was abrogated in the orthodox (not mystical) Jewish and Christian concepts. No longer could spirit be *seen-beheld* in stones, waters, springs, trees, groves, animals—and eventually not even in human beings. Instead, spirit became an ethical abstraction. Revelation belonged to the historical past, not the living present.

Mythological identification, the living out of the myth, was terminated by separating the human from the divine. Dogmatism was substituted for conscious myth-making. Symbolic imagination was likewise curtailed by limiting the sacred to nonsensory concepts that cannot be seen and felt but only taught. Therefore they must be *believed.* Faith is no longer *pistis* ("trust in one's own experience") but henceforth blind acceptance, divorced from subjective personal experience.

As symbolic imagination was banished, the All-Mother, the mistress of heaven, was no longer a living pulse within all that is.[4] The *daimonion* of earth, nature, and the cosmos was replaced by what Alan Watts called the "cosmic idiot." John Lilly refers to it as "God as the simulation, the model." The heavenly father is a remote abstraction separate from his creation.[5]

At the Council of Constantinople in the year 869, it was proclaimed that man consisted not of body, soul, and spirit but of body, soul and a *spirit-like reason,* only. Since even soul increasingly became identified with reason, that term too became superfluous. Eventually, man is seen as merely a body automated by *reasonable* reflex responses to the environment. This is the psychology without the psyche of early twentieth century vintage. Everything can be understood through rational mechanics. Knowing has been replaced by intellectual reductionism, sterile positivism, the split between subject and object.

The secularization of the cosmos inevitably brought with it the secularization of all aspects of life in this world: of working, loving, fighting, and playing. Work is no longer sacred in itself, but only insofar as it serves an end, such as financial security, or a comfortable retirement. We race to *save* time in our ungratifying jobs so we can *kill* time in our leisure. Pleasure has been turned into the joyless labor of compulsively doing something that's useful or good for us. Joy and pleasure which serve no useful purpose are considered frivolous. In the inner city, playgrounds with cement floors and chain fences give a grim work-out space to keep young bodies functional, and out of trouble.

The lust for life once served the gods in the spontaneous dance of existence, Kenge's dance. Now it exhausts itself in meaningless rituals for *winners* or *losers*. But gods banished from the high altar have a tendency to creep in through seamy back streets. As a result we find ourselves caught by waves of compulsive hedonism, living it up, or drowning ourselves in liquor and drugs. For while modern man is free to ignore mythologies and theologies, his ignorance will not prevent his continuing to feed upon decayed myths and degraded images.

During medieval times, enjoyment of the everyday realities of instinct and flesh, became tainted with the smell of guilt and damnation. Independent thought and research were suspected as heresy. The result was an ever-increasing gulf between theology and actual life, and between theology and that trend of independent thought which eventually resulted in modern science.

Profane society became convinced that unless the fullness of life were to be strangled, living in sin was unavoidable. Secular life was thus overhung by a cloud of damnation and fear of death, which was expected to bring judgment and the retribution of hell. Death was no longer conceived as a transition to another state of consciousness after a life of meaning. At best it meant extinction, at worst, an advent of wrath. It is impossible to live constantly in the presence of a condemning authority without attempting to overthrow it. Psychologically, condemnation equals repression. Self-condemnation means self-repression and is a mortal threat to one's sense of existence and self-value. It fosters unsatisfied neediness, impotence and resentment of one's fellow beings. It becomes an act of psychological self-preservation to overthrow the seeming source of this condemnation, the external superego authority. Since this process occurs more or less unconsciously, it is usually overlooked that the condemnatory external value system has been internalized. What formerly was outer or heavenly authority now functions as an inner accuser who condemns one to self-rejection. This goes on even

after the outer divine judge has been overthrown by the would-be athe-
ist: superego values become standards of the ego. Thus, while God is
dead and the heavens are empty of spiritual meaning, the judgmental
patriarchal archetype remains unconsciously as part of our ego complex. Our collective morality is still largely based upon standards of
two thousand years ago. In the very fashion of the stern unforgiving
Lord of Hosts of the Old Testament, our finger implacably points at our
own shortcomings, no less than at the faults of our neighbor.

However, since we no longer believe in existence beyond the ego's rational material world, our alienation and guilt feelings are largely unconscious. Whatever is unconscious is subject to projection: this is the
basic law of preservation of psychic energy. As a result, both divine superiority and human guilt are projected onto other people. The scapegoat complex takes over. Society, state, and nation are divinized or satanized. Society is either the divine fatherland that can do no wrong, or
it is corrupt, sick, and alienated from what it ought to be.

This trend is furthered by the transformation of the mythologically
oriented village or town into the more abstract and impersonal state,
nation, or political organization. Such systems are extensive organiza-
tional structures held together by a collective idea. They engender no
sense of personal contact. Organism is changed to organization. Within
such structures, personal needs, values, and assertive capacities of necessity recede. The individual sense of ego personality gradually increases, but so does the sense of disconnection, alienation from nature,
and victimization by the increasingly remote and impersonal social
structure of the state. The increasing sense of individuality and individual rights is coupled with individual impotence in the face of impersonal state and government. The group is no longer felt as containing,
but rather as threatening individual rights, while failing to satisfy individual needs. The extremes of asocial, indeed antisocial, individu-
alism and fanatical identification with and deification of state and political organizations, go hand in hand. In the face of this isolation the
ego frantically labors to create its own meaning. This it tries to achieve
by striving for goals to be accomplished, deeds to be done. It wants to
put its mark upon the world, to fulfill history or a mission. A sense of
apparent freedom and self-fulfillment through accomplishments is
thereby gained, along with responsibility and guilt for one's acts of
mission as well as commission. The "unease in our culture," as Freud
called it, steadily increases. The eschatological outlook conjures up the
image of heaven, hell, final judgment and damnation and, in our time,
of total annihilation, absolute nothingness. God and Devil, good and
evil fighting for the human soul replace the paradisiacal life of containment in natural cycles and rhythms.

The male god—whether still anthropomorphized or embodied in the idea of rightness, goodness, duty, or another ideal—makes demands upon *man,* challenges him, pronounces him a success or failure, and disregards the feminine world and women. The individual faces this stern maker alone, but can find him nowhere. Each person faces emptiness alone, with only intellect and will to rely on. Yet intellect can show only lifeless riddles at every step of understanding. Therefore the person exerts will in the attempt to prove self-worth and to assuage guiltridden anxiety. The world is to be *made* a better place in which to live. Unhappiness, injustice, poverty, illness, even death are to be eradicated as engineering faults in the mechanics of things rather than as intrinsic aspects of the human condition.

We find the culmination of this trend in the Puritan work ethic, regardless of its religious or secular level. This work ethic fathered industrialism in its capitalistic and socialistic forms. The ethics of both are based on the premise that we are economic beings only. Our welfare and life goals rest upon work achievement, upon restructuring the object world to suit our desires for more and more material comfort. Within the Puritan ethic, work and purposeful striving constituted a secular religion. It still does. Life is valued in terms of what is produced. An unproductive life is a wasted life. A capital investment is expected to show a profit. Work and profitable business take the place of spiritual calling. Economic prosperity is taken as proof of God's blessing. Material success is the reward and sign of moral superiority. ("No question but it (*riches*) should be the portion rather of the godly than of the wicked, were it good for them; for godliness hath the promise of this life as well as the life to come.")[6] Eventually the gross national product is held to be the guarantor of social and human well-being, regardless of needs and ecological devastation.

In the course of this schizophrenic development, theology was divorced from real life experience. It became increasingly empty, abstract and irrelevant. Hence, eventually, intellectuals felt that they had to divorce themselves from religion to maintain intellectual integrity. Or they had to compartmentalize life into a Sunday and a workday philosophy. Science became the new religion, for the religious archetype itself is indestructible. With the living spirit discredited, matter became the new god. Alone in an abstract, quantified, and meaningless universe, an orderly chaos, the individual is still helplessly driven. Only now, we are at the mercy of the newly arising divinities of matter. Failing to perceive their numinosity and without a *modus vivendi,* we fall, inevitably, victim to the sheer force of their energy. Unless we can come to recognize the living spirit in nature and matter we may perish.

CHAPTER 9

The Scapegoat

Agnus Dei qui tollis peccata mundi . . .

The fundamental difference (between the Pagan and the Christian religion) is that the Christian believes that God died once
and for all whereas the more primitive belief is that the god is per-
petually incarnate on earth and may therefore be put to death
over and over again.

MARGARET MURRAY, *The God of the Witches**

In the patriarchal world, propitiation of aggression through the sacrificial rite had to come under the rule of ethics. It had to be justified by
principles of right and wrong. We find the mythical expression of this
fact in the Jewish scapegoat ceremony. Its later elaboration is Christ's
offering. The principle common to both of them—guilt and atonement
for guilt—are still the basis of ethics and of justified aggression in the
modern world. Aggression is turned against the guilty self, or against
another person onto whom we project the guilt. The scapegoat motif
reinterprets the older matriarchal and mythical view in which the representative of life-manifest, the Dionysian god (whatever his name in
any particular culture), and his human substitute victim, die in order
to be reborn. This expresses renewal in The Great Round, the maternal
cycles of flowing and ebbing.

Instead, the *new Dionysus*, Christ the "true vine" (John 15:1), is now

* (New York: Doubleday, Anchor, 1960), p. 30.

the son of the Father. He dies in order to atone for those who have "sinned through ignorance" (Lev. 4:2).

In the "Lamb of God that carries the Sins of the World," the scapegoat motif is central to the Christian religion. The Imitatio Christi is enjoined upon the believer. Yet, an authentic and genuine ego transcendence that could accept, endure, and, hopefully, transform rather than act out and project evil was not yet possible in a culture that still had to foster ego growth and firmness. It could be accomplished by some dedicated few. For the many, it became an unattainable ideal at best, an empty presumption at worst. Unattainable consciously, the scapegoat archetype besets and haunts us unconsciously and obsessively.

Sin, guilt, and ethical condemnation of human nature are basic to later Christian theology and to medieval and postmedieval Western culture. As man is now declared a sinner before God, we all have become scapegoats. We are weighed down with guilt and self-rejection, not only for what we do, but also for what we are, for our "bad" desires and instinctual urges, for the foibles of human nature. We cannot accept the facts of our authentic natural being—our desires and instinctual needs, our aggressive, destructive, and power urges. But what we deny we cannot discipline either. Wanting to be seen and seeing ourselves as good only, we reason away our antisocial and selfish urges but are quick to see them in the other fellow. The accusing finger always points at someone else for not living up to the sentimental utopianism of how one should be and feel. When we do the pointing, we feel self-righteous. When blame is pointed at us, we are guilty and defensive. Guilt and defensiveness are the hallmarks of the scapegoat psychology of our culture. Every one of us is a victim.

Constantly on the defense against the scapegoating self-righteousness in ourselves and in our fellow beings, we are prevented from dealing realistically with the shadow aspects of our human reality. These include our natural greed, envy, power drives and selfishness. They are as intrinsic and given as love, caring, and cooperativeness. Hence we continually are forced to act out the very asocial tendencies which we so much decry and so eagerly deny.

The patriarchal propitiatory way of dealing with nonconforming instinct and aggression may be seen in the ancient Israelite scapegoat ceremony:

... he (Aaron) shall take ... two goats and set them before the Lord at the door of the tent of meeting. And Aaron shall cast lots upon the two goats, one lot for the Lord and the other lot for Azazel. And Aaron shall present the goat on which the lot fell for the Lord and offer it as a sin offering; but the goat on which the lot fell for Azazel shall be presented alive before the Lord to make atonement over it, that it may be sent away into the wilderness for Azazel. (LEV. 16:7—10)

A sin offering is a burnt offering (Lev. 4:29) which shall be accepted for him to make atonement for him (Lev. 1:4) who has sinned through ignorance. (Lev 4:2). A sin offering is an animal (usually a bull) substituted for the sinner; at this solemn occasion on the Day of Atonement for the whole community, it is two goats. A much older archaic symbol is evoked here. The goat symbolism at once takes us into the realm of the Dionysian divinities. Azazel indeed, is a Semitic shepherd goat-god. Originally the goat represented an embodiment of primal, creative energy, life in its indestructibility. It passed through the metamorphoses of dying and returning, of the God (Dionysus) "who dies but does not die."[1]

In this original form, the scapegoat ritual recognizes two equivalent principles, the Lord and Azazel. They are the new Apollinian God of thou shalt and the older Azazel, the Dionysian entity. The latter, at first Jehovah's opposite, later becomes his antagonist. Each is still given one share of the life energies. But the god of law requires his to be a "burnt offering." The Greek term for this is a *holocausted* offering. The one belonging to the god of wildness and spontaneity is to be presented before the Lord and atoned for, but sent away alive.

What may be the psychological significance of this rite for later generations? Formerly—in the matriarchal, magical phase—sacrifice was an acknowledgment of the premoral fact that whatever comes into being also has to cease, that death means at-onement and rebirth. Exaltedness called for sacrifice as a means of compensation. Now the life force, or at least one half of it, is to be offered up as atonement for sin, for transgressions which are deliberate but committed in ignorance, as part of living life as it is.

Sin cannot be avoided. It is part of being alive. Yet it deserves punishment. After having lost paradise, the primordial oneness in the maternal cosmos, humans must live in a state of sin. And "the wages of sin is death" (Rom. 6:23). Hence life is to be a sin offering, lived in penitence, humility, and fear of punishment. The tenor of the Yom Kippur prayers, no less than the *Dies Irae* of the Christian Requiem Mass expresses this mood: confession of sin, wittingly or unwittingly committed, dread of punishment and damnation, and prayer for forgiveness.

By making man morally responsible for his actions, instead of seeing him as passively subject to the changing tides of good and evil forces beyond his control, the basis is laid for a society of law and for further ego development. Self-control and mutual trust, personal relationships and personal commitment become possible. Respect for the rights of others, the basis of our present culture, would be unthinkable without this new value of justice embodied in law. Authorization comes from the God-King besides whom no other gods are permitted and to whom all available life energy is to be dedicated. Since no positive can exist without a negative, however, that one-sided stress on the law—though unavoidable and necessary—was bound eventually to bring forth negative results. The guilt offering became self-mortification and condemnation of self and others.

The sacrifice of the Jehovah goat represents the fact that desire, spontaneity, and the lusts of the flesh were to be mortified for the sake of the law. Nature is felt to be treacherous now, the source of sin and temptation. Only God, the God of the law, is deemed good. Therefore all evil must come from natural man, as the church fathers asserted. Moreover, all guidance for goodness must be sought for in God's word and law which is outside of man, and not in natural instincts or urges. Hence before the all-good and all-wise God "out there," every man is a priori a sinner. Religion becomes a grim and penitential business. Innocuousness, submission, and conformity become the prerequisites of piety. These are seen in the attitude of Abel (*habel* means vainness, emptiness).

If existence is ruled by goodness and justice, then suffering and destruction have no meaning except as punishment, mistake, or waste. They are not credited with any creative significance. Our common reaction to painful difficulty, consciously or unconsciously, is "what have I done to deserve this?" "How can I get out of this?" "How can there be a God if this is allowed to happen?" Rarely do we ask, "What new dimension of experiencing does this try to teach me?" "Wherein am I being challenged?" Suffering as proof of wrongdoing carries the additional burden of shame and guilt (see the Book of Job). Insult is thereby added to injury. Suffering means failure and must be denied and avoided at all costs; it is a threat to one's self respect and to the integrity of one's personality. Since pain leads to self-condemnation it cannot be accepted as part of normal life. In order to avoid pain, every desire must be satisfied; since that is not possible, feeling must be blocked off. One must live with a stiff upper lip, doing only what is right, and stifling all genuine feelings. In their place we gorge on things, sex, fun, drugs and alcohol, and last but not least, violence. In what has been called the "aspirin age," life is reduced to a hunt for the most readily available pleasures to drown out the underlying sense of unease, meaninglessness and guilt. For every dis-ease we seek a quick cure without stopping to ask what message, other than guilt or penance, it may offer if we only would or could listen.

We overlook the fact that difficulty, failure, and hurt are as indispensable to growth and the sharpening of awareness as success and joyous ecstasy. We do not value pain, but neither do we trust joy. It tastes a bit too much like the forbidden fruit of Dionysus and Azazel. It is sus-

pected deep down of bringing about the danger of divine retribution—
no matter in what nontheological terms this may be rationalized.

Ecstasis—the state of being outside of oneself—is increasingly suspect as a form of self-undoing. The Romans coined the word *superstitio*
as the Latin equivalent for the Greek *ecstasis*. They thus expressed
their distrust of the nonrational, uncontrolled state of mind, particularly in religious experience. Pleasure and lust, like sexuality and violence, are deemed outside the religious domain. They are at best secular,
at worst Azazel's or the devil's.

Thus Saint Chrysostom's sermon on a passage from Matthew:

This world is not a theater in which we can laugh; and we are not assembled together in order to burst into peals of laughter, but to weep for our sins. But some
of you still want to say: "I would prefer God to give me the chance to go on laugh-
ing and joking!" Is there anything more childish than thinking this way? It is not
God who gives us the chance to play but the Devil![2]

Yet there is still the other goat to be banished, yet allowed to live. It
is given over to Azazel. This *escape* goat was the original scapegoat.

This other power is still allowed for as an aspect of life, but it is to be
atoned for and sent away. Not all of the life force can be mortified and
devoted to the observance of the law. There are unacceptable urges
which cannot be rooted out. One must separate oneself from them and
send them away. Here we can see that the original myth had an instinctive wisdom which was lost in the later course of patriarchal development. For eventually it was the *holocausted*, not the living *escape* goat,
which came to represent the scapegoat. The difference between destroying and banishing is the difference between repression and discipline. Repression attempts to kill an impulse by rendering it unconscious. Discipline recognizes and acknowledges the impulse, but chooses
not to act it out. It is allowed to live, albeit banished to the desert, in its
own domain, until a time comes when it can be appropriately expressed
through Dionysian festivities, orgies, or other violence-discharging
rites. The banishment of the Azazel goat can be understood as disidentification. It implies a conscious separation of impulse and volition, an
ethically responsible choice of action in awareness of its consequences.
When angry, I may take notice of my anger, for instance, but choose
not to show it. Or I may give it expression under the particular circumstances. To repress my anger would mean to blame myself for getting
angry in the first place and to decide never to get angry again; to blot
out the emotion from existence. This corresponds to the practice of *holocausting* the Jehovah goat. Carried beyond a certain point, it leads to
psychopathology and the paranoic scapegoating complex which marks

our culture. The repressed impulse lives on in a distorted, unconscious fashion. It is projected upon our "guilty" fellow man and woman.[3]

For the still primitive ego of the European Christianized people, the differentiation between impulse and action was not yet possible. Disidentification and conscious choice require a minimal ego strength which the medieval European did not possess. Repressive destruction and self-mortification prevailed. The Jehovah goat became *the* scapegoat. Azazel/Dionysus was no longer the other god acceptable under some circumstances. He became unconditional evil, Satan. That which is deemed culturally unacceptable (and therefore evil) can no longer be in the domain of the Good God who originated the law and who created only what is good. Urges that were formerly, under ritualized conditions, hallowed to the God of lust and violence, are now unconditionally damned as belonging to Satan, the antigod who, paradoxically, also embodies a principle of nonexistence (*privatio boni*). Hence spontaneous instinctuality is treated as though nonexistent and relegated to a limbo of unconsciousness.

Thus repressed, Dionysian violence is subject to projection and infiltrates the conscious position. In the form of righteous zeal, repressed violence becomes fanatical do-gooding, intolerant destructiveness toward the unreformed and unreformable self, or toward the wrongdoing others. Based on the current dictates of the cultural superego, the ego arrogates to itself the authority of being able to decide what is good or bad for itself, for others, and for the world at large. Learning by trial and error is excluded. The result is the godlike inflation of modern people, the intolerance of creeds and convictions other than one's own. We are unwittingly and unconsciously fulfilling the serpent's predictions (Gen. 3:5) that "you will be like God, knowing good and evil" without heeding the subsequent warning that Goethe put into the mouth of Mephistopheles: "Just follow that old saying and my cousin, the snake / And you will surely tremble for your God's likeness' sake."[4]

The unruly side of one's instinct nature, the shadowy opposite to the bright, rational ideal of virtuous, godlike perfection, is not now being accepted as an ineradicable aspect of the wholeness of human existence. Nonacceptance of our *shadow* opens us to its incursions and deprives us of creative potential. Cain becomes the restless wanderer. The energy cannot be killed or transformed. Neither can it find a suitable place for acceptable expression. The individual who is beset with socially unsanctioned urges, ideas, or feelings is likely to live in a state of alienation from self, as well as from the community. Our superego standards became part of our moral conditioning as children. Through them we automatically identify with communal standards as bases of moral valuation, no matter how much we intellectually oppose them. Our wayward urges are as unacceptable to this introjected standard of our own as they are to the community at large. We are ashamed of ourselves, we label our feelings and urges bad or despicable, and we detest and hate ourselves for being what we are, rather than what we have been made to feel we should be. And moral devaluation automatically means repression. Whatever we despise or deprive of value is rejected and expelled from conscious adaptation. This tendency plays havoc with our human relationships.

In love and close personal relationships basic incompatibilities, negative feelings or the need for distance are inevitably bound to occur to varying degrees and at various times. In an atmosphere of scapegoating it is next to impossible to accept or confront them honestly. One would then have to admit that either one or one's partner is guilty. Hence the difficulty must be denied and repressed from consciousness; one cannot admit that along with the areas of attraction and compatibility, such problems are parts of the reality of the relationship. Yet whatever is denied and pushed out of consciousness does not disappear; it continues to smolder beneath the surface and makes for ever increasing unease and resentment. For a while this may remain unconscious. But eventually, as more is added, the charge increases and on the most unexpected and trifling occasions, the accumulated bitterness and resentment may explode into consciousness with mutual accusations and recriminations, much harder to contain now than if aired in the beginning.

This polarization into accuser and guilty culprit as a generalized psychological attitude, socially as well as individually, is the core of the modern Western scapegoat psychology. Our "enlightened" and agnostic world view still rests upon the ancient theological premise of the good creator whose created world of goodness must be purged of the alien, ungodly forces, the scapegoats, who misuse their God-given freedom, thereby diminishing the good and bringing about a semblance of evil. Everyone's self-respect and sense of personal integrity, then, rest upon approximating perfection in terms of the collective ideal, or at least striving for it. When difficulties occur—as they must—a natural defense reaction is to pin the blame upon others. A culprit has to be found; a scapegoat has to be put on the block, or at least banished. Righteousness as an ideal constantly necessitates the existence of a sinner to whom one can feel superior. This adds a genuinely paranoic coloring to the fundamental psychic dynamic that every unconscious tendency is of necessity always projected; it appears as though it belongs to the other person.

Per se this tendency to projection would be a neutral error of perception. As a collective phenomenon, the compulsive habit of perceiving one's own repressed violence as originating in the other person is a threat to personal relatedness, to religious, racial, and international peace, and to the survival of mankind.

The godlike conviction of rightness, of knowing good and evil, appears to justify ruthlessness against differing attitudes, ethics and ways of living. While giving perfunctory lip service to the remote possibility of receiving superpersonal guidance (as it is still preached by traditional religion) one takes for granted that human destiny depends exclusively on our personal human knowledge and upon the application of our personal beliefs. Every belief system is hell-bent upon making the world safe and happy according to its own God-given formula. The God-given system may be called theology, history, science, sociology, normality, dialectic materialism, blood-and-soil, racial superiority, or whatever.

Our culture glares with excesses of sanctimonious morality, dogmatic perfectionist imperatives, rigid legalisms, and hypocritical preaching about how life should be, rather than facing up to what it is. Conservative and radical alike, we condemn the unworthiness of our own nature as well as that of the wicked others who do not live up to our biased notions of reality. The extremes of Puritanism and Victorianism especially, still quite alive beneath the progressive surface of our modern life styles, have created a tyranny of *shoulds* in the face of which human reality falls short.

Right planning (e.g., genetic engineering) *should* eliminate social ills, poverty, physical illness, perhaps even death. Whenever and wherever those evils occur, they can be explained as human failures; misery is our own fault.

Paradoxically, or perhaps predictably, for those who understand the tendency to polar balancing, the opposite feeling persists as well. There is also a tendency to ego inflation for bearing burdens and pain. It testifies to the fact that one carries one's appropriate burden as the virtuous Jehovah goat, that one has efficiently banished the Azazel goat from one's life. The self-appointed sufferer then carries the halo of godlike responsibility and righteous mortification of self and others. "Suffering is deserved." "It serves you right." "It cannot be good unless it hurts."

Our own beliefs and convictions are considered to be validly religious or scientific. Those of other groups (cults) are held to be superstitious. Our customs justify violence. Those of other groups do not. Our wars are for liberation or for preservation of people's rights. The other side fights to enslave. God, justice, progress, and historical process are always upon one's own side. A relatively trivial example, yet poignant in

its absurdity, was reported in the *New York Times*.[5] The police raided a
voodoo sect and impounded lambs designed for sacrificial slaughter.
They were liberated by the police and summonses were issued for cruelty to animals. To slaughter an animal for the sake of a religious belief
is held to be absurd and cruel. A voodoo belief and ritual cannot be anything but a silly superstition, as we know. Yet to slaughter thousands of
lambs and other animals because we *believe* in eating meat as a staple
food is obviously not cruel to animals. Our righteous convictions completely justify that slaughter.

The ancient demon of evil is still unconsciously concretized and projected into the guilty ones. They are sacrificed or banished as scapegoats for the edification and purification of the righteous. Justice has
then been done, and all is right with the world again. Goodness shall
now reign until the next impasse comes as a quite unexpected surprise.

Thus, our virtue is constantly threatened by those who do not fit in
with our bias; by libertines, homosexuals, capitalists, socialists, *goyim*,
blacks, Jews, Yankees, "honkies," or whatever your favorite evil. This
threat calls for purifying crusades, wars of liberation, defense of sacred
values, and the imposition on others of the values we cannot live up to
because they are so unrealistic.

The most skillful and vociferous accuser becomes the great political
leader, a Duce or Führer. Nothing is as effective in coalescing the tribe
and arousing popular support as the pointing finger, blaming the wickedness of another for the despoiling of the wonderful, perfect world. Inevitably the charismatic accuser evokes the traditional Western image
of the zealous god and judge, mobilizing religious fanaticism, the most
dangerous tool of all.

In our small, private lives also, guilt and justification of guilt are
mainsprings of psychological and interpersonal functionings. They affect the ways we judge and accept others and ourselves. Since valuation
and acceptance depend upon conformity and obedience to standardized
communal values, any deviations from them, whether intended and
conscious or unconscious and unintended, draw blame, censure, ostracism, or punishment from ourselves or others.

From earliest childhood on, our lives are based, inevitably, upon
judgments of right and wrong, innocence and guilt. Our ideas of maturity presume a knowledge of the difference between what is collectively
deemed right and wrong. Indeed, our self-awareness rests upon having
undergone such a right-wrong discipline. It is impossible to raise children without such a standard, that is, without a measure of admonish-
ing and scolding. The experiencing of guilt cannot be avoided. Where
permissiveness has become excessive in the bringing up of children, a

confusion of values and damage to the personality tend to occur. Growth and value orientation without standards of right and wrong are as impossible as cultures without value systems.

Value systems, however, are the esthetic and social feeling expressions of the chief cultural myths. As the myth changes the right-wrong and esthetic systems change as well. Different cultures tend to hold different things, acts, and attitudes to be beautiful and good. Thus Tournier observes that among the poor in Italy, prostitutes do not feel guilty about their occupation.[6] They are not held in contempt by their community; but they do feel guilty if, for lack of customers, they do not earn enough to support their families.

Beauty and goodness are basic categories of human discrimination, hence of differentiation of consciousness. They are fundamental principles upon which every culture bases itself, even though their specific contents vary. Value judgments cannot be avoided. They express the collective feeling climate. However, it should be kept in mind that values are not final. They shift as the psychological climate shifts. Spontaneity, for example, at one time labeled wrong per se, is now in some circles an absolute good, to be practiced whatever the price.

The scapegoat-identified person—and this is now practically everyone in our culture—feels ashamed and guilty for what she or he *is*. Yet we cannot directly and willfully change what we are; we cannot alter the materials that went into building our individuality. We can only control what we do in respect to what we are. We can use or misuse our inborn drives or talents, but only when we accept them as unalterably existing can we properly use them. The scapegoat-identified person finds this hard or impossible to do. Shame and self-rejection make him or her a stranger and restless wanderer in an alien universe, a modern Cain. A sense of personal value can be procured only by identifying with collective rules and by seeking tribal or family approval, based upon usefulness, achievement, and acquisition. One's own reality, when recognized at all, must be hidden from society and even from one's dearest ones. For if they but knew, they would have to condemn. Indeed, that all too often is just what they do. To add insult to injury, one feels ashamed and guilty for not being happy and perfect. Isn't everybody else?

Even professed agnostics and atheists labor psychologically under the scapegoat standards of the Lord God, however they may be inclined to rationalize them. We all feel guilty, no matter what we do or fail to do. The sense of blameworthiness extends from the most important to the most trivial aspects of our lives.

In former times children were punished for not being well-behaved and good. Progressive education and modern psychology reject that standard, only to pronounce judgment if children do not now show spontaneity, personality, sociability, or maturity, whatever these may mean. Next to and perhaps even prior to, survival, everybody's greatest concern is to be right and to be justified; that is, guiltless. Even those we deem most immoral, even criminals, are concerned with justifying themselves before themselves, if not before others. We judge ourselves and others for making mistakes, for being too pushy or not being pushy and successful enough, for getting angry or for being indifferent, for being too slow or too fast, late or overpunctual. We feel guilty and judge others for their inadequacy as fathers, mothers, teachers, or as businessmen or professionals. We feel guilty for certain feelings or for their absence. We feel guilty for what has been pronounced abnormal behavior or perverse sexuality—namely, patterns at variance with current culturally approved norms of conduct. We feel guilty or fearful about expressing our natural impulses, be they hostility or affection, and then, again, about not expressing them. All this, very often, regardless of the real needs of the situation. X is approached by friend Y with a request. X feels this request to be an imposition. And yet before knowing it, X feels impelled to agree in order to avoid feeling guilty for denying a friend. Now X feels guilty for not having had the strength to say no. Again guilt arises, as resentment vents itself in projected form upon the friend—now seen as having forced X to comply. This causes X to react angrily rather than graciously, as one should. And finally, assuming that X perceives all this, X feels guilty about feeling guilty and about being unable to stop feeling guilty.

Even though we claim to have freed ourselves from the "God superstition," our cultural standards still feel like the "word of God." The archetype of the divine scapegoating judge, gone underground since the old God image no longer consciously commands universal respect, has turned into social and ethical fanaticism. It has inflated the modern ego with a sense of almighty personal power and a mission to improve the world according to its own image and rather limited lights. The payoff for this modern hubris of assuming unlimited freedom of will is an equally unlimited sense of guilt and of false responsibility. We are all scapegoats now. We blame ourselves for actions and omissions which are simply facts of our nature that we cannot help. In thus blinding ourselves to the real facts of our natures, since they conflict with our self-images of assumed goodness and righteousness, we tend to rationalize our worst actions and shun genuine responsibility. Caught up in the scapegoat complex and defensiveness, we all too easily fail to hear the voice of genuine conscience, which arises. "Not from the traditional moral code but from the unconscious foundations of the personality or individuality . . . and which possess that compelling authority, not unjustly characterized as the Voice of God."[7]

As long as we are cut off from those spontaneous feelings and intuitions, existence feels drab and pointless, a tooth-and-claw battle of all against all for survival of the fittest, a wasteland rather than a sacred cosmos.

We have painted here a picture of the social and psychological effects of our cultural scapegoat tradition which may seem one-sidedly bleak or exaggerated. Yet it is really but the underside of progress, enlightenment, and differentiation of consciousness. The phenomena described are familiar to the practicing psychotherapist as background problems encountered in practically every case of personal difficulty or psychopathology.

They are the price exacted for developing self-control, ego discipline, and intellect, and for building a culture based upon rational control, reason, and law. For perhaps forty centuries these stringent necessities were the sacrifices required for the sake of the next step of consciousness development. For many people they represent standards of value still in need of achievement.

We must not lose sight of the fact that the discipline of the superego is still essential for those individuals who have not yet achieved modern consciousness, namely full ego stability. For such people group conformism (and that includes the scapegoat pattern) helps to build personality through endurance, frustration, and self-discipline. A good measure of that is still needed by many in our time. This fact is testified to by the initiation ceremonies of all times and nations, including "hazing" rites of today. Yet by and large, the stern, patriarchal voice of the superego is becoming counterproductive in our day. This has evoked the call for avoidance of rejection in any form and loving acceptance, particularly of children by their parents. But we must beware of extremism and dogmatism even here. While it is true that rejection and disregard of need and self-entitlement, as well as demands made by parents, interfere with adequate ego development in growing children and become a threat to individuality, this was apparently not always the case. Perhaps even now it may be a matter of how much and when. We have again, with perfectionist absolutism and but little discrimination, set up extreme standards of parental and societal love, permissiveness, and nurturance. The children of other times, who had to endure harsher standards, also grew up to balanced maturity no less so than our own. It is, precisely, this apparent paradox which sheds light upon the nature of the transition in our time—"the return of the scapegoat."

In antiquity and the Middle Ages the effects of the prevalent guilt-bestowing scapegoat psychology must have been predominantly favorable to ego building. Children were reared under circumstances we now would consider harsh and even cruel. They lacked direct, loving contact with their parents. Often they were raised by preceptors and strangers. They were treated and expected to perform like little adults. Noble children were sent at an early age to become pages in another household and had to accept what amounted to adult responsibilities, hardships and punishments.

Yet, evidently, in the past, the absence of parental pampering and even of loving nurturance was counterbalanced by the protective sustainment by the patriarchal community of law and order and by the assurance of having one's God-given place in its hierarchical (hierarchy means rules of the sacred) order. The individual felt contained in an extended family group, a clan. In turn, this was a unit in what was felt to be a sacred social body protected by a king who ruled by God's grace. Personal identity was defined and sustained by trust in the God-given rule of the superego. The individual received his or her definition by virtue of, and through fulfilling an appointed role in the social structure.

Law, social order, and reason were stand-ins for the magical sense of security formerly provided by containment in the natural order. Abraham's bosom replaced the womb and breasts of the Mother Goddess. As the patriarchal epoch draws to its close, this group sustainment no longer operates.

The death-of-God feeling of our day means that superego guidance has largely lost its viability as a psychological dominant. Law and social order no longer feel God-given and sacred. Social structures are held to be ego determined, hence arbitrary agreements, subject to caprice and also to abrogation. The discipline of repression and mortification of self has ceased to sustain personality growth. Once our average present level of ego firmness has been reached, repression appears to be more of a threat than a help. Compliance with law and social order, far from assuring us of a place at Abraham's bosom, are felt increasingly to be matters of personal decision and agreement. Social conformity now stifles and is felt to be insufficient for personality growth. Moreover, concurrently, the former society with its extended family clans has been fragmented into ever more separate and unconnected units. We now have small families consisting of parents and children. Divorce of parents increasingly breaks up even these—separate interest groups, parties, and organizations abound. These are held together by personal interest and advantage only as long as coherence serves purely selfish needs. Industrialization bent upon saturation of material ego needs has thus completed the descent from the magical and mythological sacred cosmos to the wasteland of bureaucratic organization. Violence rampages freely in such a culture, since there are no archetypally effective channels to contain it. In this world of alienation and insecurity—our modern world—the average person plays at social games or plays at individuality, but lacks a real social or individual identity. The person is a lost wanderer in the desert; truly the *escape* goat. Escapism has become a prevalent attitude toward existence.

This development marks the psychological turning point of our time. Where is the escape goat, the desert wanderer, to turn to for help and sustenance but to its appointed master, Azazel-Dionysus, the force of life indestructible, *life as it is*, regardless of what it *should* be?

The awakening call of the new conscience in our time is the call to selfhood or individuation, as Jung has called it. It is the call to be what you are. But Dionysus-Azazel cannot come alone. He is the god of the Feminine, the consort of the Great Goddess. She was banished with him, and with him she also must return. The way of the phallus alone, without the personalizing and integrative attitude of the Feminine, its sense for wholeness and containment, would fail to satisfy our growth needs. Today's power threats, indeed, arise from the unrecognized and as yet unconscious epiphany of Dionysus when he inflates an unprepared ego sense, which then goes upon a rampage of *me, me, me*. Without the reassimilation of feminine values, Azazel would be truly Satan. We shall return to this important point in discussing the Grail myth and its perversion by Hitler.

But individual self-assurance and assertion, plus a sense of containment, place a new importance also upon the relationship between a child and its individual, personal family. Containment in an individual family now fulfills the function formerly assigned to clan and society. Children today need to learn discipline, but also to be lovingly accepted by family and especially by parents, for what they are, not just what they should be.

Children cannot be raised without learning discipline and responsibility. Value judgment and superego authority cannot be dispensed with. Yet if scapegoating or stigmatizing rigidity are to be avoided, those value judgments and rules will have to be offered as models, not prescriptions, to be observed in their spirit not followed by letter and rote. One may reject what one *did* or does, but not what one *is* or desires. Only thus can a genuine ego responsibility be taught. The inevitable failure to be equal to the new demands is typical for a period of transition. In child rearing, the old psychological habit of exercising either repressive discipline or undiscriminating permissiveness continues. Rather, what is needed is the loving affirmation of individual needs and talents. The imbalanced swinging between repression and permission partly accounts for the current psychological epidemic of what is being called narcissism. This term is really a misnomer. The state we speak of is not one of too much but rather of too little self-love. Narcissism is the psychology or psychopathology of the outsider, of Dionysus-Azazel, still a wanderer in the desert. The scapegoat is seeking to return and to be accepted. His asocial and at times even antisocial self-preoccupation is a beginning attempt, vain and inadequate as yet, to turn inward in order to discover his authentic self.

Today, the scapegoat state is universal. In our culture every person has to carry a burden of guilt and of alienation. The attending sense of unease, disease, and insecurity can be seen as the ultimate consequence of an intended development of personal autonomy. The independent *I* is no longer embraced in the all-containing maternal. This is the expulsion from paradise. It first marks that stage of evolution of consciousness which makes us know good and evil. It makes us all into lonely wanderers in a wasteland, feeling cut off from a transpersonal divine origin and forever subject to "sin." That is the price of ego development in its first patriarchal phase. With it goes the compensatory reaction, the power drive or power complex. The inferiority complex, as first described by Adler, is indeed a reaction to a sense of bodily inferiority, to the inadequacy of the embodied *I*. The source of the complex is not so much a personal defect, as Adler assumed. Rather it is a universal phenomenon. Feeling isolated in a threatening cosmos and collectivity, in which there is no sense of loving commonality, filled with a neediness for love and support which can never fully and adequately be satisfied, even under the most favorable conditions, an individual instinctively reacts with anxiety and insecurity. The result is the inferiority complex. The compensation for this is the power drive, the attempt of the *I* to shore up its position by increasing its sense of importance and by attempting to build protective fortifications and defense measures. In our time this drive has reached a peak. Dionysus's revenge for his repression is to set man against man, women, and the world, driven by guilt and an unslakable thirst for power. We have convinced ourselves that our consciousness and reasoning make us superior to everything else on the planet. We claim to be the self-appointed lords of our universe, purporting to manage, control, and improve the world and the nature we live in through our superior resources. We try, every one of us, to dominate and manipulate our life and circumstances by our free will. Likewise, we seek to control and manipulate the behavior of other people in order to secure our needs and shore up our insecurity. While a certain measure of all of that again seems to be part of the intended evolution, it also threatens us with further personal isolation, mutual conflict, global warfare, and ecological disaster. We can no longer afford to treat our world and fellow human beings as passive objects of exploitation.

As Dionysus-Azazel returns from his *e-scape* goat state, he endeavors to bring with him and reestablish the feminine space alongside the masculine order. He seeks to integrate discipline, aggression, and bravery with natural rhythm, affirmation of personal values, play, and a sense of the unfathomable mystery of nature and existence.

As Dionysus returns, the repression of the Feminine can no longer continue.

CHAPTER 10

The Feminine and Its Repression: (Femininity and Masculinity)

Heaven is mine, the earth is mine
I am warrior am I
Is there a god who can vie with me?

The gods are sparrows—I am a falcon
The gods trundle along.
I am a splendid wild cow.
                              Song of Inanna*

Blessed art Thou, Lord our God, King of the Universe, Who made me not a woman.
                    Morning blessing to be recited by men*

Blessed art Thou, Lord our God, King of the Universe who has made me according to Thy will.
                  Morning blessing to be recited by women*

Woman is the confusion of man, an insatiable beast, a continuous anxiety, an incessant warfire, a daily ruin, a house of tempest, a hindrance to devotion.
          The Speculum of Vincent De Beauvoir, 13th Century

The devaluation of femininity is an intrinsic feature of the dominant culture during the epoch of patriarchal ego development. Women have been regarded as second-rate human beings at best, and often as some-

---

* S.N. Kramer, ed., *From the Poetry of Sumer* (Berkeley: University of California Press, 1979), p. 97. Morning blessings from *The Siddur: Traditional Prayer Book for Sabbath and Festivals.* Trans. D. de Sola Pool. Authorized by the Rabbinical Council of America. New York, 1960, p. 108.

thing less than human. Owing to its religious nature, this devaluation has characterized woman's own self-image as strongly as it has men's views of her. And women have been as guilty of repressing their own feminine nature as men have been of repressing the feminine component of their psyches. To see the problem only in sociological terms would miss the core of the issue.

Indeed, none of the sociological explanations can really satisfy when looked at closely. The inferior status of women has been explained by the transition from plant to animal oriented societies. But even in later social structures such as Rome and Greece that relied heavily upon agriculture, women's status was subordinate; indeed, if possible, even more so than in earlier more primitive societies. The greater reliance on warfare cannot satisfy either, for among Germanic and early Celtic tribes women fought alongside men. The stories about Valkyries and Amazons testify to this fact. Moreover (quite the opposite of what one would expect) many of the early prehistoric divinities of warfare were female: Sekhmet in Egypt, Inanna in Sumer, Anath in Uruk, the Morrigan in Ireland, Bellona in Rome, to name but a few.

Women were never a minority group to be discriminated against by virtue of that status. At all times and everywhere, women were the majority. This was simply due to women's greater biological strength and the reduction of the male population through warfare. If sheer physical strength, regardless of mental abilities were the decisive factor, lions and tigers would easily have gained ascendancy over humans. As to mental capacities, women are equal, and in the ability to manage interpersonal relationships are, if anything, even superior to men. Industrialization is not an explanation. Women's inferior status preceded industrialization by about 6,000 years. When the need and opportunity arose, such as during the two world wars, women performed as well as and better than men at the workbench and the assembly line.

The classicist Jane Harrison came closer to an explanation. At the same time, because of her own sociological and unconsciously androlatric bias, she failed to understand fully her own point.

The shift (from matriarchy to patriarchy) is a necessary stage in a real advance. Matriarchy gave women a *false, because magical* [italics mine] prestige. With patriarchy came inevitably the facing of a real fact of the greater natural weakness of woman. Man, the stronger, when he outgrew his belief in the magical potency of women proceeded by a pardonable practical logic to despise and enslave her as the weaker.[1]

The "natural weakness of woman" we now know to be a fiction. It is not true biologically or psychologically. Like the "falseness" of the magical prestige, it has been a bias of the androlatric view. Now it is gradually being dispelled. Yet the transition from the magical to the mental world view necessitated both the fiction of the spuriousness of the magical dimension and the greater value given to sheer muscular strength. This fiction underlies the androlatric value system of the patriarchy. It caused both sexes to devalue, not so much women, *per se,* but the feminine, and the entire magico-mythological dimension. Since women are by and large more feminine than men, they were declared inferior by mutual consent.

Maleness and femaleness are archetypal forces. They constitute different ways of relating to life, to the world, and to the opposite sex. The repression of femininity, therefore, affects mankind's relation to the cosmos no less than the relation of individual men and women to each other. Sociological solutions serve some purpose, but lack a basic understanding of feminine psychology. They do not even ask the very question which in the medieval myth saves Arthur's life and thus restores the realm. Centuries later, it reappears in Sigmund Freud's puzzled statement: "The great question that has never been answered and which I have not been able to answer, despite my thirty years of research is, What does a woman want?"[2]

Freud's puzzlement is the more significant in view of the fact that the old myth has already answered it. We shall come back to this in the chapter on the Grail myth. Furthermore, the father of psychoanalysis derived his basic insights from predominantly feminine patient material. Despite that, he came to the conclusion that woman's highest achievement might be perceived as functioning as "ministering angel to the needs and comforts of man."[3]

To achieve the exalted status of her "whose price is far above rubies," the "virtuous woman" had to confine her activities, and even her dreams, to the sphere of motherhood, family life, child rearing, or perhaps, if circumstances forced her to enter the world, to a career as an elementary school teacher. In the rearing of children, competitive self-assertion and aggression were fostered in boys but prohibited to girls. Limited to mostly domestic routine, any concern with personal authority and satisfaction of their own needs was repressed in girls even more than in boys. I remember a middle-aged woman who continued to have severe difficulties in personal and career situations, owing to her inability to stand up for her convictions. Eventually, in the course of psychological work, a rather painful early childhood memory was elicited. (Early childhood memories are diagnostically important because the very fact of something's being remembered from a period of which most is forgotten makes it a sign post that points to a traumatic situation or complex.) She remembered how at age three or four she had gotten into a fight with her little brother about who was to sit in the front seat of the family car. In the ensuing push and shove she had punched him and thereupon was severely reprimanded by mother for behaving in such an "ungirlish" fashion. Girls, she was sternly told, must always be sweet and yielding and never compete or contest with boys and, indeed, *never, never* show any overt aggressiveness whatsoever. Women had to learn to blunt their urges within the narrow culturally acceptable ways that made them more often than not excessively vulnerable to shame and self-loathing. At a gynecological congress at the beginning of the century the question was seriously debated as to whether women do or do not have any sexual feelings. And indeed the overwhelming consensus of the learned pundits was that the *good* woman does not have any sexual feelings. Psychologically at least, women had to be bland and innocuous in order to be good.

Yet, where Freud expresses confusion, earlier masculine reactions to the problem are far less generous. St. Augustine declared that women have no souls. So medieval scholars debated whether they might not first have to be changed into men by God in order to qualify on the day of resurrection. Most revealing is the "witches' hammer," the *Malleus Maleficarum*. Compiled by two Dominican friars, this book was explicitly authorized by Pope Innocent VIII as *the* judiciary standard, binding upon judges and princes, for adjudication of witches. Between 1486 and 1669 it reached thirty editions from the leading German, French, and Italian presses. It was implicitly accepted not only by Catholic but also by Protestant legislatures. Hence it was the standard of judgment from the fifteenth to the seventeenth century.

According to *Malleus,* women are moved predominantly by intensity of affect and emotion. Their extremes of love or hate are generated by the "lust of the flesh," by possessiveness and jealousy. "More carnal than the man," they are, in fact, sexually insatiable, vain, pleasure-seeking liars and seducers, bent on deceiving in order to achieve their own ends. They are mentally and intellectually inferior, deficient and "feeble in mind and body"; of poor memory, "intellectually like children," over-credulous, superstitious, over-impressionable and suggestible, of "slippery tongue," undisciplined; indeed, altogether like an "imperfect animal."

Since the first corruption of sin by which man became the slave of the devil came to us through the act of generation, therefore greater power is allowed by God to the devil in this act than in others. . . . For though the devil tempted Eve to sin, yet Eve seduced Adam. And the sin of Eve would not have brought death to our soul and body unless this sin had afterwards passed onto Adam, to which he was tempted by Eve, not by the devil. Therefore she is more bitter than death. More bitter than death again because death is natural and destroys only the body;

but the sin which arose from woman destroys the soul by depriving it of grace, and delivers the body up to judgment for its sins.

It is worth noting that for the *Malleus* sin is practically identical with carnality, literally "fleshliness," especially sexual pleasure. This "call of the flesh" is taken to be "embodied" in women and is the core of all evil.[4]

But it is not only Western cultures that have dreaded and rejected the feminine. The law of Manu, which forms the basis of Hindu culture, states that "woman by her nature is always trying to tempt and seduce man . . . The cause of dishonor is woman, the cause of enmity is woman, the cause of mundane existence is woman—therefore woman must be avoided."[5] Conversely, "no matter how wicked, degenerate or devoid of all good qualities a man may be, a good wife must also revere him like a God."[6]

The religious trends which characterized the era of patriarchal ego development were based on the devaluation of natural life and matter, of mundane existence, and of the body. Concrete reality, as we encounter it, was increasingly considered devoid of the spirit and opposed to it. The inwardness of being in the world, which is the realm of the Feminine, was rejected.

Misogyny and androlatry, then, are indissolubly intertwined with the religious convictions and beliefs that were held during the last two to four thousand years or more. These religious ideas have become accepted standards. By sheer suggestive power and cultural consent they have imposed themselves even upon those who are made to carry the projections of purported inferiority, women themselves. Degradation leads to self-rejection and to identification with the image of inferiority and self-hate. The image of the mentally inferior but deceptive and wily serpent, in need of atonement by virtuous containment and sterile self-effacement, has been bought by women as much as by men in our past cultures. Had this not been so, that image could never have maintained itself as a lasting cultural standard.

The devaluation of the Feminine, then, has its roots in more basic dynamics of the psyche than passing fashions or prejudices of the mind. Regrettable and even destructive as this attitude may have been, nevertheless it was apparently necessary for the development of ego consciousness itself.

In the evolution of religions, it is a common and recurring fact that the gods of one religious phase become the devils of the next. Androlatry and misogyny reflect the masculine overthrow of an older order in which the divine was felt to be manifest in feminine forms and values. Divinity then was conceived in the images of the Great Goddess—virgin, mother, harlot, and destroyer—whose reign extended over heaven, earth, and the underworld. The Old Testament abounds with warnings and misgiving about the recurring tendency towards the worship of Astoreth and Baal. This Mother Goddess of the Canaanites and her consort repeatedly penetrated (and probably even were indigenous to) Hebrew religion.[7]

The same concern is expressed in the Decalogue's insistence, already referred to, that "thou shalt have no other gods beside me," and probably in the warning against "graven images." The Golden Calf, object of the wrath of Moses, was but another representation of Isis-Hathor, the Egyptian Great Goddess. The apocryphal saying ascribed to Jesus, "I have come to destroy the works of the female,"[8] as well as the condemnation of the "great whore of Babylon," the "great beast" in the Revelation of John, reflect similar sentiment.

Why, we may ask, was the feminine felt to be so antithetical to the developing new consciousness that it had to be judged as evil incarnate? Before attempting to answer this question we ought to pause and clarify what is really meant by the terms feminine and masculine in the symbolic archetypal sense. Is there really a basic, that is, not merely culturally and socially induced, difference between women and men? How do the symbolic genders relate to actual men and women? Most assuredly cultural and environmental value systems do have a profound effect upon self-image and self-evaluation of women and men. The understanding of the nature and meaning of these cultural influences is the point and purpose of this chapter. However, brain research has produced increasing evidence during the last few years that fundamental differences in the functioning of brain and mind really do exist as a priori primary sex characteristics. They are not just environmentally induced.

For example, the *Brain/Mind Bulletin* of June 2, 1980, reported on animal experiments, the findings of which we may assume to parallel human patterns:

In a series of recent experiments, neuroanatomists at the University of California have demonstrated that the left and right hemispheres of the rat brain are not symmetrical. These asymmetries are different for males than for females. Removal of the ovaries at birth causes female brains to develop the more exaggerated left-hemisphere growth typical of males.

By young adulthood, females who had had their ovaries removed at birth showed the male pattern—greater left-right differences than those seen in normal females.

The question that still remains is why the removal of the ovary (in newborns) causes the cerebral cortex to increase in dimension.

Judging from a variety of recent experiments, sex differences in the brain may be initiated and maintained by sex hormones from birth. The hormones are also essential for the development of brain regions controlling adult sexual behavior.

Moreover, the very existence of culturally insisted-upon differences between male and female is psychologically significant. Prevalent as the distinction is in all cultures and at all times, it expresses the fact that for the collective psyche the polarity between maleness and femaleness does exist as an a priori datum. For culture is not an arbitrary invention but a precipitate of archetypal dynamics, of the "just so"-ness of psychic experiencing. In saying this we simply express a state of affairs which happens to exist, like it or not. We do not excuse or explain away the devaluation of the feminine, or discrimination or depredations against women. Rather we attempt to understand the dynamics of this attitude in order to be better able to deal with it.

This brings us to another point: the ready confusion between sexual and archetypal gender. Failure to make this distinction leads us to overlook the psychological in favor of the sociological factor. It makes us see discrimination against *women*, primarily, where we must deal with a repression of femininity in women *and* men.

For too long we have failed to notice or give value to the evidence that each sex carries within itself the qualities of its opposite. Jung was the first in the West to point out this polar unity, namely that maleness contains recessive feminine traits, psychologically as well as biologically, and femaleness contains masculine traits.

Masculinity and femininity as a priori archetypal traits are to be differentiated, then, from individual male and female persons. Thus we can avoid the confusion inherent when we fail to distinguish personal and psychological problems from their religio-cultural determinants.

The worship of a divinity as male or female expresses an existential value system and a mode of perception in which one archetypal gender prevails over the other in psychological relevance, being as convincing and determinative for women as it is for men. In gynolatric cultures, masculine characteristics are given secondary value by both men and women. In androlatric milieus, women look up to masculine traits no less than do men. Male and female characteristics, hormones, organs, archetypal tendencies, complexes, and personality traits are intrinsic to both sexes. Whether a given person is a man or woman, we now know to be decided by the relative predominance of one gender over the recessive other. The predominant one imprints itself upon consciousness, basic psychological structure and bodily sex characteristics. The recessive traits operate unconsciously as potentialities rather than actualities. According to the terminology originally introduced by

Jung, the term *animus* expresses male traits in women, and *anima*, female traits in men. Owing to the relative predominance of one gender over the other, men and women differ psychologically no less than biologically. However, this difference is relative and moves along a flowing spectrum of transition and merger. It is not absolute.

But why speak of masculine and feminine at all if we merely mean traits shared to varying degrees by males and females? This seems to make for very confusing terminology. At the risk of being repetitious we must stress again that the male-female differentiation is deeply ingrained a priori; it is an archetypally predetermined perception, patterned in the unconscious psyche. Opposition and complementariness of male and female belong among the most basic representations of the experience of dualism. They underlie the polarities of solar and lunar, light and dark, active and passive, spirit and matter, energy and substance, initiative and receptiveness, heaven and earth. In everyday language the imagery of male and female describes the penetrating bolt and the enclosing and holding nut. Among the oldest symbolic representations of cosmic polarities is a phallic shape standing in a containing vessel, representative of the female genital: spear or sword and Grail in the West, *lingam* and *yoni* in the East, refer to the archetypally male and female principles. These depict the patterns or themes of which the manifest bodily organs are only specific physiological expressions. Ancient Chinese philosophy spoke of Yang and Yin as cosmic principles. All existence expressed their interplay in varying proportions.

By and large we have come to think of the masculine Yang as creative and the feminine Yin as receptive. This appears too narrow to me. Perhaps a more adequate rendering might be the idea of exteriorization, diversification, penetration and external action for Yang and inherence, unification, incorporation, activity and existence for Yin.

R. Ornstein sees an analogy between the functions of the right and left brain hemispheres and the Yin-Yang dynamic. He presents a tabulation "for purposes of suggestion and clarification in an intuitive sort of way, not as final categorical statement. . . ." Here is some of it[9]:

Yang—Left Hemisphere	*Yin—Right Hemisphere*
Day	Night
Time, History	Eternity, Timelessness
Intellectual	Sensuous
Explicit	Tacit
Analytic	Gestalt
Lineal	Nonlineal
Sequential	Simultaneous

Focal	Diffuse
Intellectual	Intuitive
Causal	Synchronicity
Argument	Experience

In Western tradition, the archetypal Yang principle has been represented under the mythological, alchemical, and astrological symbolism of the Sun, Mars and Saturn; the archetypal Yin by the moon and Venus. The solar stands for spirit, logos, creativity, and self-conscious awareness; the striving for consciousness and separateness, purposefulness and authority. Mars, the Roman god of war (and his Greek counterpart Ares), embodies initiating, active energy, courage, determination, desirousness, and the impulse toward both work and aggression, including brutality, recklessness, and destructive hostility and violence. Less commonly appreciated is the fact that in astrological symbolism Mars stands also for Eros, sexual attraction and desire. The Saturnine factor is disciplined and principled, bent upon separation and systematic order, repressive, tyrannical, and bullying; conducive to egotism and ruthless use of power in its less pleasant manifestations.

On the Yin side, the moon embodies actualization. In opposition to the sun's potentiality, it receives the imprint of the solar *logos,* the *noumenon,* bringing it to manifestation as phenomenon. Perhaps one of the oldest symbols of the senses and of sensuality, of soul and body, the moon is matrix for fantasy and dreams. It is container and holder of the life energies, the world of the senses as they relate to physical reality. The moon represents the collective both in terms of outer world and inner consciousness. It implies an approach to life that focuses not on planned striving, but rather on playfulness and imagination, seeing the world of fantasy and reality as but opposite sides of the same coin. This emphasis upon sensuality and bodily experiencing over abstract thinking and rationalism permits greater openness to the intangible, as well as a greater susceptibility to the realms of the magical, mystical, mediumistic and psychic. Positively this can lead to a broadening of awareness of new realms. Negatively, such susceptibility may carry with it the danger of regression to atavistic primitiveness; to mass and mob psychology, *isms* and fads. When carried beyond an individual's capacity to integrate, borderline states, addiction, and/or the loss of a viable connection with reality may be the result.

To the feminine, or Yin element, are ascribed in addition those qualities associated with Venus or Aphrodite: joy, pleasure, artistic expression, and the appreciation of beauty and harmony. On the negative side we find vanity, dawdling, and sheer hedonism.

However, Yin and Yang stand for cosmic rather than specifically

psychological principles. It does not seem obvious at all why a trend toward ego development should have to be inimical to the Yin principle.
A further excursion into and reassessment of the mytho-psychological
aspects of the respective archetypes seems called for.

During the early thirties, Jung attempted what he then considered a
preliminary characterization of the female and male predispositions.
He termed Eros the tendency to relatedness, and deemed it fundamentally expressive of the Feminine. The male attitude was to be typified
by *logos,* spirit, creative and ordering intelligence, and meaning. Unfor-
tunately, this first preliminary attempt has been treated in Jungian literature as though it were the final word for the intervening fifty years.
In the light of women's increasing awareness of themselves, more and
more evidence has been accumulating that the Eros-*Logos* concept is inadequate for covering the wide range of feminine and masculine dynamics. Moreover, it is also terminologically and psychologically inappropriate.

For one thing, mythologically, Eros is a male phallic deity. An aggressive hunter, he represents the urge to connect, to touch and to possess. He motivates the human quest for humanity, for the beautiful, the
good, and the divine. He expresses outgoing aggressive libido, striving
desirousness, and the insistent urge to join and to penetrate. As patriarchal cosmogonic Eros, the first divinity emerging from the world egg,
he is kin to a primordial light or *logos* coming from the womb of nonbeing. He is a son of the Great Mother. He imposes his own order of
connection and desire upon what, prior to him, was primordial dark
void. The birth of Eros is akin in this mythological representation to
the biblical "Let there be light." In the gospel of St. John this same
light is from the *logos* and is life and love.[10] An identical vision is expressed in the medieval invocation of Hrabanus Maurus: *"Veni creator
spiritus"* ("Creator spirit come"). This calls upon the Holy Spirit as a
male creative entity to "bring light to the senses and love to the heart"
(*accende lumen sensibus, infunde amorem cordibus*). *Amor* is the
Latin equivalent for the Greek *Eros.* Both terms are of male gender
grammatically.

Language, in its phonetic and etymological context, often expresses
the hidden wisdom of the unconscious. Thus, we are struck by the closeness of *Eros, Eris* (the goddess of strife and dissent) and *Ares* (the
Greek god of war); love, dissent, and strife. The similarity is as phonetic as it is psychological and mythological.[11] Indeed, as the Roman
Mars, Ares shows his close relation to Eros. *Mars gradivus* represents
the life and love-engendering genius of spring. Astrologically, Mars expresses aggressive activity as well as erotic desire and sexuality. His
symbol is an erect phallus (♂).

Eros thus represents an aspect of the archetypal Yang; outgoing, aggressive maleness. The ruthless soldier, striving hero, and often ruthlessly desirous lover are expressive of the Eros-Ares dichotomy. By no stretch of the imagination can they be seen as *logos* figures.

In myth, Eros is the son, Ares the lover, of Aphrodite. Together they are the Twin Suitors, Dionysian son-lovers of the Great Goddess, Eros and Thanatos, the life-giving and life-destroying aspects.

Their Apollinian complement, *logos* aiming at material manifestation, is Saturn-Jehovah, the fourth aspect of masculinity. He concretizes, creates, and preserves by establishing limits, order, and law. He is maker and ruler, the jealous, sick, or wounded king or crippled craftsman; ever striving for perfection, he suffers from and tends to deny the flaws of his creations and of existence as it is. Creativity begets woundedness or rests on woundedness.

It may be argued that, no matter how much we split hairs about proper terminology, and regardless of which mythological name we call it, the Yang-Yin polarity is still one of spirit and order versus relatedness. This argument overlooks the fact that words *are* literally *logos*. Words, particularly those hallowed by age-old tradition and the power of mythological fantasy, are pregnant with and generate meaning. Improperly applied they have the power to confuse.

Relationship and relatedness, no matter by what name we call them, are by no means exclusive qualities of the Feminine, any more than spirit is an exclusively male property. Relationship is a principle of order—in space or time. Order pertains to the masculine and the feminine principles, though in differing ways. In turn, relatedness, as a psychological concept, has come to mean *awareness* of relationship. This includes attraction and connection as much as repulsion, rejection, and aggression; mutuality as much as separateness; inner feelings and thoughts as much as outer interaction; rhythmic and lawful order as much as play or even chaotic confusion; discovery of meaning as much as acceptance of meaninglessness.

Relatedness is not to be confused with the longing for personal involvement and empathic identification which, indeed, is a quality typical of the feminine consciousness. Such empathic involvement, however, does not necessarily constitute relatedness. Without a corresponding awareness of the separate identity of each partner, it may be no more than symbiotic identification or just sentimental mush. Relatedness involves a willingness and ability to perceive and appreciate the other just as she or he is, while maintaining one's own genuine position. Conflict is an aspect of relatedness as much as rapport and communication. It calls for acknowledgment of the other's displeasing and unacceptable as well as agreeable characteristics. The particular relationship needs to be seen in its separating no less than its sharing aspect.

Relatedness, then, is a conscious achievement to be worked for as an aspect of individuation by both sexes. Neither relationship nor relatedness characterize the feminine any more than the masculine consciousness. They are involved in the feminine urges to personalization and involvement as much as the masculine drives for distance, control, possession, competition, and meaning.

Moreover, in defining the Feminine primarily in terms of relatedness, we overlook its depth dimension. This is active, transformative, and devoid of any relatedness concern. To equate Yin simply with relationship reduces the feminine to a relatively passive re-active and responding complex, never an initiating one. I believe that such has been the intent of the patriarchal cultural bias. However, prior to working consciously on her relationship problems, the average woman is no more genuinely related than the male who, driven by his erotic libido, is *in love.* By virtue of the cultural training which requires her to be attentive, sensitive, and receptive, she may present an appearance of relatedness, yet this is but a gesture of her persona, her social mask. Other tendencies may enhance the misleading impression of relatedness as an a priori function of the Feminine: women may show emotion, perceive and react in concrete and personal terms rather than abstractly and impersonally as men tend to. Women may nourish, mother, and protect.

Unless consciously worked through, these very tendencies merely serve to make a woman cloying, self-centered, possessive, and egotistically unrelated, though in a personal fashion. The corresponding Eros-Ares driven male is self-willed, determined to conquer and to have what he wants. He is inconsiderate of personal values, egotistically unrelated in an impersonal way.

The lover who is motivated only by his need to conquer and to satisfy erotic appetites fails to *see* and to accord individuality and human dignity to the object of his desires. In turn, the over-mothering or over-protective female likewise acts primarily for the satisfaction of her own needs, regardless of those of her partner. She is experienced by the man as suffocating and devouring. His instinctual, most often unconscious, response is to love her and leave her, to take flight after he gets what he wants and to discount her as a person. Indeed she acts out of unconscious possessiveness and the need to express her urge to give and to contain, regardless of whether what she gives is wanted or can be assimilated by the other.

In both cases, the lack of appreciation of the other as a separate and different person, with different needs, prevents genuine relatedness.

Unless she is in touch with her own disconnected Yin tendencies, it is difficult for a woman to be conscious of her center, her source of instinctual wisdom. Genuine relatedness requires connecting with that source.

If not Eros then, what are the archetypal forms of expression of the Yin in both sexes? We can find excellent descriptions of feminine consciousness in E. Neumann's *Moon and Matriarchal Consciousness*[12] and S. Perera's *Descent to the Goddess*.[13] Both renderings deserve a full reading in their original versions. I shall hence limit myself to a short summary, a masculine abstraction. In Neumann's description, feminine consciousness is seen as intuitional and impulse-dependent, unsystematic and given to fantasizing, dreaming and wishing. In spiritual or creative activity it is inspired rather than analytic. It is receptive toward what is felt, the impulse, or even invasion, by the spirit. That sense is stronger than the sense of self as originator. Insights have to mature, to be assimilated into a total organic feeling experience if they are to be real. The feminine experiencing is thus given over to, or interconnected with, the processes of growth and decay, the natural cycles of living, ripening and dying, and the rhythms and periods of nature, spirit and time. Thus, we designate it moon-attuned. Feminine consciousness experiences time as quality, not as an abstract measure of action. As a result, it is attuned to the mood, meaning, and favorable or unfavorable quality of the given moment. It is able—nay compelled—to wait more patiently than the male for the right moment in which an event or impulse may be given birth.

The stress in the Yin-anima world is upon expectant perception and openness to the *call*, which is to be responded to rather than preempted by ego-will oriented action. This outlook may be called meditative and oriented toward the existential and experiential mystery. It is less impressed by the analytic and by ready intellectual verbalization. Consequently the archetypal feminine attitude is more empathy- and involvement-oriented than the more abstract masculine attitude. It is part of an extended natural field, where all elements are interwoven in circular rather than linear fashion.

Yet paradoxically the Feminine, for this very reason also, shares in the very impersonalness and playfulness of nature in its more ready acceptance of suffering, of cruel necessities, of severance and destruction and the necessity to inflict them. Natural to the Feminine, too, is a fundamental relation to sexuality as to a lustful, changeable ephemeral play that can be devoid of feeling for a particular individual or personal relatedness.

Written by a woman, Perera's study of Inanna's descent into the underworld gives us a personally authentic, in-depth view of that night

side of the Feminine that is so frightening that it had to be repressed by
the patriarchy. Even in her lighter, day aspect as queen of heaven, life,
and fertility, Inanna's symbolism is not an expression of static reliable
security but "like the radiant erratic morning and evening star . . .
awakening life and setting it to rest . . . she represents energies that
cannot be contained or made certain and secure." She represents a consciousness of transition and borders . . . creativity and change and all
the joys and doubts that go with a human consciousness that is flexible,
playful and never certain for long. As a judge . . . to decree fate" she
presides over the ups and downs of destiny, which is both unpredictable
and inexorable and necessitates acceptance of life as an ever changing
process.

According to the Sumerian poem, Inanna is also a lion-goddess of
war and a dragon slayer, "the heart of the battle," "the arm of war-
riors," "all-devouring in power and angry heart . . . and awesome face,"
ambitious, regal, and powerful. Equally passionately she is goddess of
sexual love. She extols the desires and delights of lovemaking, invites
her lover, her "honey man" to her "holy lap to savor her life-giving
caresses and sweetness of sex with her." "She craves and takes, denies
and destroys and then grieves and composes songs of grief. She does not
. . . arouse desire from within but claims her need assertively and cele-
brates her body in song. *Her receptivity is active.*" She is goddess of
courtesans, called harlot, bridesmaid, and *hierodule* ("ritual prostitute") of the gods, loving, jealous, grieving, joyful, timid, exhibitionis-
tic, thieving, passionate, ambitious, and generous. But she is also virgin, eternally youthful, dynamic, fierce and independent; embodying
the playful, self-willed, never-domesticated aspect of the feminine.

If the embodiment of this fierce and untamable range of affects was
bad enough, the dark, underworld face of Ereshkigal, her *other side*, appears even more frightening to the emerging potential ego of both sexes.
Ereshkigal rules over everything that seems opposed to life: death,
nonbeing, annihilation, emptiness. "She is the root of all, where energy
is inert and consciousness coiled asleep. She is the place where potential
life lies motionless—but in the pangs of birth; beneath all language and
distinction, yet judging and acting. . . ." full of fury, greed, the fear
of loss and even self-spite, rage, sadomasochistic destructive violence,
"raw instinctuality split off from consciousness . . . the perilous
ground upon which consciousness treads as inevitable aspects of the archetypal underworld," a state of energy comparable to a black hole
where energy is inverted and thus transformed. Hence this state entails
also rot, decay and gestation, "which work upon the passive stuck recipient invasively and against his or her will, . . . like impersonal forces

[that] devour, destroy, incubate and bring to birth with implacable pitilessness, thus bringing about a hopeless empty sense of barrenness, void or loss, an abysmal agony, suffering and helplessness and futility, a loss of individuality," yet also a "sense of uncaring coldness like the 'eye of death' that refuses closeness, relationship and even pity." Here is that black maw and terror of existence that we have previously described as having to be propitiated by *holocausted* sacrifices.

As Perera says (p. 24):

> Ereshkigal's domain, when we are in it, seems unbounded, irrational, primordial and totally uncaring, even destructive of the individual. It contains an energy we begin to know through the study of black holes and the disintegration of elements, as well as through the processes of fermentation, cancer, decay and lower brain activities that regulate peristalsis, menstruation, pregnancy and other forms of bodily life to which we must submit. It is the destructive-transformative side of the cosmic will. Ereshkigal through time and suffering pitilessly grinds down all distinctions in her indiscriminating fires—and yet heaves forth new life. She symbolises the abyss that is the source and the end, the ground of all being.

In the Greek myth we meet Ereshkigal again as Gorgon, the Medusa (the name means "ruleress") with terrible face and tusks like a boar, head and body girdled with serpents; her sight makes the beholder lose his breath and on the spot turns him to stone. She is slain by Perseus, the solar hero, under the tutelage of Pallas Athena. Still later in the Grail cycle we encounter her as Kundrie the Grail messenger and the Ugly Dame or Goddess who is to be honored and given sovereignty again if the Grail is to be restored. In the Greek version (which is already patriarchal) her cut-off head is given over to Pallas Athena who wears it on her breast and on the *aigis* ("goatskin"), her shield, thus reminding us that the goat god Dionysus is associated to the underworld, indeed *is* Hades, death. Athena also was addressed as "Gorgonfaced" or "she who petrifies," a goddess of fierce battle as well as a protectress of arts and civilization.

Brought into the daylight of consciousness through strife and conflict, the forces of the abyss can become elements of creativity.

Yet for the emerging patriarchal consciousness the Ereshkigal aspect of existence is utterly terrifying. It is rejected as a "rape of life," a violence to be feared, avoided or at least controlled as much as possible.

We believe in order, reason, and progress and assign change, destruction, and transformation to the unconscious. We prefer not to look too closely at the awesomely dissolving and destructive, yet also dangerously attractive, abyss of the dark side of the goddess. Hence, of the vast range of feminine qualities, only the lifegiving and protecting motherly qualities came to be acceptable to the patriarchal ego. The free expression of feminine instinctuality had to be restrained and reduced, subjected to patriarchal breeding purposes. This transition is typified by the change in the meaning of "virgin"and "virginity." Formerly, in the gynolatric cultures, virginity denoted that aspect of the goddess or of her priestess which mediated the mystery of existence through body and sexuality. A virgin was a woman who belonged to herself, not to any man. The term had nothing to do with sexual abstinence or chastity. Aphrodite was called a virgin, yet was anything but chaste. The virgin was *hierodule* (Greek: servant of the Holy; from this we coined the term temple prostitute). She was to be beholden to and answerable only to the goddess and the ecstatic Dionysian darkness within. She did not submit herself to any man but sovereignly bestowed upon the supplicant the renewing power of the divinity through sexual union.[14] In our discussion of the Grail Goddess in chapter 11 we shall meet this theme again.

In the androlatric system "virgo" came to mean "virgo intacta": a chaste or celibate woman. Intact means "untouched by anything that harms or defiles, uninjured, unimpaired." In order to be suitable and limited to continuing a patriarchal family lineage a "good" woman had to be a "good breeder" and limit the "use" of her body to her lord whose property she was to be. (Hence Exod. 20:17: "You shall not covet your neighbor's house; you shall not covet your neighbor's wife or his man servant or his maid servant or his ox or his ass or anything that is your neighbor's.")

Henceforth woman was to renounce the threatening power of her "dark moon" side, be chaste and humble and cease tempting man with lust and passion, lest the abysmal power of the feminine dissolve his firm will and render him over helplessly into the maelstrom of transformation.

A symbolic grand image of this threat to the patriarchal, male-identified ego as an elementary fact of nature, can be studied in the dynamism of the sexual and reproductive organs. This exploration is meant symbolically. It does not intend to suggest that feminine and masculine dynamics are *derived* from anatomical structures or biologic functioning. Quite to the contrary, I regard anatomy and physiology as analogical manifestations in the realm of form and structure of the very same archetypal patterning which likewise manifests itself psychodynamically.

The feminine sex system, and the behavior of the egg cell especially, on first sight convey an image of passive, receptive, and engulfing behavior. There is a quiescent openness, ready to receive. In dramatic contrast to this static, quiescent immobility are the thousands of rest-lessly swarming spermatozoa, aggressively seeking to penetrate. How-ever, this is only an external view. As soon as the action shifts inward, after penetration into the egg cell, the dynamic is reversed. Now the masculine is no longer aggressively active, but, having spent its energy, becomes passive; the feminine, from its inner depths, now moves forth and takes charge. The sperm cell is dissolved, annihilated by the en-zymes within the ovum. Its constituents are utilized by the ovum to build from its own structure a new organism, the embryo. At first this is always female, not sexually neutral as was formerly believed. In dis-solving and transforming, the feminine is itself transformed. Although outwardly the feminine receives and submits to aggressive penetration, in the inner invisible mystery of her being she actively dissolves and dismembers in order to re-create, whereas the outwardly aggressive male, in this inner sanctuary, experiences the bliss of surrender to a dif-ferent kind of wisdom.[15]

In turn, the fear of the transformative ability to overpower and de-vour can create pathology. Underlying the psychology of frigidity and impotence is frequently an over-identification of the male with his dy-namic and aggressive side, and of the female with her passive needs and receptive side. They are then not able to permit themselves the experi-ence of their own duality, of their own receptive-aggressive polarity. This experience is absolutely necessary for sexual ecstasy and full po-tency.

The male orgasm leads to an experience which may, in its extreme form, carry the quality of a deathlike surrender. (In French it is called *petit mort*.) Among some animal species, such as the praying mantis, the male is literally killed and eaten by the female in the act of copula-tion. Conversely, for the woman the orgasmic experience has an arous-ing or even electrifying character that leaves her with a sense of full-ness, strength, and power. The sense of the surrendering, collapsing penis after climax has been described by some women as being as plea-surable as was the previous erection.

The transformative dynamic of the Feminine, when not understood, can also be felt when it erupts in relationships, as a seemingly disturb-ing factor. This is most likely to occur when the woman, consciously or unconsciously, feels that the relationship has gone stale, perhaps owing to the man's tendency to settle down into nicely regulated and assigned roles and expectations, everything neatly tied in a bundle of routine.

Seemingly without any external provocation—or in response to a relatively minor one—and commonly independent of any conscious in-tent, something suddenly erupts from the woman's unconscious. She over-reacts, starts a fight over a small issue, feels a need to withdraw, to stop being sweet and loving, acts moody and "bitchy." She groundlessly and irrationally upsets a calm and smooth relationship. A trifling matter results in a major emotional blow-up and shatters the sweet peace needlessly—or so it seems to the bewildered male. He becomes ever more convinced of woman's unfathomable irrationality. Worse still, the unleashing of feeling has seemingly given her a profound emotional satisfaction. It "turns her on" sexually. If her partner has not fled from the fracas, he is likely to end up in bed at the end of the fight and find her unusually loving and passionate. This may be as incomprehensible to him as her former "bitchiness." On the surface everything seems the same as it was before the storm. The bewildered male shrugs it off as "one of those things." Yet it is not the same. Emotionally at least, some readaptation has occurred. Something has changed or been challenged for eventual transformation in the psychological relationship. Some feeling quality has shifted regardless of whether the partners are aware of it. What appears to the surface view as merely a wanton disruption can be seen, by a psychologically sensitive observer, as a phase of needed transformation.

Needless to say, such a psychological attack may also strike the man from the depths of his woman within, the anima. In this case, since the attack strikes his inner receptive side directly, he is even more helpless and less able to react in a related fashion. He may externalize the conflict by projecting the disturbance upon an external situation or person, probably his mate or close associate. But this is a shot in the dark. It is of little help emotionally. A successful career or a period of calm activity is suddenly broken by unexplicable moodiness, wild passion, a profound depression, or a totally irrational sense of meaninglessness and a "to hell with everything" feeling. Such spells when attended to receptively portend basic changes in outlook and creative potential. They can mean dangerous and destructive—indeed self-destructive— crises when disregarded and repressed. In either case, whether originating from the woman without or the anima within, what appears to the superficial view as destructive eruption is the expression of an inexorable trend for transformation in terms of the inner dimension.

The transformative Ereshkigal-Medusa dynamic is an expression of the deepest mystery of the life force, in which creation, destruction, change, and re-creation are but variations of a unitary process of form and play of form. This central life-play of the transformative dynamism carries a sense of inexorability. In the midst of the pain it inflicts, it instills its own peculiar ecstatic satisfaction. It gives birth to the forces of the dark twin, of Dionysus, aggression and destruction, that were to be contained in the ancient sacrificial rites. Hence it is closely akin to, and often indistinguishable from, the rapture of religious exaltation or sexual frenzy. This fact is well known to us and documented by the phenomenology of sadomasochism, with its tendency to seek expression in sexual and religious violence as well as in revolutionary outbreaks. The latter are but secularized religious eruptions. It ranges from the menadic frenzy of ancient and modern religious ceremonies (Dionysian celebrations, orgies of the Russian Chlysts or some Black Masses) to the cold pervertedness of torture chambers of the Inquisition and contemporary concentration camps and acts of terrorism and crime. It is the more inhumanly destructive the more its mania is rationalized and secularized by ideological explanations. Only when we can recognize its origins in the transformative dimension of the Feminine which has been repressed in the awareness of both sexes, can we hope to discover acceptable, new, and more humane channels for these otherwise atavistic and dangerous urges.

Bachofen has given an apt characterization:

That Bacchic mania which Euripides portrays and whose physical manifestation is represented in so many works of art is rooted in the depths of woman's emotional life, and the indissoluble bond between those two mightiest forces, religious emotion and sensual desire, raised it to that frenzy of enthusiasm, that reeling drunkenness, which was bound to be looked upon as an immediate revelation of the glorious gods. . . . The intensity of the orgiastic passion compounded by religion and sensuality shows how the woman, though weaker than man, is able at times to rise to greater heights than he. Through his mystery Dionysos captured the woman's soul with its penchant for everything that is supernatural; by his blinding sensuous epiphany he works on imagination that for the woman is the starting point of all inner emotion and on her erotic feeling, without which she can do nothing, but to which under the protection of religion she gives an expression that surpasses all barriers.[16]

This transformative frenzy operates in the depths and with the dynamism of the magical and mythological dimensions described earlier. Under conditions of repression, within an ego-system which seeks stability and fears change and transformation, it is reduced to functioning subversively and to evoking grimness, bitterness, and self-hate. Moreover, under repression, this smouldering is bound to constellate an atmosphere in which blindly destructive events are likely to occur.

It is the ego's fear of the transformative dimension which has deprived women of what was for them, during the gynolatric era, a chief transformative function and source of meaning; namely, their roles as priestess, seeress, prophetess and magical healer. In all of these manifestations they have been ruthlessly persecuted wherever the Christian church has set foot.

It is obvious that no woman, even were she free from cultural bias, could possibly consciously assimilate, integrate, and give expression to the whole range of affect and behavioral qualities of the feminine archetype. Nor can any man give adequate expression to all the possible masculine traits. In addition to the contrasexual, some of the basic drives and affects of one's own gender are bound, therefore, to remain unconscious and unassimilated in both sexes. They operate like inferior functions, that is, in what frequently amounts to primitive and even obsessional ways compensating or opposing the conscious adaptation. This fact bears upon the issue of psychological typology and animus-anima dynamic.

Typology can be helpful as an ordering system. It can also become a system of restricting pigeonholes. Bearing in mind this danger we may utilize our insights now to enlarge Toni Wolff's typology of the Feminine[17] (Mother, Hetaira, Medium, and Amazon). Wolff's types have been criticized, and rightly so, for characterizing the feminine primarily in terms of relationship to the male, hence making it dependent or secondary to the masculine. Her approach seems justified and logically consistent, as long as the premise holds that the feminine equals Eros, which equals relationship or relatedness. This we can no longer uphold. Yet these types can also be seen as special, personalized aspects of the Great Round expressed in the Inanna-Ereshkigal polarity. Then Mother and Hetaira would be expressions of the creating, nourishing, protecting, and lustfully, erotically, and virginally playful aspects of being. I propose the name Luna ("moon") and Lila (Sanskrit for "play") respectively for those types. They represent what Neumann called the elementary aspects of the Feminine; Medium and Amazon can be seen as personalizations of Medusa and Pallas (Athena) respectively, the abysmal strife-and-civilization-generating, transformative aspect of the Feminine. I shall attempt a very sketchy characterization to encourage further study.[18]

Luna supports the claims and needs of reality. She can be wife and mother but also competent administrator and creator of a congenial atmosphere and living space, of home and *soul.* She is attuned to the rhythm, tides, needs, and possibilities of concrete life expressions. She has the capacity to structure and order her environment. She is aware of measure, limitations, and proportions. Luna has a sense of natural rhythm, tactfulness and timing and the capacity for empathy. Her way is the way of attunement to the logic of feeling, and of personal response to the needs and possibilities of people. She responds to practical and concrete rather than abstract situations, and to the requirements of the moment. She listens, receives, carries, gestates, nests and nourishes, protects and promotes growth. She identifies with pattern, process, and form, and with the needs and tides of the body or bodily existence.

The way of *Lila* is the way of lightness, playfulness, charm, attraction, and voluptuousness, the dance of the senses and of the Muses. She is attuned to beauty, pleasure, and enjoyment, the play of love and life. She can be woman's girlishly youthful aspect, shy and evasive, touching, escaping, yet wanting to be caught and touched, or sensuously alluring and indulging. She gives lightness, playfulness, and poetic inspiration, enjoys and grieves, loves and rejects, connects and repels, dances and plays with a life that for her is but game and illusion.

Pallas creates and strives; she is ready to fight for her own needs and rights, for cultural achievement and human dignity and causes. For the sake of her convictions and needs she is willing also to disregard relationships and destroy old patterns that have outlived their usefulness. She inspires the career and pioneer woman. It is Pallas, not the Hetaira as Wolff implies, who is concerned with personalization and the possibilities or limitations of personal relationships.

Medusa is the abyss of transformation, the seemingly chaotic riddle that woman is to herself and to the puzzled man she leads to the dread of unpredictability and seeming emptiness and depression and annihilation. Hers is the way of the medium priestess or healer, the inspired artist, or an erratic, hysterical devouring borderline personality. A *femme fatale,* and *belle dame sans merci* or witch. At her best, she connects with the abyss, she challenges and inspires. Hers is a realm to which every woman and anima must periodically descend for renewal, like Inanna to Ereshkigal. When this happens life comes to a standstill according to the myth. Paralysis, inertia, or depression seems to reign. Interest in work and human connections, even to those closest to one's heart, may be lost temporarily in a haze of indifference.

Interestingly enough, the myth of Inanna depicts a conscious and deliberate descent and eventual return for the Feminine, but a sacrificial death—as the price for her return—for Dumuzi, her beloved, an Eros figure. Apparently the required waiting, the receptive introversion necessary in this phase, is somewhat easier for a woman to accomplish than for a man, since by virtue of her Luna side she is more consciously attuned to her tides, including her darkness, than the man. For him the experience is one of temporary loss of soul. It is a deathlike threat that exacts a sacrifice of Eros, a letting-go of one's expectations, demands, and desires.

Woman's sacrifice occurs on the animus level when she gives up being the *beloved one* at any price, as the patriarchal culture has taught her to be. The price for her transformed rebirth is to accept her own reality and to commit herself to what she discovers herself to be, even though by the prevailing collective standards this may be regarded as ugly and repulsive.

In the light of these insights I propose now to reexamine also the traditional Jungian ideas about anima and animus as they apply to consciousness and sexual gender. Jung limited anima and animus to the unconscious dynamics of either sex. On the strength of clinical experience accumulated since his early formulation, this no longer appears valid. The evidence does not justify the contention that anima exclusively embodies the nonpersonal unconscious of men and animus of women. Nor can we still maintain the dogma that consciousness in both men and women is masculine and that unconsciousness is feminine.[19]

Only during patriarchy did masculine values, patterns of perception, feeling, and behavior shape the structure of consciousness. They did so *because* they were given supreme value. Feminine standards were then devalued and rejected. As a result, they were repressed and reduced to unconscious determinants. Masculinity therefore represented consciousness.

In our time, we are witnessing a reemergence of feminine Yin and anima qualities in the collective value system. They are becoming cultural determinants again and coshapers of a new consciousness for both sexes. Consciousness-determining ("psychopompic") figures appear in dreams and fantasies as frequently in feminine shapes as in masculine ones, if not more so.

Consciousness is difficult to define. The ancient languages do not have a definite word for it. In the Latin root word, *conscientia,* from which both the English and French terms are derived, conscience and consciousness are not yet separated. *Conscientia* means "joint knowledge," "being privy to," "having a feeling or sense of." We could formulate it as "being in touch with a significance." Hence it is a perception of relationship between a subject and an object. Consciousness is a mode of relatedness; relatedness a mode of consciousness. This perception of relationship can occur in two ways, in Yang or Yin fashion. The Yang way, utilizing primarily the left hemisphere of the brain, strives from center to periphery. It is separative, analytical and abstracting. The Yin way, corresponding to right brain activity, draws inward toward the center. It moves toward unity, identity, patterns, and analogy. The former represents a male and animus consciousness. The latter constitutes the feminine and anima consciousness which we are now more and more recognizing as equal in importance to the analytic male trend.

Applied to men and women, the most we can claim is that somatically at least, male trends preponderate in men and female ones in women. I do not know whether or not such a preponderance has been established in terms of hemispheric activity, and in the ways in which men and women "get in touch with" and relate to the world and to themselves. Apparently hemispheric functions are not as dichotomized in women as in men. However, even if we do assume a preponderance of Yang or Yin trends psychologically in men or women respectively, these are by no means uniform. While some may be dominants of consciousness, others may remain unconscious in either sex.

We have grown accustomed to reserving the terms animus and anima for contrasexual drive elements, male traits in women and female traits in men. Yet neither the qualities they represent, nor their specific animus-anima compulsivity, nor their capacity of relating us to the Self is limited to either sex.[20] Men can be as animus-ridden, dogmatic, belligerent, busybodying and power hungry as women; women as anima-possessed, moody, seductive, unrelated, and depressed as men.

In the original Latin, the two terms were used synonymously, with some preference given to anima in poetic usage. They both cover a wide spectrum of sentiment, affection, disposition, courage, spirit, pride, arrogance, desire, will, purpose, resolve, inclination, pleasure. Jung tended at times to define animus in terms of or equivalent to spirit, and anima as instinct or soul. Yet as instinct, soul, or spirit they pertain to both sexes equally. Men are not necessarily more spirit-oriented than women. Nor do women have a monopoly on soul and instinct. The notion of spirituality as a predominant male characteristic and soul as a female property is an heirloom of nineteenth century romanticism. Dominant in Jung's day, it is no longer valid for our generation. Women can and always could be psychologically determined in their conscious outlook by *logos,* yet be out of touch with their affects. Men can be immensely sensitive to instinct, feelings and affect, and quite at a loss in respect to *logos* or any other of the masculine archetypes.

Much more in keeping with word meaning and the clinically practical is to use the words animus and anima to denote archetypal masculinity and femininity respectively, regardless of whether they apply to women or men. We would thereby avoid the terminological confusion of gender and sex, and having to explain over and over again the differences between masculinity and men, and femininity and women. We would also be able to use indigenous Western words for psychological dynamics and leave the Chinese Yang-Yin for the cosmic and biological principles which they were intended to denote. And once it is agreed that men can be as animus-ridden as women and women as anima-possessed as men, another issue of contention and confusion would be resolved.

A question we will not examine in detail is the bearing one's own mother has upon one's perception of one's relationship to the archetypal Feminine. This is a complex issue, especially relevant to the therapeutic process but beyond the scope of this study. In general, however, one's mother constellates the archetype of life with its wide ranges. Hence, unconsciously, mother equals goddess. The more rejecting and ignoring of the child's needs the mother has been, the more the Goddess's death aspect is prevalent in that child's mind, and adaptation, even into adulthood. The more the mother has been nurturing and accepting, the more the Goddess is seen in her life-supporting qualities. The parental figures of our early childhood experience more or less represent or distort the great universal archetypes. Thus also our basic apprehension of the Father God archetype may range from the severe judgmentalness or moral support of Jehovah to the anarchy or life-affirmation of Dionysus depending on how our own fathers related to us.

In summary, the devaluation of the Feminine, the Yin, the anima, and consequently also of women during the patriarchy, was a result of the need to separate the nascent ego from the encompassing field-consciousness of the magico-mythological world of need and instinct with its transformative (hence ego-threatening) dynamic of existence. This sense of separateness is illusory; yet this does not change its validity for a mind that believed in it. A sense of individuality and freedom were to be achieved through reason, will, and obedience to the Father God's rational law.

The price for this achievement was twofold: the loss of connection with the life-death continuum of existence; and the experience of self as a stranger in a senseless world. We also now face the threat of collective self-destruction, as the instinctive sadomasochistic urges of violence and aggression can no longer be propitiated by appeals to law and reason.

This critical point in time marks the turn of the tide again. The Goddess and her consort, banished and seemingly lost through the past millennia, make their epiphany again in modern consciousness. The question we must now answer is: What myth do they bring with them that could show us the psychological channels of their intended expression?

Isis. Egyptian, Ptolemaic period.
Bronze statuette. Walters Art Gallery, Baltimore, Maryland.

Part 4

A MYTH
FOR OUR TIMES

The spirit of the fountain never dies.
It is called the mysterious feminine.
The entrance to the mysterious feminine
Is the root of all heaven and earth.
Frail, frail it is, hardly existing.
But touch it; it will never run dry.

LAO TZU, *Tao Teh Ching**

* Trans. John C. H. Wu (New York: St. John's University Press, 1962), verse 7.

CHAPTER 11

The Grail

The land was dead and desert
So that they lost the voices of the wells
And the maidens who were in them.
     "Elucidations," Prologue to Chrétien de Troyes' *Perceval*

Lully lulley; lully lulley
The falcon hath born my mak away

He bare hym up, he bare hym down;
He bare hym into an orchard brown.

In that orchard ther was a hall
That was hanged with purpill and pall

And in that hall ther was a bede;
Hit was hangit with gold so rede.

And in that bed ther lythe a Knyght
His woundes bledying day and nyght.

By that bedes ther kneleth a may,
And she wepeth both nyght and day.

And by that beddes side ther standith a ston,
'Corpus Christi' wretyn theron.
     The Knight of the Grail, ANON., Eng., 16th Cent.

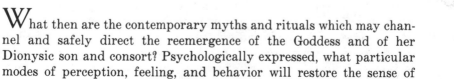

What then are the contemporary myths and rituals which may channel and safely direct the reemergence of the Goddess and of her Dionysic son and consort? Psychologically expressed, what particular modes of perception, feeling, and behavior will restore the sense of

meaning and unity between world and man, overcome the alienation of
the modern mind, and give us an aggression-control ritual and resul-
tant new ethic?

The modern myth is no longer sung by bards in the halls of kings, nor
told by grandmother in the glow of the fireplace. It has to be pieced together from the jottings of news commentators and editorial writers,
social ideologists, and political candidates; from what is believed to be
true and taken for granted by the *Zeitgeist,* and from our expectations
for a "better" tomorrow. Among those hopes, demands, and assump-
tions, three key motifs stand out: the hope for liberation, the theme of
research and discovery—whether of the secrets of nature or of the inner
self—and last, the restoration of a lost Golden Age of freedom, human
dignity and fulfillment. Even behind today's cloud of marijuana smoke
these themes continue as major motivational factors. They shape our individual and collective unconscious underneath the observable surface
of seeming cynical resignation. Our modern ideologies are the ways
that the unconscious imagery of the Grail theme structures the
rationalizing tendency of the modern collective consciousness.

Liberation

The call for liberation presupposes that something is enslaved or at
least imprisoned. Is this only a miscarried social structure? The political nature of the lack of liberty has fascinated our minds for the last
two hundred years. We rarely consider its possible psychological significance. Paradoxically, the increase of outer social and political freedom
has gone hand-in-hand with ever-new forms of oppression. Moreover, it
has accompanied an increasing sense of alienation, emptiness, and dissatisfaction, what Freud called the *Unbehagen,* "unease" of our culture.

Viewed in its inner dimension, liberty is freedom from those restraints that inhibit expression of one's genuine being. Yet these restraints are not only external and material. That was erroneously assumed by a generation which identified individuality with the
conscious ego personality—which in turn, was assumed free to be whatever it wanted. The conscious personality, however, is not psychologically free. We are limited by our given nature, which is largely unconscious. We are mostly unaware of our true individuality, hence
prevented from experiencing it. And finally, we are prevented from
genuine self-expression and forced into inauthentic pretense by repressive bias, habits, and conditionings. "We can do what we want but
we cannot want what we want," as Schopenhauer put it. The expression
of intense feelings or the showing of softness and tears, for instance,

were held to be incompatible with true manhood during the late Victorian epoch. During this same period, women were not free to show too much initiative, independence, intellectual brilliance, or awareness of their erotic desires. This is largely true even today. While cultural patterns shape and inhibit individual self-awareness and self-expression, they also express the evolving collective consciousness. A common denominator of this has been the inhibition and devaluation of the feminine Yin trends in favor of masculine Yang modes of competition, combative control, and exploitation. Hence in the political arena, yesterday's champions of liberty have tended to become the new oppressors. The external tyrants have been overthrown, but the inner aggressor has taken command and restructured external relations in terms of new restraints.

Likewise the present cry for women's liberation tended at first to overlook the unconscious repression and devaluations of the Yin elements in the attitude of women feminists themselves. Like all archetypal determinants, this attitude remains choiceless and compulsive, hence an obstacle to liberation, as long as it remains unconscious.

The political and social goals of the women's movement deserve fullest endorsement. They are vital in establishing equal human rights and dignity on the social level. However, an egalitarianism that disregards human differences, and deals with sociological problems as though there were no difference between archetypal masculinity and femininity, is a remnant of the repressive, monotheistic, and monolithic patriarchal outlook. It prevents the liberation of the devalued and repressed Yin nature.

The disrespect for genuine feminine dynamics will have to be sought out and discovered as an unconscious factor in the psyches of both men and women, feminists included. Men express the androlatric bias that devalues sensitivity and inwardness when they project their own rejected femininity upon the supposedly over-emotional, stupid, or exploitative *femme fatale*. Women do the same when they repudiate differences between masculine and feminine, and imitate standardized androlatric male behavior, with its pushy competitiveness and abstract intellectualism. They project their own unconscious patriarchal self-rejection as women upon the repressive tyrant. In scapegoating men and identifying primarily, if not exclusively, with competitive achievement and external reforms, some part of the feminist movement, at least, runs the danger of perpetuating the worst features of the androlatric, patriarchal heritage.

Quest

Search is an expression of the urge to discover what "holds the world together at its inmost core" (Goethe, *Faust*) to establish an order and meaning for our place in the cosmos. As with liberation, our view has been too much limited to external, spatial reality. The quest motif is embodied as much in Columbus's search for new shores as it is in the Arthurian knights' quest for the Holy Grail, in Demeter's search for her kidnapped daughter, or in the scientists' attempt to solve the riddle of matter. The pursuit of happiness is a quest. So is the Horatio Alger journey from rags to riches, and the alchemist's search for the Philosopher's Stone, which seeks to unravel the mystery of soul no less than that of matter. Behind man's thrust into outer space looms the yearning to find an answer to the how and why of our existence. It is the counterpart of the quest into inner space in search of integration and fulfillment.

The Myth

In summing up the search and liberation mythology of our time as a coherent whole, the following version of the story suggests itself. Our cultural development has reached a critical period, a point of danger, sickness, and stagnation. Industrialism, technology, and capitalism have turned our planet into a wasteland. The resources of the earth, formerly plentiful, are being exhausted. Mankind is threatened by ecological disaster and by self-inflicted destruction. Suffering and oppression prevail. Large masses of people—indeed society itself—are in need of liberation from the illness of industrial, technocratic or capitalist repression of the natural flow of life. Likewise, women have been repressed and deprived of their individuality by the prevalent male-dominated society. They need liberation. Humanity is alienated from the wholeness of nature. Yet we are at the threshold of a new age. In the coming age of Aquarius, the water-bearer, the "flow of the waters" will be restored. Life and spirit will be renewed. Peace, happiness, love, and wisdom will be regained. The way into this new age is the object of man's quest. This is to be found by increasing research into the hidden secrets of nature and mind.

This Utopian myth of our day is a slightly disguised secularized version of various redemption and messianic myths of paradise lost and found again. Visions of such a Golden Age, to be restored through a divine redeemer, have moved countless minds and hearts prior to and during the Christian era in the West. These have found a final and increasingly effective formulation in the Grail myth. They all reflect the growing sense of isolation and alienation which attended the development of ego and the rational mind during the rise of the patriarchy. The Grail version, however, is the most significant and most modern form of the redemption myth.

The Grail myth has replaced the original form of Christian messianism in terms of psychological effectiveness. From the late Middle Ages on through our present post-Christian days, it has had a most powerful effect. It is also an integrative myth. It unifies pre-Christian with Christian and modern post-Christian elements. The ancient cauldron of the Great Goddess is filled now with the blood of Christ and awaits redemption of the redeemer through human search, through the conscious effort of a seeker who dares to ask the socially forbidden question "Whom or what does it serve?" and "What is the meaning?"

I wish to sum up the overt core elements of the Grail myth, abstracted from its numerous versions. Yet this is not an easy task. For "... there is no single, clearly defined image of the Grail, nor indeed evidence that it ever existed; opinions differ widely about the origins of the stories that have circulated in written form since the beginning of the twelfth century."[1] The very centrality of the Grail symbol has exerted a magnetic pull. Many images cluster in orbit around it. Just as the legendary knights had to seek out the true Grail by overcoming many obstacles, so too the modern reader cannot expect easy access to the heart of the mystery. We inherit a complex past. "An amalgam of many things gave rise to the symbol of the Grail. Traces of alchemical lore and classical myth, of Arabic poetry and Sufi teaching, of Celtic mythology and Christian iconography are all to be found in the final image."[2] Before turning to a consideration of this rich imagery, I shall paraphrase one narration.[3]

Joseph of Arimathea was entrusted with Christ's body for burial. At the Last Supper, he had obtained the cup from which Christ drank. This was the Grail. While washing the corpse, Joseph caught in this vessel some blood flowing from the wounds. After the body's disappearance, Joseph was accused of stealing it and imprisoned without food. In prison, a radiant Christ appeared to him and left the cup to his care, revealing to him the mystery of the Mass and other secrets. A dove flew into Joseph's cell every day to bring a wafer to the cup. This nourishment kept Joseph alive.

In the year 70 A.D., Joseph was released from prison. He led a small group into exile overseas. They constructed the First Table of the Grail, in memory of the Table of the Last Supper. Twelve could sit around it. A fish was placed in Christ's place. A thirteenth seat, the place of Judas, swallowed up the one who tried to sit in it, so it had to be left empty and was called the Perilous Seat.

Joseph then sailed to England and founded the first Christian church at Glastonbury. It was dedicated to Christ's mother.

The Grail itself was the chalice for celebrating the Mass. Then, on the Mountain of Salvation, a temple was built to house the Grail and an Order of Grail Knights created to protect it. A sacred feast from the Grail was shared at a Second Table. The Grail Keeper was called the Fisher King. He was priest for the mass. Soon afterwards though, he received a spear wound, either on the thighs or genitals. The cause was either loss of faith, violating his vow of chastity a blow from a stranger (the *stroke doloureux*) or a wrong done to a woman. Then he became known as the Maimed or Wounded King. His country fell barren and was called the Waste Land. The land's desertification and the King's wound were intimately linked. The wound was inflicted by the Lance of Longinus, which had pierced Christ's side on the cross.

At King Arthur's court, Merlin the Magician set up a Third Table, the Round Table. Under the rules of chivalry, Arthur met with his knights around it. At Pentecost, the Grail appeared to them in a beam of sunlight. They pledged to quest for it. Each set out on a separate path and went through initiatory trials. Among these knights were Lancelot, his son Galahad, Gawaine, Bors, and Parsifal, nicknamed Perfect Fool for his innocence.

The knights barely caught a glimpse of the Grail. Each of them had to search alone. Often they wandered through deep woods. There they met hermits who helped them understand the tests they were undergoing. Their failure to attain the Grail was due not so much to external circumstances as to their own deficiencies. For example, Lancelot was turned away and temporarily blinded because of his adulterous relationship with Arthur's queen. After a first failure to find the Grail, Parsifal wandered five years through the Waste Land. He again reached the castle of the Fisher King. This time, by asking the prescribed ritual question, he healed the King. The question was "Whom does the Grail serve?" or "What ails Thee?" Finally healed, the King was permitted to die. The Waste Land was restored to fertility.

The preceding gives a continuous narrative of the late Christianized version of the Grail myth, much simplified of course, to serve às guide through the bewildering richness of Grail imagery, with its deep psychological resonances. The Grail is a wondrous vessel, a wellspring of life-giving, life-restoring waters, and a cornucopia of nourishment, a cup made of Helen's breast: it is a miraculous stone, or a man's head, or the secret primeval tradition of the mysteries. It is in the care of a goddess or a beautiful maiden. It is guarded by heroic knights in a magical castle in the land of *yonder*, in paradise, the land of the spirits, or of fairies. As an ancient cauldron, it renews life and restores youth. It is an endless source of food and sustenance, of joy, pleasure, and feasting, as well as of the ecstasies of Venus.[4] As a vessel, it is the cup from which Christ drank at the Last Supper. It received his blood as it poured out of his wounds at the Crucifixion. As a stone, it is a jewel from Lucifer's crown, brought to earth by those angels who took no part in the conflict between God and Devil. In medieval lore, vessel, Grail and womb, as well as *lapis* ("stone"), were still synonymous images for Mary, the mother of God.[5]

The Grail is associated with a spear, purportedly the one thrust into Christ's side on the cross. It is also associated with two kings, one younger, the other older and ready to die; or with a king suffering from an incurable, ever-festering wound on his genitals, or with a stag-headed shamanic figure or magician[6] who is kin to the Celtic Cerunnus, the Norse Odin, or the Roman Pluto, the Greek Hades, Dionysus, and the Chaldaic Dumuzi or Tammuz.

In the latter figure, we readily recognize the Dionysian companion of the Goddess. Another figure associated with the Grail is a woman with boar teeth, hair like pig's bristles, doglike nose, bear's ears, a hairy face, and fingernails like a lion's claw. This creature of terrifying ugliness reminds one of the Greek Medusa or the Sumerian Ereshkigal, the dark death aspects of the Goddess or of the Sphinx. She is the sister of Malcreatiure, who again is another version of the horned Shaman-Dionysus figure. In many Celtic stories, it is through this terrifying Medusa that the Grail or the kingdom or the wellspring is finally encountered, and only he who can accept and kiss her can achieve kingship in her timeless realm.

The Grail and its castle and guardians are bewitched owing to an act of disrespect. This is variously represented as insult, rape, assault on its maidens, disrespect of the sovereignty of the Grail itself or of its law through an improper attitude to *Minne,* or love. In Wolfram von Eschenbach's *Parzival,* the bewitchment befalls through falsely serving the maiden Orgeluse whose name means "anger and pride." In other versions, it comes about through competitive fraternal strife, a *stroke doloureux* ("painful blow") administered to one of the brothers who is henceforth the Wounded King; or it is due to the influence of a power-hungry evil magician, Dionysus satanized. As a result, the Grail and its castle and keepers are bewitched and removed from human reach. Its King suffers, yet cannot die. A blight is upon the lands. The waters no longer flow. Food no longer grows. A Waste Land prevails "where the myth is patterned by authority, not emergent from life; where there is no poet's eye to see, no adventures to be lived, where all is set for all and for ever."[7]

Anxiously awaited is the questing hero who will remove the spell, re-

store the blessed state, make the waters flow, heal the King and help
him to die, and thereby achieve kingship himself. He is to accomplish
this by asking the magical question which is given in varying accounts
as "Whom does one serve with the Grail?" or "What is the meaning of
this?" or "What ails you?"

In the best-known Middle European version, Wolfram von Eschenbach's Parzival reaches the castle. Having been trained in courtly manners, which forbid questions, he fails, at first, to ask. Apprised of his
failure after leaving the castle, he himself becomes a wanderer in the
desert. He loses his faith and at this point we lose sight of him. Unac-
countably, he is given a second chance and succeeds, but not until after
Gawain has successfully dealt with Orgeluse and Malcreatiure, redeemed a bewitched castle of women and finally confronted Parzifal in
combat. We will return to these adventures later on, for they offer the
key to understanding the hidden implications of the myth.

The Grail legend is closely related to the imagery of Aquarius and to
the myth of paradise and the Garden of Eden. The "Elucidations," a
prologue affixed to Chrétien's *Perceval,* describes the Grail country as
formerly abounding in damsels, food, and plenty until a ruthless aggressor, Amargon, puts an end to the Golden Age. "The land was dead
and desert . . . so that they lost the voices of the wells . . . and the maidens who were in them." Originally when a traveler approached the well,
"there issued out of the well a maiden, they could not ask a prettier, she
carried in her hand a gold cup, with rolls, pastries and bread, the food
he had asked for, who had come there for it. At the well he was very well
received. . . ." Yet King Amargon "did violence to one of the maidens,
against her will he violated her and took away from her the gold cup
and carried it off with him . . . therefore . . . never anymore from the
wells did appear maidens, nor did they serve anymore . . . the realm
then turned to ruin . . . the realm then turned to waste, never did a tree
have a leaf, the meadows and flowers dried up, and the streams shrank
away. Then no one could ever find, the court of the Rich Fisher, who
made splendid the country." (In this version, incidentally, Gawain, not
Parzifal, redresses the wrong done to the maidens of the well, finds and
restores the Grail.) We are reminded of the desecration in the story of
Eden, the lost paradise and the biblical "Accursed shall be the ground
on your account. With labor you shall win your food from it all the days
of your life. It will grow thorns and thistles for you, none but wild
plants for you to eat" (Gen. 3:17–18).

Campbell reproduces several ancient Mesopotamian seals showing
the serpent, in male as well as female forms, holding a cup or attended
by a water-carrier, an *aquarius,* in the presence of a world tree or *axis*

mundi, offering a boon of fruit to a petitioner.[8] "There is no sign of divine wrath or danger to be found in these seals. There is no theme of guilt connected with the garden. The boon of the knowledge of life is there, in the sanctuary of the world to be culled. And it is yielded willingly to any mortal, male or female, who reaches for it with the proper will and readiness to receive."[9] Another seal represents the goddess and a serpent sitting on one side of the tree facing her horned god partner, her beloved son-husband Dumuzi, "Son of the Abyss, Lord of the Tree of Life, the ever-dying, ever-resurrected Sumerian god who is the archetype of the incarnate being."[10]

The images of Aquarius also refer to this prebiblical Golden Age paradise. This constellation is to rule the coming age. It is pictured as a male and/or female divine guardian alongside a well, container (the medieval term for Aquarius was Amphora), or spring at the root of the world tree or world *axis* from which flows life, enlightenment, and wisdom. Even in Norse mythology we still find the Norns (goddesses of fate or destiny) at the foot of the world ash and Mimir (a guardian of wisdom) at its roots, guarding the well from which Odin (the supreme deity) drinks wisdom at the price of hanging on the tree for nine days and nights, an initiation sacrifice of himself to himself. And from the Garden of Eden, according to biblical tradition flow four rivers in the four directions of the compass, thus constituting a world cross of waters.

In the pre-Judeo-Christian primitive myth, the end of the Golden Age, the coming into the world of death, crying, and misery, is associated with the killing of the serpent or the woman or both, and with the growth of food-bearing plants from the buried head or body of the victim. In the patriarchal redaction of the myth, the killing of the serpent or of the woman is replaced by the woman's and the serpent's disobedience to the now exclusively male creator god. In a similar story, Lilith, supposedly Adam's first wife (and the mistress of the world), is banished because she refused obedience to him. In the patriarchal version there are two trees, one of life and one of knowledge. Knowledge is separated from life. A *stroke doloureux* replaces renewal through sacrifice. It is administered by Cain (the original Son of God)[11] to his brother Abel. The lord of the tree of life and of reincarnation, Cain or the horned god becomes a scapegoat. The Golden Age "in which fear and punishment were absent since everybody of his own will did the right thing," according to Ovid's *Metamorphoses,* is now to be replaced by forced obedience to externally imposed law in a world in which the earth no longer gladly offers its food. Misery reigns. We are in the Grail story's Waste Land.

The Grail/Aquarius myth, then, implies nothing less than reversal of the patriarchal trend through which the paradise of magical all-oneness was lost. This is to occur through restoration of the wellspring and its maidens, that is, the world of the goddess, and through asking the question and/or kissing the ugly damsel.

In this realm life and knowledge were one; there was one tree only. Knowing was experiential, akin to sexual union, a merging-with. In Latin, the word *sapere* still means both to *taste* and to be wise or discerning. The separating of the trees, along with the injunction against eating or *tasting* the fruit, put abstraction, obedience, and the notion of the sinfulness of sexual knowing in place of the experiential unitary discovery. Similarly, the injunction against graven images separated imaginal experiencing from spirit. This split was an act of violence against the unitary nature of the Goddess, a crime against the maiden of the well. With the patriarchal ego's left brain sense of separateness and responsibility were also born competitiveness, fratricidal power strife, guilt, and the scapegoat attitude. It is the modern wasteland of man against man. Small wonder then that the yearning for the lost unitary reality, for the golden days of containment under the rule of the Goddess, grew like a nostalgic background melody throughout the patriarchy. The yearning was expressed in the various redemption myths. It culminated in the Grail myth which, with ever-increasing intensity, has haunted the unconscious fantasies of the last millennium.

The Grail Myth and Hitler

Joseph Campbell was the first to draw attention to the likely significance of the Grail myth for our present time, as attested by the flurry of preoccupation with it by writers, artists, and anthropologists ever since Wagner's *Parsifal.* It was, however, the discovery of Hitler's and some of his forerunners' obsession with the Grail myth that confirmed for me that this myth, though distorted and sentimentalized in our time, may indeed be a major motivational factor which, unbeknownst to us, shapes our collective consciousness for better or worse. If we can understand the myth, we may avail ourselves of its constructive possibilities. While it remains unconscious, however, we leave ourselves open to its obsessive and destructive dangers; to a repetition of Hitler's madness.

I do not claim that Hitler's political ideas are to be explained simply as attempts to put a Grail program into action, although even this possibility cannot be ruled out. What is obvious however, is that the messianic renewal idea—the idea of a restoration of an ideal order that has been lost and the literalistic renewal of the blood rites of the pre-Chris-

tian mystery (Hitler quite astutely perceived the pre-Christian significance of the legends) was an idea which obsessively haunted Hitler's
outlook as well as the nationalistic and pseudospiritual movements that
preceded him.

Adolph Hitler's passionate and lasting preoccupation with the Grail
quest and its mystical significance, in both Richard Wagner's and Wolfram von Eschenbach's versions, has been attested to by various people
who knew him personally. Prior to Hitler's and Wagner's re-rendering,
Wolfram von Eschenbach's *Parzival* made the myth a part of middle-
European cultural thought and fantasy from the middle of the nineteenth century on. But it is not generally known that its basic premise,
the quest for the lost sacred object, sacred tradition, or sacred service,
Christianized or pre-Christian, has run like a red thread through medieval and modern culture and history ever since the beginning of the second millennium.

We find it in the impulse of the Crusaders as well as in the establishment and rituals of the order of the Knights Templar, suppressed in
1314 on the grounds that its members were heretical, blasphemous, sod-
omists who worshipped a strange Dionysian god called Baphomet,
identified with the Devil by the church. Otto Rahn (in *Kreuzzug gegen
den Gral*, 1933) has speculated as to the likely reference to the Grail
story in the worship and rituals of the Albigensians. He even went as
far as identifying Montsegur, the central sanctuary and last fortified
stronghold of the Albigensians, with Montsalvat, the Grail castle. We
may remember also that the Albigensians were suppressed in the
bloody Crusades that laid waste what is now southern France on
charges similar to those invoked against the Knights Templar. A continuation of the tradition of the Knights Templar has been claimed by
Masonry, especially Scottish Masonry, and later in the 1700s by the
Strict Observance, a quasi-Templar order which claimed to possess secret documents dating back to the fourteenth century and to work
under the direction of a mysterious unknown superior.[12] This tradition
purportedly made a mark upon masonry and influenced Madame Blavatsky, the founder of the modern Theosophy and the Order of the
Golden Dawn in England, which led to the O.T.O. (Ordo Templis
Orientis) in the 1880s. It does not matter for our purposes whether
these claims are historically valid or spurious. The very fact of their
being made expresses a mythological identification and attention to the
vitality of the Grail myth. Both Golden Dawn and O.T.O. represented
profound cultural influences, counting among their members such people as Yeats, Aleister Crowley, and Rudolph Steiner, the founder of
Anthroposophy.

While in the process of finalizing this text, I came across a new best

seller, *Holy Blood Holy Grail,* by M. Baigant, R. Leigh, W. Lincoln.*
This book undertakes not only to confirm but also to document the fact
of a living Grail tradition reaching back to the beginning of the Christian era and continuing into the present day. This tradition is presented as vested in a Prieuré de Sion in France, an esoteric society
which stood behind the Crusaders, Knights Templar, some Masonic
branches and Rosicrucian and Hermetic societies. According to the
records of the Prieuré among its Grand Masters are counted Nicolas
Flamel, René of Anjou; the artists Sandro Botticelli and Leonardo da
Vinci; Robert Fludd, Robert Boyle, and Isaac Newton; Maximilian of
Hapsburg, the protector of Haydn, Mozart, and Beethoven; Victor
Hugo, Claude Debussy, and Jean Cocteau.

According to the authors, the objects of the Prieuré de Sion are spiritual and political, the latter the establishment of a United States of
Europe as a constitutional monarchy under a priest-king who is to be a
descendant of the Merovingian dynasty. The Merovingians are represented as Grail Kings by virtue of descending from the womb of Magdalene (the Grail), purportedly the wife of Jesus.

I am in no position to judge the validity of these claims. But no matter how realistic, the fact of their being made at all and the continuing
existence of Grail societies bears eloquent testimony to the vitality and
continuing relevance of the Grail motif for our time. Regardless of, indeed even because of, its possible external political applicability, this
fact emphasizes the necessity of our concerning ourselves with the psychological impact and significance of this myth.

An amalgamation of the Grail and Thule lore apparently is part of
the secret teaching of eighteenth-century occult tradition which is alluded to in Goethe's *Faust,* Part One, in Gretchen's song of the Thule
king's lost gold cup, an old folk song, purportedly, which comes to her
after the first entry of the forbidden world of Faust and Mephistopheles into her bedroom. It is an artist's allusion recognizable only
by the initiated one, analogous, perhaps, to the Masonic allusion in the
text of Mozart's *The Magic Flute.*

However, the most drastic and dramatic surfacing of the Grail temple motif occurred in Austria at about the turn of the century. At the
very time Freud published his first basic book, *The Interpretation of
Dreams,* a New Templar order was founded by D. Lanz von Liebenfels,
a former Cistercian monk. The expressly stated purpose of the New
Templar order was to be the continuation of the Grail tradition. The
order purchased and maintained several castles in Austria. It had a
definite system of grades: novice, magister, Covenal, Familiar, Prior,

* (New York: Delacorte Press, 1982.)

Presbyter, etc. Every Templar was assigned to a specific castle. The order carried on public activities and celebrations, but for initiates only it also had a system of secret rituals and services. These included a *legendarium, evangelarium,* and *visionarium,* assigned readings and a *biblio mysticum* (a "secret bible"), and prescribed prayers and invocations. All this purportedly constituted a Grail liturgy dedicated to reviving the ancient forgotten mysteries of the old sacred tradition (ascribed to a legendary Aryan Thule) from which the whole Indo-Germanic culture was supposed to have originated.

The central symbol of the Thule Grail mysteries was represented by a swastika, the ancient symbol of renewal, flanked by two horns of the moon (the horns of the old Celtic shamanic god Cerunnus). It is held within and over a moon sickle, as in a cup. Such a symbol was represented as still to be found upon ancient Gothic spearpoints.

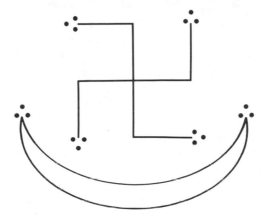

This emblem was now said to be the most secret symbol of the Armanentum Armandom, the name given to the order by its high priests and spiritual directors. These new Templars claimed to guard and serve the Grail of the racially pure blood and the Thule mysteries of the ancient Aryan root race.[13]

The central teaching of the new Templar order was the rabid racist nationalism and anti-Semitism in which Hitler later excelled. It stressed the cultivation of the racially pure blood, the "furthering of the sense of the sacredness of the blood and the laws of inheritance," and of pure "Asic" or Aryan breeding. It held the original paradisal state to have been that of the pure race. The fall of man was due to the mixing of blood. The coming appearance of Jesus, the redeemer and supposed advocate of racial purity, will signal the first battle and final victory of the blond, blue-eyed race which will bring back the Kingdom of Heaven. Needless to say, in this rendering Jesus is Aryan, not Jewish.

He is referred to as Frauja, the word for Jesus used by the Visigothic bishop Ulfila in his translation of the Bible, obviously because it sounds more Germanic.

According to Liebenfels, the Grail is the "god in man carried and supported by the pure woman of higher breeding."[14]

For the public, the religion of the order was promulgated by a periodical called *Ostara*, named after a conjectured Germanic earth goddess of spring and beauty. From her name also the word Oster, "Easter," is supposed to be derived. *Ostara* dwelt upon Aryan superiority, spiritual and physical. It propagandized the racial pseudotheories of the superiority of blond, blue-eyed, Aryan, Nordic strains over the inferior Mediterranean, Slavic, Jewish and Negro races, with their supposedly undermining effect upon the nobility of culture and spirit.

According to Daim's research, the readers of *Ostara* apparently belonged to the most influential circles of old pre–World War I Austria. They included the chiefs of staff of the Austrian army and navy, members of the House of Lords, the inventor of synthetic rubber, and no less a person than Karl Lueger, the anti-Semitic mayor of Vienna, as well as Franz Ferdinand, heir to the throne, whose assassination sparked the First World War. In one of his letters, Ferdinand makes use of the subsequently worn slogan denouncing Jews, Freemasons, and socialists as undermining the state.

The most important member and disciple, however, is referred to by Lanz von Liebenfels (alias Fra George ONT) in a letter to Brother Aemilius (a Mr. Emile): "You were one of our earliest followers. Do you realize that Hitler is one of our disciples? I shall still live to see that he and through him also we shall be victorious and shall unleash a moment that will set the world atremble. Hail to you."[15] This letter is dated February 1932. And in 1934 he speaks of his initially small nucleus as the "first carrier of the movement which at the present by the judgment of God irresistibly rolls across the world as the most powerful movement of history."[16] Hitler was quoted by Rauschning, the *Gauleiter* of Danzig, as having said:

You ought to understand Parzifal differently from the way it is generally interpreted. Behind the trivial Christian dressing of the external story, with its Good Friday magic, this profound drama has quite a different content. It is not a Christian, Schopenhauerian religion of compassion, but the pure and aristocratic blood that is glorified. To guard and glorify this is a task for which the brotherhood of initiates has gathered itself together. There the king suffers the incurable sickness of corrupted blood. There the ignorant yet pure man is led into the temptation of yielding to the guile and ecstasy of a corrupt civilization in Klingsor's magic garden, or else he may choose to join the knight elect who guard the secret of life: the pure blood. We, all of us, suffer from that sickness of contaminated mixed blood. How can we purify ourselves and atone? Take heed: the compassion which leads to knowing is only for the inwardly corrupt one, for him who is split in himself. And this compassion knows only one course of action: to let the sick one die. The eternal life which is the gift of the Grail is only for the truly pure and noble ... How is one to stop racial decay? Politically we have acted: no equality no democracy. But what about the masses of the people? Should one let them go their way, or should one stop them? Should we form an elect group of real initiates? An order, the fraternity of templars around the Grail of the pure blood?[17]

Hitler eventually answered this question in the affirmative: the *Ordensburgen* of the S. S. were formed as Grail castles for the purpose of cultivating a pure race for the *perfecti* in a holy marriage of the racially select. Hitler's extermination of minorities, notably Jews, may well have been intended as a ritual offering; the *holocaust*, the burned sacrifice to his Holy of Holies. His mode of operation unleashed gruesome Dionysian orgies of destruction. A myth disregarded, forgotten, and repressed, erupted and immersed the world in a cataclysm of destruction.

The Hitler phenomenon presents us with an example of obsessive, indeed psychotic psychopathology of a collective nature. But its basic dynamics are not essentially different from the similar invasions of transpersonal, mythological, or archetypal material as they flood the psyche of single individuals. In fact it would seem that individual and collective obsessions mutually sparked each other in Hitler's National Socialism. Such dangerous possibilities, not at all limited to that one-time event, have been far too little considered. We looked at an example of individual Dionysian obsession (our "downtrodden housewife") in an earlier chapter, and noted the dangerous tendency toward destruction or self-destruction, the loosing of the beast, which arises when the force is not properly understood and received. As collective phenomena, brutality and devastation are rampant in our time. They are not limited to Hitler, Stalin, and the Ayatollah Khomeini.

We have noted already that the horned god, the consort of the Great Goddess, is an integral aspect of the Grail dynamic. In the pre-Christian blood rites, he is slain in the form of the old king (represented by his predecessor or other sacrificial scapegoat victims), dismembered, and reborn.

Strabo writes that among the Germanic Cimri "when prisoners were brought into their camp ... priestesses apprehended them, sword in hand, and after wreathing them in flowers, led them to a great copper bowl large enough to contain twenty amphorae, against which a kind of ladder had been erected ... One of them climbed up until she stood over the bowl, pulled each prisoner up to the edge, and cut his throat."[18]

The archetype of horned god and Shaman, involving madness, death, and rebirth appears also in the rituals and in the liturgy of the Templar orders, both medieval and new. No inside information is available about the secret rituals of Liebenfels' new Templar order, but the rituals of the OTO, claiming to carry on the traditions of the old Templar order, explicitly, repeatedly, refer to "our god Baphomet, the unutterable one, the bearer of the holy Grail."[19] The old Templar order was broken up, ostensibly, because their worship of this Baphomet, depicted as a hermaphroditic horned god figure, was heretical. In medieval witches' cults this figure appears as the horned attendant of the goddess. Called the Devil by the church, he was known as the Lord of Reincarnation by the witches. As with Dionysus's death and renewal, blood rites were undoubtedly associated with this figure in pre-Christian pagan cults.

Consciousness and Myth

It is important to understand the difference between creative possibilities and regressive pathology in the expression of a myth. In order to do so, we need to note that the barbaric blood renewal rite through killing has undergone a process of symbolic evolution. In the medieval Christianized version, the renewal of life through dismemberment and spilling of blood is replaced by a symbolism akin to the mass. The Grail contains the blood of the one-time crucified Christ. It renews itself through the devotion of its community, that is, through a psychological act of loving dedication and commitment. In the Hitler psychosis, the *archaic element* resurfaced; not loving dedication but *murderous frenzy* were acted out in the National Socialist paranoia.

Whether creative possibilities or regressive destruction shall prevail then depends not upon the nature of the archetype or myth, but upon the attitude and degree of consciousness. This is the most important and least understood fact of psychic dynamics. It is valid collectively no less than individually. Any autonomous archetypal or mythological element which strives to become activated must become integrated and somehow constructively and creatively channelled into conscious living by reconciling its current demands with the degree of consciousness, ethos and morality already achieved by the community and the individual. To fail to understand this can be very dangerous. This was the problem faced by our patient in Chapter 1, but missed by the would-be assassin of President Reagan. Whenever, owing to unconscious disregard or impatience, this painful maturation process is short-circuited, the energetic core emerges in an archaic, primitive, obsessive form, more often than not with paranoic projection, and leads to dangerous, often destructive, acting out. We encounter the most tragic instances of such event patterns, of course, in periods of individual and collective transition. Then the conscious orientation is still unprepared and incapable of assimilating the new trends. Consciousness can not comprehend the new. It reacts, in a backlash response, by fortifying and hardening the old position. In public life, we have come to know this phenomenon well enough. The attempted integration of Blacks into formerly all-white public schools, and the ensuing violence in many places, is an example. The individual also tends to react to the threatening inner stirrings with increased rigidity. Then the new tendencies are acted out unconsciously in terms of the old habit patterns. The result of this is not only ambivalence, self contradiction, and deadlock, but also bizarre or even outright destructive action. Thus the patient we described in Chapter 1 responded to the shamanic, Dionysian music teacher with self punishment and the danger of killing and dismembering her child, rather than by giving herself to her "inner music" and "dismembering" her rigid behavior pattern; the young man felt he had to kill a president, any president, in order to serve his goddess.

Hitler did not understand the call to transcend and sacrifice the patriarchal stance of combativeness, conquest, and self-aggrandizement. Instead, he became obsessed by the great shaman redeemer god. In paranoic identification, he believed himself to be the god of renewal and blessing. The flip side of the coin, the unacknowledged ego trip with its selfish power greed, he projected upon his scapegoats: the Jews and other enemies.

The following quote is given as a quasi-clinical demonstration of this identification-projection dynamic and its paranoic danger. It is taken from the *National Socialist World,* number two, Fall 1965, published and released quarterly by the World Union of National Socialists (international headquarters, Arlington, Virginia). The title is "Bolshevism from Moses to Lenin: A Dialogue between Adolph Hitler and Me," by Dietrich Eckhardt, translated by William Pierce.

The truth, Hitler said, is indeed as you once wrote: one understands the Jew when one knows what his ultimate goal is. And that goal is, beyond world domination, the annihilation of the world. He must war down all the rest of mankind, he persuades himself, in order to prepare a paradise on earth. He must make himself believe that only he is capable of this great task, and, considering his ideas of paradise, that is certainly so. But one sees, if only in the means which he employs, that he is secretly driven to something else. While he pretends to himself to be elevating mankind, he torments men to despair, to madness, to ruin. If a halt is not ordered, he will destroy all men. His nature compels him to let go, even though he dimly realized that he must thereby destroy himself. There is no other way for him; he must act thus. This realization of the unconditional dependence of his own existence upon that of his victims appears to me to be the main cause of his hatred. To be obliged to try to annihilate us with all his might, but at the same time to suspect that that must lead inevitably to his own ruin, therein lies, if you will, the tragedy of Lucifer.

In a fashion as uncanny as it is totally unconscious, Hitler here describes his own psychology, driven as he is by the Aquarian myth. It is quite obvious that when, in this text, one replaces "Jew" with "Hitler" or "National Socialism" or simply "I," the wording constitutes a most accurate self-description, not only of Hitler's own personality and goals, but also of the nature of the Dionysian, shamanic impulse that drove him inexorably to the Holocaust and self-destruction. The tragedy of Lucifer, the light-bringer, drove him to act obsessively rather than consciously and responsibly.[20]

How then can we channel the impulses of the Aquarian Grail patterns if we are to avoid another Holocaust psychology? In a way Hitler was correct in holding that the Grail myth, in its popularly known fashion, hides a deeper mystery. He was catastrophically wrong of course, in naively acting out his power-greed in terms of racism and in the attempt to renew ancient blood sacrifices, scapegoating and *holocausting* in concretistic terms. Instead of moving into a new awareness, he regressed into barbarism and madness. But the evolution of consciousness has moved from mythological identification to symbolic ritual, from actual slaughter to the Eucharist. It is now moving further toward interiorization of ritual and myth in the form of psychological meaning for the way we live and function. Teilhard de Chardin defines evil as ontological inferiority or unconsciousness.[21] In this sense, as well as to our feeling values, Hitler embodied evil. It is from the angle of psychological significance and of a new evolutionary step that we have now to look at the Grail myth.

There is an increasing consensus among anthropologists that the extant forms of the Grail legends, including Wolfram's *Parzival,* are but exoteric versions of initiation rites, or perhaps secret teachings revealed only to the elect.[22] The continuity of the Grail theme in later esoteric societies as discussed above, makes such an assumption even more probable. Moreover, a psychological evaluation of the story, particularly Wolfram's, leaves us with the feeling that probably a main, perhaps decisive, point has been omitted or suppressed in the extant versions. What finally enables Parzifal to achieve the Grail after his initial failure is never explained. Presumably the deliverance of the Grail depended upon his asking the question, "What ails you?" or "Whom does one serve with the Grail?" After he is apprised of his failure he loses his faith, becomes Christianized, is told about the Grail, and becomes a wanderer in the wilderness, a scapegoat. The fault was not his in the first place, as he was instructed in the code of knighthood not to ask any questions. But now there is a gap in the continuity of development. Parzifal is lost sight of inexplicably. Equally inexplicably, when he appears later on he is called upon to assume the kingship of the Grail. We are not told what change or initiation he underwent that would qualify him now for that election. Instead the story has turned to the exploit of Gawain, who liberates the *castel merveil*, the bewitched castle of women, and successfully serves Orgeluse, the woman who brought ruin upon the Grail king. Might this be the initiation?

We have learned from our work with dreams in analytical psychology that the intervening, seemingly irrelevant motif frequently presents us with an unconscious key to the problem. Could the exploits of Gawain be a disguise for Parzifal's initiatory experience? Once considered, the evidence is both convincing and amazing. For one thing, there is evidence that Gawain is Parzifal's original name. In the Welsh version, the *Mabinogion*, Pryderi's (Peredur's), Parzifal's earlier name is Gwri Gwalt Adwyn, meaning bright hair, which eventually becomes contracted to Gawain.[23] Gawain is also called the Fountain of May, "he of the bright hair," "he who is given eternal youth" (in *diu krone*). On his shield he wears the pentagram, the endless knot, the emblem of Venus Ishtar. He is both an Irish solar hero,[24] and the new year's god who heals and renews the old god, who has guarded the cauldron and now must die.[25] Gawain is a healer and is the lover of the Grail goddess. In Wolfram's version he redeems the castle of women, the world of the Fée or mount of Venus, which is the hidden aspect of the Grail castle. He serves Orgeluse who, like the ancient goddess, has caused many men to lose their lives and the Fisher King his wound. In her service, he challenges Gromoflanz, who killed his predecessor, her former husband. He does so by breaking the branch from the sacred tree, comparable to the Golden Bough. In support of our thesis, at the end of the same story Parzifal carries that same branch, and discovers his Gawain side in an episode described as combat to a standstill.

Gawain's initiation and liberating deed occur in the space of the castle of the goddess, represented in the medieval versions as Kundrie, Morgan Le Fay, Lady Ragnell, or the Grail maidens. The Grail goddess is the heroine of a seasonal abduction story, mistress of the moon and vegetation, who transforms herself from the most hideous animal forms into radiant beauty and is a guide to the other world. With the knowledge of her husband she embraces a youthful god and her husband interrupts them with his lightning stroke. Finally, she is associated with a cult in which a priestess bears a vessel adorned with lights in an initiation ceremony intimately connected with the healing of the maimed god.[26]

Gawain and Parzifal are initiated, then, into the mysteries of the feminine. We can glean the details from a similar Hindu legend of the Great Goddess, which closely duplicates the main features of Gawain's initiation, and from two popularly known medieval stories: the stories of the Green Knight and of Lady Ragnell. They contain the gist in a psychologically comprehensible form which is veiled in the official Grail legends. I shall give a short rendering, since they are less well known today than the Parzifal story.

On the new year's day, King Arthur is holding court at Camelot; as is his custom on such a day, he will not sit down and touch food until he has heard some strange tidings or until some adventure has happened. Suddenly a huge knight enters the hall on horseback. He is splendidly attired and armed with a battle axe. His face, hair, beard, coat, mantle and accoutrements are all green. In one hand he holds a holly bough "that is greatest in green when groves are bare." He challenges the court to contend with him in a Christmas game: he will receive a blow from the axe, without resistance, provided that a twelvemonth and a day hence, his opponent will receive from him a stroke in return. Only Gawain accepts the challenge, and smites off the green knight's head with one sweep of the weapon. The green knight picks up the head, mounts his horse, identifies himself as the knight of the green chapel, and enjoins Gawain to fulfill the compact by presenting himself on next year's moon at the green chapel, the location of which he refuses to define. It is to be found by setting out upon a quest into the unknown.

The next year Gawain sets out on the quest from which he may never return. After long and toilsome wanderings through wild and unknown lands, a fine castle appears on Christmas night, suddenly and unexpectedly, out of nowhere. He is auspiciously entertained by the lord of the castle, a stalwart knight of "high age," a broad beard, and a face "fell as fire." His wife is of great beauty, and there is another lady in the household, old and very ugly, but held in high honor. The host urges Gawain to stay on, since the object of his search, the green chapel, is no more than two miles hence. Gawain agrees to stay until the new year's moon.

For the last three days of his stay, his host proposes a merry bargain which Gawain accepts. Wearied by his hard journey, Gawain is to lie in bed till mass time and spend the day indoors in the lady's company while the host goes hunting. In the evening, they will exchange what they have won during the day.

On the morning of each of the three days Gawain is visited, while still in bed, by the lady of the castle, who pleads with him to accept her love. With great difficulty to himself and great courtesy to her, he withstands the temptation, but agrees to accept one kiss the first morning, two kisses the second, and three kisses and a green lace, which she avers will protect him from death in fight, for the third. The kisses he faithfully renders up to his host while protecting the lady's secret. Only the green lace he keeps for himself and says nothing about. In return he receives from his host a bounty of deer the first evening, a huge boar the second, and a fox on the third.

On new year's day he is led to the chapel but warned by his guide that he faces certain death. As he rides down into the valley, Gawain at first can see nothing of the chapel. At last, by the side of a roaring stream, he perceives a mound overgrown with turf and having a hole at the end and on either side. It seems to him "an old cave or the crevice of an old crag." Perhaps this is the green chapel, says Gawain to himself. "It is a place where the devil may say his matins at midnight. It is a chapel of mischance. It is the cursedest kirk that ever I came in." He hears a noise as of a scythe being ground, and presently the green knight approaches. Gawain bends his head and the axe is raised. As it first descends, he shrinks a little with his shoulders. The green knight pauses and upbraids him with cowardice. The second time the green knight makes a feint with the axe and Gawain holds firm. The third time the axe comes down but instead of striking off Gawain's head it merely scratches his neck. Gawain, now having fulfilled his obligation, wants to fight, but the green knight refuses. He reveals himself as identical with Gawain's host at the castle. At his instigation his lady has wooed Gawain to test him. The first two blows had been harmless because on the first two days Gawain had faithfully lived up to the bargain between them and rendered up what he had received. The third blow injured him slightly because he had concealed the green lace, yet since fear for his own life is natural for a human, the injury was but a slight scratch. The green knight also reveals his own name as Bernlak de Haut Desert and tells Gawain that the ancient lady at the castle is Morgan le Fay, who had planned the whole adventure, purportedly to strike fear into Arthur's court. Gawain returns to the court and recounts his adventure but he is ashamed of his all too human shortcoming, the mark of which is his scar. "For no man can hide his scar, nor rid himself of it; when once fast upon him it will never depart." Arthur, however, has high praise for Gawain and proclaims that henceforth all knights of his table are to wear a green lace like Gawain's.

A second story, that of Gawain's encounter with the ugly dame, Lady Ragnell, sheds further light upon the pertinent psychological factor. In defense of a wronged lady, Arthur meets in combat a "loathly knight," the most terrible man he has ever seen. This giant of demonic power defeats him by magic. The lady then identifies herself as the servant of Morgan Le Fay, and the knight, Gromar, as the lord of the "wicked goddess castle." To redeem his forfeited life, Arthur is now given the task to go where he will and ask of all he meets what thing it is that women most desire in this world. After a year and a day, he is to return with the right answer or have his head struck off. He sets out on his quest with Gawain, but after a year they have failed to come up with a convincing answer. On returning sadly to the bewitched castle they meet the loathliest lady that ever the eye of man rested upon. Her face is red as the sinking sun. Long, yellow teeth show between wide, weak lips. Her head is set upon a great thick neck; she is fat and unshapely as a bell. Yet the horror of her lies in something more than the hideousness of her looks, for in her great, squinting, red-ringed eyes there lurks a strange and terrifying shadow of fear and suffering. She offers to tell Arthur the true answer which would save his life upon condition that a knight of his court shall be her husband this day. Horror-stricken, Arthur refuses, but Gawain offers himself as willing to accept the loathsome sacrifice. Returning to the demonic knight who is ready to strike off his head and bring it to Morgan Le Fay, Arthur redeems himself with the answer: what women desire most is to have sovereignty over men. Now Gawain's wedding with the loathly damsel is celebrated. The whole court pities his horrible lot. When bride and groom are alone in the bridal chamber, the bride demands to be kissed. In spite of his revulsion Gawain manages to oblige her. She then changes shape, and he holds in his arms the loveliest maid that ever his eyes beheld. She reveals to him that by his noble act he has freed her from enchantment, but yet not entirely, for half of the time she still must wear her hideous form. He is to choose whether by day or by night she is to be foul and ugly, whether to endure either the shame before the court or the revulsion at night in their intimacy together. This Gawain declines to do but feelingly leaves the choice to her, willing to abide by her own decision. By thus giving her the sovereignty, the enchantment is broken entirely and she henceforth appears beautiful by day and by night.

A Hindu story, coming from a different culture (even though not necessarily from a different time), contains in a coordinated form the chief elements of the Grail motif. It demonstrates too that indeed the Waste Land, and the injury to male creativity (the wound of the Fisher King), are owing to the disregard of the great Feminine. Restoration of land and man depends upon restoring homage to her.

One Vishnu was riding through the air on the sunbird Garuda. Both of them, filled with their sense of self, saw in Vishnu the highest, most irresistible and universal being. They flew past the throne of the Great

Goddess but gave her no heed. "Fly on, fly on," said Vishnu to Garuda. Then the Great Goddess poured rigidity upon them, and they could not stir from the spot. Vishnu in his rage shook her seat with both hands but could not move it. Instead he fell and sank to the bottom of the world ocean. Unable to stir, he lost consciousness and became rigid, defenseless, and lifeless. Brahma, the creator, went in search of him and tried to lift him, but he also fell under the same enchantment and grew rigid. The same fate befell all the other gods who went with Indra in search of the first two, and tried to raise them from the bottom of the sea. Only Shiva, the consort of the Goddess, understood what had happened and led them all back to do homage to her and obtain her grace. In order to do so, he taught them to fashion in their own flesh the magic "defense" or "armor" of the "mysteries of all desire and joy." Thus they released themselves from her *maya* and saturated themselves once more with her strength. It was this "armor" that protected Shiva against her enchantment. He who fashioned it in undivided devotion could behold the Goddess. Then as they worshipped her, the Goddess revealed herself in the flesh and bade all gods drink of the waters of her womb and bathe therein. "Then will you be free of imprisonment in your ego, and thus will you move to your place in the senate of heaven."[27]

This story is paralleled by a modern dream brought by a very "macho," successful business executive. He had reached the wasteland phase in his life, with a sense of sterility and meaninglessness. He dreamt that a bunch of robbers kidnapped a girl and were tearing out her heart. She muttered, "You must drink my water. You must drink my water."

Through all these versions, including the "elucidations," we can now discern the chief elements of the hidden myth: the angry or insulted Feminine, hidden away in a bewitched, grim and joyless *yonder,* is to be redeemed by a quest into the threatening, roadless "other" land. The quester is to offer himself to the rite of renewal by besting the terrible shaman, the horned companion with the power of death and renewal. Through reverence for the sovereignty of the Goddess in her repellent no less than her beautiful aspect, the quester thereby receives her boon and may drink again of the ever-flowing waters.

Bernlak de Haut Desert means "shepherd of the high desert," hence of the Waste Land. He represents essentially the same figure as the Fisher King who suffers from a wound on his genitals. In another form, he is the castrated magician, guardian of the *castel merveil,* the castle of the captive bewitched women which Gawain frees, or he appears as Sir Gomer Somer Jour ("growling, sinister day"), the sinister guardian and brother of the dreadful Morgan la Fee. She in turn is called "Ruleress," Gorgo, Medusa, and represents the abysmal terror of the

depth dimension of the Goddess, the dark mysterious womb of the un-
born. She is the loathsome well maiden who was goddess of the land.
Rejected by the patriarchal ego's pride and fear, she waits to be redeemed, accepted, and accorded homage and sovereignty. Both the Goddess and her dark companion guard the *amphora,* the Aquarian Grail,
source of life and renewal. Its waters flow from underneath the roots of
the world tree or world *axis,* the tree of life *and* knowledge.

In the Western "paradise lost" myth, the tasting of the fruit, the experiential knowing of good and evil, led to the loss of Eden. In the patriarchal ethic, the activity of the serpent—instinctual, natural action—was accounted evil, and was no longer to be "tasted." Natural
action was to be regulated by law, no longer by instinct. The channeling
of violence and of natural destructiveness into human sacrifice, as embodied in Cain's deed, was decreed murder and is now unacceptable to
us. Killing was to be meted out legally (and only to scapegoats) in retaliation for the evil they did or whose projection they carry. In the patriarchy, ethics and goodness were to be preserved by obedience to the
law.

Are we to assume then that the opening of the amphora is now to le-
gitimize evil and destructive violence? This was Hitler's implicit assumption. His man of the future, bent only upon conquest, was to be
ruthless, cruel, and lacking any compassion or respect for human suffering.

Yet the old cauldron of renewal has been filled with the blood of
Christ, the god-man, who consciously and voluntarily offered himself to
crucifixion, according to the medieval form of the myth. The blood is no
longer that of involuntary scapegoats, nor of an equally anonymous racial collective.

The vessel containing the blood of the Crucifixion, which ever and
again renews itself, points to a contained inward, psychological renewal
through conscious bleeding and crucifixion. This means awareness and
acceptance of inner, emotional, and psychological conflict. No longer
safely guided by the collective rules of the superego, we must, as we risk
individual choices, now discover the conscience that speaks through our
individual selves. This scene is amplified and elaborated in Gawain's
trials and the motif of the question.

Gawain's trials are not ones of conquest. The capacity to conquer and
be brave is taken for granted; it had to be acquired previously. The new
challenge is one of acceptance, as in the Hindu story. This acceptance is
to occur from a position of loyalty and of strength, not weakness. The
trial demands the strength to sustain awareness and suffering of conflict, and to be able to surrender oneself to it. Gawain consciously expe-

riences the conflict of fear versus bravery in relation to the green knight, of honor versus desire in respect to the *chatelaine,* and of loyalty and affection to Arthur versus his revulsion for the ugly hag. He acts but does not *act out.*

He offers himself to the beheading. This archetypal motif is as old, if not older than, crucifixion. Thus he becomes "like the serpents [who] abandoning their inveterated skins move on, put off death, and become the sun ... putting off the old man [the head is considered the seat of the soul] and assuming the new."[28] Likewise, he surrenders to the ugly witch, who is a Grail damsel and guardian of the well. These are different manifestations of the earth mother, who controlled the plot.[29] Thus he proves his readiness to deal with life and power. In the drinking of the Goddess's waters the ego's personal claim to power is renounced. Indeed, the ego acknowledges itself as but a recipient and channel of a destiny flowing from a deep, mysterious ground of being which is the source both of terror and revulsion as well as of the beautiful play of life. This power flowing from the sovereignty of life is to be handled in a reverential fashion if the protection of the Goddess is to be gained. That protection is symbolized by the "armor of the Goddess" and the green baldric of the lady.

In most of the Grail stories, a question must be asked if the waters are to flow again and the Waste Land is to be redeemed. But it is significant that while the importance of the question is emphasized over and over again, when finally it is asked no answer is forthcoming; indeed the matter is passed over.

This paradoxical state of affairs can be understood in two ways, each really complementary to the other. What matters most is the asking itself—regardless of what the answer might mean, or even whether there is an answer. For the question is about the reason for the suffering and about the nature of the Grail mystery. Whom or what does it serve, what is behind the mystery of wound and pain? To these questions, indeed there are no standard answers of universal credibility; at least not for our postecclesiastic culture. Only individually can answers be discovered; not only by means of asking, but more than that, by living and suffering the question. Apparently for our times, life demands to be lived as a Koan question, as a continual searching; not, as before, in accordance with a dogmatically prescribed pattern of behavioral and moral codes. No longer, as in the Oedipus myth, is the riddle asked of man. We are no longer (or at least not only) to endure being questioned by life (the Sphinx). In addition, we ourselves are to ask the question, and try to discover, in our individual ways, by our own trials and experiments how and when the mystery of our life's calling or destiny speaks to our individual selves. Thus, as Campbell pointed out, Arthur's knights set out together on their search for the Grail, but each one chooses his own separate and individual way through the forest.

In the older Irish sources, an answer is suggested which accords with the above. In pledging the royal cup, the ceremonial question was to be asked, "Whom does one serve with this cup?" The answer was, "the sovereignty of Erin."[30] This sovereignty was represented by the Queen Priestess. While on the face of it the answer seems to refer to a political sovereignty, we are also reminded of Lady Ragnell and the question she embodies: namely, the acceptance of woman's sovereignty, the acceptance of the ugly with the beautiful, the dark with the light. There are many tales extant in Celtic lore of the ugly maiden who bestows the sovereignty of the land upon the knight who has accepted and kissed her in her ugly form. The Queen Goddess Priestess represents life itself; to be accepted as it is, in its darkness as well as lightness, in its ups and downs, its tides of destiny. Not only is she to be accepted, she is also to be responded to.

And this is what Gawain does, both with Lady Ragnell and with the Lady of the castle of the green knight. He does not reject her and her temptation, but allows himself to be moved and touched by her. He maintains his own integrity, but responds to her, her need, and her game.

But there is still another aspect of the answer which is implied. Whatever he received Gawain had to render up to the green knight, to the Dionysic shamanic power of death and renewal. In return he receives a deer, the animal of Artemis, representing youthful, playful sensitivity; a boar, standing for the strength and power of maturity; and a fox, symbol of the cunning and wisdom of advanced age. The deeds of living are not to be regarded as our property or as achievements to be gloried in. They are to be rendered up to the gods, to the power of life. They serve change, growth, transformation, and experience. Ours is the action but not the fruit of the action, as the *Bhagavad Gita* has noted. Or, stated differently, not our action but our motivation, our way of experiencing, and consciousness gained, are what matter as we suffer and work through our conflict between our desires and our deepest conscience. This is what is served by life and living. Hence it is psychological significance, not the committing of heroic acts in themselves, that matters, in the Aquarian epoch.

Asking the question also implies an admission that the position one happens to hold, namely the ego position of objectification, and reliance on superego rule and rational "head" control, could be unsatisfactory or sterile. One realizes one's Waste Land. In the Indian version, Shiva asks, "How did you become rigid and lifeless, shorn of consciousness like substance without animation?"[31] Confronting the Dionysian raging force, the demonic hunter, the dark mother who stands behind, and offering oneself for beheading implies a renunciation, temporarily at least, of "head" control, of the objectifying sense of order and collective rule upon which the ego has relied. One faces into the dark maw of one's own nature, into one's needs and hurts, one's affects and instincts, including the two demonic aspects of "devouring passion and bestial stupor," in their tempting as well as destructive forms; and seeks an individual, morally satisfying answer.[32] One does this, however, in order to play with them without being swept away by them; to experience rather than act out. (We shall return to this difference between acting out and experiential enacting in Chapter 14.)

What is the nature of this "play," as it is intimated in Gawain's dalliance with the lady of the green knight? Surely the better part of three days spent in bed was not taken up entirely with moralizing, philosophical or Platonic discourses or with just one to three kisses. This is even less likely in view of the fact that in Wolfram's *Parzival* Gawain is assaulted by a wild beast while in his bed in the castle of the ladies. In order to gain an understanding of this encounter with the chatelaine who is surely another version of the Grail goddess, we have to consider the symbolism of courtly love, in terms of which the encounter is described. The cult of courtly love, regardless of the extent to which it became actual practice, embodies the first notion in the Western patriarchal space of an enhanced value of the feminine. Indeed, courtly love was a means of educating and transforming men, a means to "make a gentleman out of a lout," and "cure the beast of his bestiality and reveal his superior humanity."[33]

Courtly love did not advocate unfleshly love but was a discipline of eroticism, like the Hindu Tantra. Possibly also like Tantra, it constituted a temporary surfacing of secret religio-erotic cult practices in the service of the Goddess. In the rites of courtly love the lady sets herself up as the supreme recompense above and beyond all earthly glory and above and beyond death.

"The longest, the most passionate part of love is the part that precedes the act of love, and it is over this period that women reign as mistresses and prophets. They force their suitors to undergo all sorts of trials, testing their fidelity, their discretion, so important in an era where secrecy took the place of virtue and discipline and their refinement. Only this long period of unsatisfied desire, deliberately prolonged by the woman, allowed her to distinguish a passing infatuation from true passion, to excite the latter, and then pass to the trial of the bedchamber.

"At this point everything does not suddenly turn topsy-turvy to the woman's disadvantage, as will happen later on in the seventeenth century; she herself sets the date of the single night that is to serve as a test, and invites the man to come to her if he so pleases, on condition that he will do 'everything I should like,' as Beatrix de Die put it. In fact, it is she who takes the initiative and gives all the orders. It is she who embraces, caresses, and asks for caresses and intimate embraces in return. The lover must be able at once to contain himself—for it would be unseemly to allow his sexual impatience to show—to give her pleasure, and to gain her confidence. This custom of the first night of tenderness and respect, entirely devoted to caresses and declarations of love, preparing the heart for the act of love, is attested to by more than one writer."[34]

Compare this with the tradition of the Indian Tantra, which is a "cult of ecstasy focused on a vision of cosmic sexuality. It proclaims everything, the crimes and miseries as well as the joys of life to be the active play of the female, creative principle, the goddess of many forms, sexually penetrated by an invisible, indescribable, seminal male. In ultimate fact, he has generated her for his own enjoyment. And the play, because it is analogous to the activity of sexual intercourse, is pleasurable to her."[35]

The Tantrica must learn to identify himself with that cosmic pleasure in play, and to recognize that what may seem to others to be misery is an inevitable and necessary part of its creation, whereas the pleasure is a true reflection of cosmic delight.[36] The Tantrica has to lead a controlled life of repeated rituals and carefully designed meditative activities of erotic discipline.

The central ritual of Tantra is carefully controlled, meditative sexual intercourse with a female power holder, whose favor the initiate has to win. She represents the goddess: the Shakti, or pure energy. The intent of the ritual is not procreation or physical pleasure per se, but psychic transformation, a transformation of the subtle body. It is a kind of erotic Eucharist. It is also a "blood" rite inasmuch as the most powerful rite of reintegration requires intercourse with a female partner when she is menstruating and her red sexual energy is at its peak. This rite may be carried out in a cremation ground among the corpses and flaming pyres. The corollary to this is the gruesome realm of the green knight in our tale.

In Tantrism the woman is considered the embodiment of the goddess, to be worshipped and communed with regardless of social caste or marital status. She channels divine energy in its beautiful and ecstatic, as well as its terrifying and ugly aspects, to the man who approaches her and submits to the elaborate ritual of communion and "chastity." Yet this chastity, like the *castitas* of courtly love, refers not to sexual abstinence but to purity of purpose, the one-pointedness of its dedication to the transpersonal in the personal encounter, to the renunciation of the egotistic, animalistic drive satisfaction, and their subordination to a spiritual goal. Sexuality and instinctual drives serve as mediating channels.

The lady of the green knight appears as Aphroditic temptress who initiates him like a Shakta or hierodule virgin. She brings the hero to an awareness of the conflicting nature of his urges and desires. She opens him to his weakness, his fears, his psychological ambivalence and splitness, all of which are incompatible with the idealized hero image. He now faces up to his conflict between honor and desire, between courage and his fear, between his code of ethics and his hitherto unadmitted and unacceptable wishes. She makes him aware of the fact that the detestable scapegoat is none other than himself. He is tempted to two extremes: either take refuge behind the established code of behavior and deny the truth of his subjective feeling by putting off the woman in the traditional way; or fall for his desire and violate his code of ethics.

Prior to facing the green knight's axe, he discovers an entirely new challenge: he is to honor desire and the instinctual urge without being overcome by them. Conscious enactment within the range of what is morally acceptable—rather than either uncontrolled acting out or total avoidance—is suggested by the "innocent" dalliance of the three mornings in bed with the lady.

The new approach, then, for our time (which is asked of Gawain in his trial), is not to avoid but to risk the encounter with the world of the Goddess and of Dionysus-Azazel-Pan, the green shepherd god. We are called on to meet their world in its ecstatic and joyful, its ugly and terrifying aspect; to risk losing our heads, and this at the price of being painfully wounded; yet to lose neither awareness nor self-control, nor caring regard for our partner.

Gawain is tested: can he receive and give love and empathy in a disciplined, responsible, and self-transcending fashion; can he respect social mores, yet not use them to avoid an honest, personal response and commitment based on affirmation of need and feeling, rather than impersonal rule and code? This entails personal risk—voluntary self-exposure to crucifixion or beheading—for the sake of progress, growth, and initiatory experience. It eschews the assignment of guilt and blame to a scapegoat, person or group, in a holier-than-thou fashion. It calls for mutual support, a sharing of responsibility, and a playful trying, as well as individual self-confrontation. The chatelaine and Lady Ragnell both risk themselves in concert with Gawain. They challenge and trust his integrity and self-control. Thereby they are able to call forth the Dionysian level, hitherto repressed, *without a surrender of basic ethical standards.* In Wolfram's *Parzifal,* Gawain's adventure consists in serving and redeeming Orgeluse ("pride and anger"). The conditions of the trial apply not only to desire but to all affect expressions; foremost also to anger and aggression.

The new Grail quest, the release of the waters or renewal of the blood, is a symbolic and psychological one. When Gawain finally presents himself at the chapel, the greater part of the test has already been passed. He underwent the real trial when he accepted the scapegoat role for Arthur when he confronted the lady of the castle, and managed to maintain the discipline of courtly love involving courteous acceptance and service to her; and discerning control of his instinctual urges, when he married the "ugly dame" and deferred to her "sovereignty"; and when he served rather than acted out the commands of Orgeluse: "Anger." Thereby he succeeded where both the Fisher King and Parsifal failed. The latter refused to serve the lady, the former "fell for" her.

The old way of avoidance in order not to fall into sin may now be moral cowardice and failure, in light of the demands of the next evolutionary stages of consciousness. Every and any external rule of behavior is open now to the question, "What or whom does it serve?" It may be disregarded or followed according to how it accords with the verdict of one's deepest conscience, the *vox dei* ("voice of God") or Self heard within. This Self addresses us through the reality and the needs of the other person no less than our own. In the new age, The Golden Rule is rediscovered as a psychological dynamic and inner experience, no longer as an external collective command. Whatever we feel toward or do to the other person we know now, has a psychological effect upon ourselves. For better or worse it modifies our own character and being. The new roles of interpersonal functioning and the new ethic through discovery of self within and without, in inner and external relatedness, will be our next concerns.

The Triumph of *Venus*. Tray painting, school of Verona.

Part 5

VISION FOR
A NEW AGE

For every thing there is a season
And a time for every purpose under heaven.

ECCLESIASTES

Labour is blossoming or dancing where
The body is not bruised to pleasure soul
Nor beauty born out of its own despair
Nor blear-eyed wisdom out of midnight oil
O chestnut-tree, great-rooted blossomer,
Are you the leaf, the blossom or the bole?
O body swayed to music, O brightening glance
How can we know the dancer from the dance?

WILLIAM BUTLER YEATS,
"Among School Children"*

* *The Collected Poetry of W. B. Yeats, p. 214.*

CHAPTER 12

New Models of Orientation

Near is and hard to fathom, the God;
yet, where there is danger, groweth
salvation as well. . . .

F. HÖLDERLIN, *"Patmos"*

Psychoneurosis must be understood . . . as the suffering of a soul
which has not discovered its meaning. But all creativeness in the
realm of the spirit as well as every psychic advance of man arises
from the suffering of the soul and the cause of the suffering is
spiritual stagnation or spiritual sterility.

C. G. JUNG*

We have seen how the patriarchal culture of necessity had to repress
what was felt to be the evil aspect of the Feminine. The compelling urge
of instincts, in unison with passionate desire, were held to be threats to
the newly felt freedom of will based upon cool reasoning. In their unpredictability, desire, instincts and emotions were felt to be kin to a
challenge from untamed nature. They manifested the destructiveness of
Satan, the "prince of this world," the antigod to the all-loving reason of
the Father God. Women were seen as daughters of Eve, the temptress,

* *Collected Works,* Vol. XI, par. 497.

or of the demonic Lilith. They were perceived as embodiments of Delilah or Salome, witches and destroyers of men.

The tragedy of the male, as he aspired to the heroic ideal, was represented as a faltering in his resistance to wily woman; letting himself be deceived or seduced into accepting from her hands the forbidden fruit of desire, passion, and bodily urges. The more the patriarchal culture came to stress the life-denying ascetic ideal, the more were the repressed passions—the vulnerable as well as the lustful sides of existence—projected upon women.

Consequently, women needed to be kept in subordinate positions, if not quarantined in harems or hidden beneath disguising or disfiguring clothes, veils, or *sheitels* (wigs worn by Orthodox Jewish women). Femininity was to be limited to obedient passivity, domesticity, and maternal nurturance. Women themselves had to learn to distrust the tides of their emotions and to suspect the voices of their bodies.

The play of sensuality and sexuality became frivolous wickedness, devoid of virtue and goodness. Bodies, bodily functions, body emanations, excretions, and odors were reprehensible, to be despised and hidden away, to be accorded no more attention than absolutely necessary for the sake of survival and reproduction.

Of the vast range of manifestations of the Great Goddess, only the unearthly Mary was acceptable to the Christian West. Through the themes of the Immaculate Conception and the Virgin Birth, she was made asexual. She became the prototype of all loving, sorrowing, good mothers and was a beneficent intercessor. Yet Protestantism would have no truck with even that little divinization of the Feminine.

Not only were women and men cut off from a part of their inner natures—but for men, such "feminine" behavior as sensuousness, playfulness, and the showing of feeling came to be judged reprehensible. The instinctual connection with nature outside was also lost. The destructive aspect of existence is at the same time its transformative and life-renewing aspect. Casting off, change, regeneration, and rebirth are all phases of the same process of life. The experience of ecstatic, orgiastic, and sexual surrender is close to the experience of dying. The denial and fear of sexuality led eventually to the denial and fear of dying; to the loss of the unitary awareness of death and rebirth. Man became trapped in that very physicality which he himself had deprived of divinity. He was reduced to material greed, hedonism, and consumerism in return for denying the creative—indeed divine—dimension of pleasure, joy, and play as manifestations of the spirit.

Males could compensate for the loss of natural and instinctual connectedness by means of increasing reliance upon ego-rationality, achievement, power and control. Women, however, were denied equal rights, in the power-competition game. They came to feel themselves more and more cut off from their natural selves and hemmed-in. Deprived of access to the transformative depth dimensions, their pent-up energy tended to utilize first the remaining channel of "feminine guile" for the sake of retaining a sense of identity and self-value. Indirect assertion by playful or flirtatious seductiveness, however, also came to be considered inferior, if not detestable, in the androlatric system. Consequently, this form of feminine assertiveness turned out to be insufficient for enhancing women's self-respect. Small wonder then, that the dammed-up energies gather themselves in the forms of depressive self-hate, of resentment against the world of men, and a competitive imitation of masculine behavior. In our own time, a situation has come to a head which leaves both sexes profoundly dissatisfied and confused. A depth dimension calls again for active expression of femininity in both sexes. The way this need is shown by the unconscious psyche is exemplified in the following dream. A man had seen a chiropractor, also male, for a period of nine months. A close rapport was felt emotionally and in terms of the body comfort of the treatment. The patient moved to another part of the country and missed his doctor. Four months later, he dreamed of being again in the treatment room. The two dream figures embraced heart-to-heart as the men had actually done on parting. Then the former patient dreamed he put his head on the doctor's chest, felt the steady heartbeat and radiating affection from the heart. Then the chiropractor grew maternally comforting breasts under his shirt which cushioned the patient's head and added to the warm accepting feeling. In this dream the chiropractor is to be taken as an *inner* figure, part of the dreamer's own psyche. He represents now the healer within who enables him to give emotional nurturance to others but also to himself. It is significant that a nine month "pregnancy" period occurred here during which time the external relationship nurtured and ripened inner development. The unconscious is highly sensitive and responsive to such rhythms.

This new form of feminine activity needs to gather itself, to grow and ripen on an interim plane, prior to making itself felt as outer activity. It is likely to be an affirmative expression of the growth and transformative dimensions, of inner psychic realities and facts of feeling. As we have discussed previously, this transformative dimension carries a destructive potential in its outward manifestations, since the birth of the new calls for destruction of the old. It is small wonder then that the smoldering pressure of this upsurge, neither understood nor integrated as yet, is charging our collective psychic atmosphere with what might well be called free-floating violence. These violent urges are born out of general vague dissatisfaction and frustration and tend to fasten upon any suitable pretext and scapegoat as a justification for acting out.

How is this potentially destructive transformative dimension, this repressed Medusa, to be reintegrated into the psychology of men and women? How can we open the door to the seductive play, equally repressed, of Lila, and thereby give space to Pallas the renewer of culture?

We shall discover that those aspects are mutually complementary and help to support one another. And we can find a clue to the overall model of integrative possibilities in the myth: our contemporary myth of Aquarius with its background stories of Gawain, Parsifal, and the guardians and seekers of the Grail.

The dynamic of the *Minne* or Tantric rites, as we explained in the previous chapter, is a conscious experiencing of the conflict between the onrush of desire and voluntary acceptance in the exposure to the dangerous play which was forbidden to the uninitiated.

In accepting the lady with both her allure and her dangerous threat to his value system, her beauty as well as her ugliness, the new man meets his fear of the Feminine, as well as his fear of life, which is the same as his fear of the totally other. That aspect of existence, of himself, is beyond his accustomed standards of comprehension and control.

This is the transformative aspect of life which woman and anima bring to bear. Ugliness, darkness, destruction, and terror demand of us a respectful, if not loving, acceptance without flinching. They are the other sides of beauty, love, nurturance, joy, and pleasure: and this in the face of the revulsion and fear which we discover in ourselves as we confront them.

Life is not good and pleasant only, and neither is one's own nature. Our ugly or evil tendencies, and desires—hate, vengefulness, and envy to name but a few—are part of our natural makeup. Even while held in check consciously, they are always ready to emerge and make existence grim for ourselves and others.

The role of the temptress then is to serve as initiatrix into the daring venture of becoming consciously aware of one's depth and of life as an undivided whole. No longer is life seen as neatly compartmentalized into inner-outer, good-bad, nice and ugly, as in the androlatric cultures. Rather, it is revealed as a living depth of ever-moving, merging balances of tensions and releases, in the constant transformation of creation and destruction. She carries this initiating challenge for the man, but also for herself. It is the challenge to have the courage to look and listen to her own depth, regardless of whether what she may discover accords with what she has been in the habit of considering right.

The temptress challenges us to forego the simplistic trust in the power of well-meaning intentions and to face into the shadow aspect of existence and self without rejecting or repressing, but also without succumbing and being swallowed up by it. We are led, thus, to discover that what we regard as evil or reprehensible rests not only in the other fellow out there, but in ourselves as well. It cannot simply be killed or expelled without destroying and rejecting ourselves. The more we protest this or that as immoral or unacceptable, the more it lives in ourselves, as well as in others. The power of what we choose to call evil is part of the living substance. We must discover how it can be integrated into what we feel is ethically or morally acceptable.

The new ego's aim will be to live fully and consciously through the experiences of fear, destructiveness, and destruction as much as through love, joy, play, pleasure, and success. This needs to be done without fighting them or acting them out, but meditatively experiencing them, psychically and somatically, while giving them as much space and consideration as our needs and duties permit. Doing so apparently connects us with a new core of selfness beyond ordinary ego consciousness. It is a dimension which, according to age-old tradition, even sees us through the portals of the physical death of the body. For this reason, Jung considered analysis an appropriate preparation for dying. This seems borne out also by the researches using LSD with terminal cancer patients. As their experience of self was widened and deepened, most of those so treated were able to accept death peacefully.

A similar level of experience is aimed for by the traditional Tantric Chod meditation on the Goddess to be carried on at a place where the dead are cremated. Many of the newer Western psychological approaches—guided imagination, psychodrama, Gestalt, treatment of anxiety by "flooding"—intend, paradoxically, to deal with problematic or anxiety arousing areas by intensifying experiential awareness of painful events. This means enacting them deliberately, within a controllable and safe context, rather than avoiding them.

What underlies all of the above is a new principle expressive of the holistic frame of reference inherent in the Feminine. It is the principle of accepting confrontation or affirmation. This is now to compensate for the still prevalent patriarchal habit of control, repression and expulsion. The new ego is affirmative. It accepts what formerly has been rejected: body sensuality and enjoyment, but also woundedness, pain, discomfort, and imbalance. It accepts what the Aspirin Age declared to be pathological or insufferable. Only the spear that caused it can heal the wound, says Wagner's Parsifal when he returns the holy spear to the Grail and to the suffering Grail King.

"That which has wounded shall heal" was the reputed answer of the

Delphic oracle to the inquiry of Telephos who suffered from a wound that would not heal from the spear of Achilles.

The formerly rejected shadow problems—our secret weaknesses, shames, "perverted" urges and feelings, everything that makes us feel "guilty"—are now to be accorded recognition and value as balance and indispensable aspects of life, aspects of the transformative power of the Goddess. They are now to be reintegrated, in a transformed fashion, into a new personality pattern which will retain the ethical or moral principles of the patriarchy—the Golden Rule. Action is still to be responsibly controlled even though desire and urge are affirmed. To abandon the moral achievement of the past for the sake of acting out without restraint would constitute a step back, not forward. It would be an attempt to avoid the experience of inner splitness and conflict, the psychological, rather than historical, experience of crucifixion, which is the challenge of the new age. The Hitlers and Stalins, the political climate of today's world, show us what this leads to. Repression of the moral dimension leads to a projection of moralistic rejection now felt from others. One becomes identified with the scapegoat and feels persecuted and martyred by the misjudging *others*. And in justified self defense, any destructive act seems permissible.

Discrimination between what is felt as good or evil, pleasurable or painful, beautiful or ugly, morally acceptable or unacceptable, is a first indispensable step in the achievement of consciousness. Scapegoating—"projecting the negative aspect of those dualities onto the other"—belongs to the patriarchal phase of this evolutionary development. Now, however, the scapegoat demands to be found in ourselves and redeemed. We must learn to live with what formerly has been rejected. We have to take responsibility now for finding a place where it can fit into our lives. It expresses a compensating balance and a rounding-out of the wholeness of our personalities. We can no longer afford the one-sidedness and stereotypedness of the person who is identified only with his virtues, with the collective ideal.

Strictness requires looseness. Courage must discover where it is afraid and needs to fear. Honesty needs to find out where it cheats and is untruthful to the needs of life. Love has to see where it hates and rejects or is indifferent to the realities of the other. Hate has to discover where it is attached, and loves. We must endure the full reality of ourselves, not only that part we wish to be. The full reality of the living being requires a *down* for every *up* just as it leads to an *up* for every *down*. That is the pulsebeat of existence.

Here is the new and contemporary form of scapegoat sacrifice: to face into one's own weaknesses, imperfections, and inadequacies—along with one's strength—as inexorably part of the tapestry of life. One must learn to accept as given the discrepancy between the wished-for and the real self. One's unique individuality is one's destiny. This abrogates the ego's claim to perfection and self-justification for being able to make oneself or things right. Thereby a new attitude is gained: one is "in tune" with life and one's fellow human beings. The scapegoat, received as the brother who is myself, ironically becomes the new redeemer. Thus Parsifal brings "redemption to the redeemer" (R. Wagner) through having the courage to seek his own individual way to salvation by accepting, temporarily at least, the role of outcast.

Integrating what formerly was repressed is bound to change radically the ways in which maleness and femaleness are being expressed. It will call for and generate new and different standards of ethics, as well, and also an existential attitude: *amor fati,* "love of one's destiny," a saying yes to one's life and selfness as a given configuration rather than an accidental hodgepodge that could or should be different from what it is.

Femininity can no longer be limited to responsiveness, passivity, and mothering. It will discover and express its active, initiating creative, and transformative capacity. This expresses itself in the readiness to demand and challenge: for example, to demand subjective affirmation and acceptance of one's being as it is, to affirm readiness to play and to be played with. It includes whatever is given, whether deemed poor or bad, and it leads to acceptance of empathy, "suffering with." Such new stirring is also bound to affect men, in the form of inevitable new demands from women, as well as from the anima, the feminine aspect of their own psyches.

For women and for the anima, the new femininity requires self-affirmation if they are to be able to give adequate affirmation to the uniqueness of others. We cannot really give what we do not have ourselves. We treat others as we treat ourselves, regardless of conscious attempts to the contrary.

Self-affirmation for women means, first and foremost, acceptance of their differentness from men, rather than identification, imitation, and competitiveness with them by androlatric standards. Only by first finding this basic feminine stance can they also claim their Yang element and give expression to their masculine drives and capacities, in their own ways, as women. Then they can call upon the rousing, ordering, and creative impulses to enter, fill, and impregnate them. They can allow themselves to contain and suffer these urges in their conflicting, nourishing as well as destructive, natures until they are assimilable into a human relationship. The raw impulses—to hurt, to possess, to make something or someone conform to one's expectation—can be destructive when vented as they occur. This is true for men no less than women. We have been trained by our culture, therefore, to deal with these impulses by means of control or disguise, by will and discipline only, or to reason them away. The male psyche, attuned as it is to repressive discipline, may partially get away with this way of dealing with impulses. Such evasion is felt as hurtful by the woman's psyche. It amounts to a repression of the transformative Yin, the Medusa aspect that needs to generate new forms and make them rise out of the depth in its own way and timing. Equally, it thwarts those who manifest this generative process: Lila, the play experimenter, and Athena-Pallas, the civilizer.

While men may wait for a strategically feasible moment, women's timing is determined by the inner experiencing of cycles and events that "fit" together because they are felt as one. The instinctual impulses need to be affirmed within until they ripen into what, on the personal level, is mutually bearable and acceptable. Then they are to be issued as the challenge of inner fact, not as manipulation by guilt or threat. Thereby woman takes on the role of an initiator and leader into a new experience of subjectivity. She initiates by arousing and yearning, by clearly stating her needs and affirming her standpoint, both to herself and to her partner.

For men and the animus, the new demands of the Yin require the courage to let go of their firm ego position of control over self and others. They have to learn to affirm what is *not I*—the reality of the other—and to respect power and needs that are beyond their control or competence. Instead of putting all of their efforts into the attempt to achieve their superego ideal, they will have to learn a measure of "letting be." This is essential if they are to become capable of genuinely affirming what they really are, rather than what they wish to be. This requires a new type of courage: namely, to live not only with strength but also with vulnerability. One will suffer the conflict between opposing drives and callings, living between the "ought to" and the "want to," without attempting a premature decision. A *tour de force* of will in favor of one or the other side will no longer do. One will need to live in uncertainty while abstaining from seemingly rational decisions until reason, wish and "gut" feelings can agree.

That means mustering the courage to enter the abyss by allowing oneself to be enveloped, temporarily, by the chaos of subjectivity, the old enemy. It means to lose oneself in order to find oneself eventually. In so doing, men and women will be called upon to try and give tentative expression to their "foolish" or "absurd" feeling urges and personally toned reactions, without losing the integrity of ethical responsibility. They will need to practice "letting go" without betraying or throwing overboard honor, self-respect or respect for the rights of others. The ethical precept "Thou shalt not inflict harm" must still be primary.

The change we are speaking of means to learn to affirm one's psychological pregnancy and sensitivity and thereby reclaim one's own femininity, the personalizing and civilizing force arising out of subjective chaos. In this way, men too can discover their relative passivity, or rather, responsiveness to the initiating challenge of the feminine without and within.

These new ego values necessitate a radical change in the masculine value system of both sexes. The heroic striving for dominance, conquest, and power, the topdog-underdog order of things, the rule of authority and rank, of right or wrong, my way or your way, will have to be modified by the capacity to endure simultaneous, seemingly mutually exclusive opposites. We must learn to appreciate shadings and a spectrum of colors rather than black-and-white systems; to enjoy intertwining polyphony rather than a single dominant melody to which the rest of the ensemble merely adds harmonizing voices. The new masculine values must respect a variety of different gods or ideals, rather than only one dominant God who is lord and king. Parliamentary cooperation is called for rather than monarchical or even majority rule. Such a value system, far from being chaotic, would initiate a new integrative, moving, and balancing order rather than the static version we are used to.

In this tentative perspective, we may now redefine the new archetypal roles of men and women. The former masculine ideal of conquering hero or king is now modified by the role of the *seeker* or discoverer. The new aspect of the feminine appears as revealer, guardian, and challenger; the mediator to herself and to the masculine of *being* as it is, the *priestess* of life's values and mysteries. Women, too, need to find the seeker in themselves. Men need to respond to the guardian revealer and challenger of personal value—within, no less than without.

The Masculine: The Seeker

The seeker is a modification of what, in the patriarchy, was the ideal of the battling hero and ruler. As a new image of maleness, it arose in the collective consciousness of the West for the first time during the 11th to 13th century A.D. We look upon this period as bringing forth the first, however temporary, attempt toward a revaluing of the feminine. Its foremost representations, mythologically, were the Arthurian and Grail legends. The hero's quest is not one of conquest but of a search for *Minne*, a new form of ritualized love. This love includes both Eros— passion and physical attraction—and *agape*, divine love and caring respect for the other. The ritual aim for the seeker is to be worthy of the love of a venerated lady, regardless of traditional social convention and marriage. He is to discover the secret of the Grail and restore its kingdom. In the light of our previous discussion we may safely assert that the Grail search is the mythological explanation for the practice of *Minne*. For *Minne* is the worship of the mystery of the divine power embodied in beauty, sensuousness, play, pleasure, and attraction as well as in the feeling of passion and the creation and destruction of forms. All this is manifested in the shape of a feminine partner. The archetypal figure of the seeker is found in the variants of the suffering errant knight, such as Parsifal or Gawain. Modern contemporary versions of the seeker or wooer of the mystery, are the pioneer, researcher, explorer of outer or inner space.

In yielding to and reverencing his lady, the knight errant was expected already to have acquired the knightly virtues of courage, enterprise, loyalty, and good manners—as well as skill in combat and poesy—if he was to be worthy of her esteem. He was not a drifter or flower child. By the same token, the new pattern of maleness requires a prior adequate development of ego-firmness and discipline, of ethical integrity, stability, and external social adaptation. An adequate psychological armor is called for: self-control, and the ability to maintain oneself on the level of combat and competition in the fight for existence. In short, the acquisition of highly developed patriarchal values and capacities is needed in addition to poetic sensitivity. None of these are ultimate goals however; they are preludes to the quest. In the presence of the lady, in the space of the Grail mystery, the armor is to be shed, the weapons left behind.

The new respectful attitude toward the feminine as the mystery of transformation requires a readiness to be attentive and sensitive to feelings, needs and to personal values, one's own as well as others.

To the question of what it is that women want of men, the answer Arthur got was: "Sovereignty." For modern women this means respect for their autonomy. They wish to be paid attention to as persons, not as functions, be it wives, bedfellows, mothers, or daughters. They want to be listened to, especially when they feel inarticulate and when they are in an unexplainable mood. They want men to take them seriously and at least try to catch on to the feeling implications and nuances which are hinted at by what may look superficially like logical irrelevancy. As one woman put it, when complaining to her husband about trouble with the washing machine, she hopes for a response from him that shows he cares about and is interested in how she has been feeling that day. Being willing to fix the machine is not enough. She wants a response to the feeling rather than to the fact of the matter. In this way, he could help her discover what she does not yet understand about herself and is unable to say except in terms of the machine. At issue here as a new form of self-awareness is the quest for the mutual unraveling of subjective feelings, and the secret of nonrational motivation. Women are, by and large, more aware than men of their emotional motivations without necessarily being able to define them. For this they often need the help of a confronting and questioning partner who can help through his sensitivity and attentive response. In the process he may also sort out the nature of his own feeling-state.

Modern woman wants her partner to take time for such mutual exploration. She wants him to experiment and play with new ways of being and interacting, and to work with her toward clarifying the possibilities, difficulties, and implications of their relationship.

The role of the explorer, therefore, requires him to be ready to move on, to move in different directions, and to avoid getting stuck in fixed expectations, ideas and demands. The explorer plays, in the hope of discovering new dimensions of significance. All of the above applies to his attitude and relation to his inner feminine, no less than to the flesh and blood woman without. When in a dark mood, for instance, it would be a matter of engaging her in inner dialogue. His technique is kin to those developed in Jung's active imagination or Perl's Gestalt approach. Thereby he could attempt to be attentive to the inner demands, even though prepared to take a stand against them, should that be necessary. In any event, he will listen and try to understand what she wants rather than fall back upon standard attitudes.

Being on the move, he may get involved with more than one partner or psychological possibility. He may risk getting caught, temporarily at least, on the horns of his own dilemmas and conflicts. He also risks incurring the sense of failure and guilt. Like Parzival, he must dare ask questions which convention has forbidden in the past. He must ask and be attentive to the wound, his own no less than the other's. He may have to do what the collective code prohibits. He must take responsibility, also, for the effects of his deeds, questions, and mistakes.

I want to stress again that I do not speak of—nor do I encourage—deliberate acting out or flouting of the laws of one's community just "for the hell of it." I speak of accepting and allowing oneself to feel—rather than merely abstractly know—that for every good that one accomplishes there is also a bad; a pain or deprivation inflicted upon oneself or another. Whatever I give I deprive someone else or myself of. Even in giving love I may have to deprive myself or another. Love for one person may take me away from another. In giving advice or help I risk and have to take responsibility for the eventuality that it may also lead to disaster. The new man cannot project responsibility for his guilt and shame upon a convenient scapegoat. He cannot even make a blameworthy scapegoat of himself. He tries to correct or mitigate the effects of his mistakes. He bears the wound of his shame or guilt as a sacrificial offering of himself toward the next inevitable step of evolution: the learning process of awareness. The acceptance and reintegration of the scapegoat, the acceptance of woundedness, pain, guilt, and shame, is the unavoidable price to be paid for being human and being in search. Growing in awareness calls for courage, and makes for humility and empathy with others who are in the same dilemma, whether they know it or not.

The questing explorer can never feel himself to be perfect, nor can he expect others to be. He is ever painfully aware of the inadequacy of even the best we can do. While accepting the ethical ideals of the patriarchy, he avoids their self-righteousness. Life and relationship are seen as processes, not as fixed forms which would enable one to demand, or even know, what should happen next. He realizes that the best one can do in any situation is to seek, ask, risk, and remain open. He accepts a state of flux and becoming rather than hoping to be right, justified, and invulnerable. He continues to ask Parzival's questions of "What ails you?" "What is the meaning of this?" "Whom does it serve?" and "How does it serve the sovereignty of life?" This also means foregoing the expectation that security can be assured by being able to control all circumstances and people. Jehovah offered the doubtful promise of security, at the price of "Ye shall have no other gods before me," of adhering to a limited and unchangeable standard. In this rigid system of order and goodness the inevitable and uncontrollable surprises and calamities of existence were blamed upon somebody's wrongdoing which, ideally, could and should have been prevented. The fictive sense of security of the "righteous man" rested upon the scapegoat system described previously: if only everybody obeyed the law of the righteous men, life would be all calm, peaceful and beneficent; there would be security and general well-being.

The explorer and knight errant, however, realizes that difficulty, pain, and troubles are part of the world we move in, and cannot be avoided. Nor can what is right in a given situation be known beforehand.

The discovery of woundedness, particularly of childhood trauma (trauma means "wound"), as an almost universal factor of human motivation and behavior, is one of the most important discoveries of modern depth psychology. By and large, however, it is still misunderstood in patriarchal terms. There is still widespread an underlying assumption that trauma could and should be avoided. It is practically taken for granted that given "mature" parents, a "stable" family life, and a "properly" functioning society there need be no disadvantaging nor trauma: it is the old promise of a good world if only everybody would but do the right thing.

But the wound underlies and motivates the search. The wound is part of that intensification of consciousness which, if it is to know the good, must also incur the pain of the bad. While striving for the good, the questing knight realizes that on the way, he cannot hope to avoid the bad. He will find it within his own soul. For it is there that the Grail is to be found. The patriarchal ego attempted to hold tight, to be perfect and guiltless, and never ashamed of itself. As a result, it became self-righteous, rigid, hard and judgmental. The searcher faces up to inner conflict and moves through pain and joy in expectation of change. Pain is accepted in self; others are allowed to have theirs.

The meaning and feeling implications of pain are explored. Depth psychology started with Oedipus, whose parents tried to avoid the wound, shame, and guilt—tried to thwart destiny. He merely responded to the question of the Goddess, and that in general terms only. Thus he blinded himself.

Yet the Grail seeker sets out deliberately to face conflict and pain. At the risk of moving beyond the sanction of collectively approved standards, he asks, rather than merely responds to, the question of life. It is his own question. He undergoes his own individual trail. Thereby he redeems the individuation principle embodied in the Christian motif of the Crucifixion. It was expressed in "My God, why has thou forsaken me?" but lost in the wasteland of the institutionalized patriarchal church. His search is about, and in relation to, the wound which cannot be avoided, try as we may.

Acknowledging the wound in oneself as well as in others leads to a clarifying of feeling and to the possibility, thereby, of discovering individual, hence genuine, conscience. Both are tasks of the new age, just as clarifying of thinking was the task of the preceding patriarchal one.

The capacity to feel is equivalent to the capacity to experience hurt. We tend to protect ourselves against getting hurt by shutting out feelings. Allowing oneself to be touched also opens one to hurt. Between the sense of touch and of pain there is a difference of degree only. There is no possibility of joy without the capacity to be hurt, no pleasure without pain, no love without anger or hurt of separation. Anesthesia (literally: "absence of sensing") lacks both poles. In turn, exploration of feeling means to touch and be touched, or hurt. The seeker, then, may wear his armor in fighting situations. But he also has to risk lowering his guard and allowing himself to see and be seen, to hear and be heard. He respects sensitivity—his own and others—and learns to live not only with the sense of success and goodness, but also with error, failure, inadequacy, shame, and guilt. All the while, he continues to try and to carry on.

It is important to realize that the denial of pain, guilt, or shame leads to callousness, insensitivity, and cynicism, hence to destructiveness. In order to defend myself I have to accuse someone else. My wrong, which I deny, appears to me as though adhering to the other; I project it. In order to defend I must attack. When I am insensitive, I am likely to inflict pain without knowing, hence also without acknowledging or being able to mitigate it. The wound which I deny in myself I may feel compelled, by unconscious compensation, to inflict upon the other.

The Grail as the cornucopia is kin to a "primal breast," a maternal source that never ceases to flow. We are made questers by our primal hunger and needs, the wounds which inevitably everyone receives as a child in never receiving enough, in never having all yearning and needs satisfied. If we can see those hurts and yearnings as gifts of emptiness—if we can endure the frustration of pain and desires and follow them to their ultimate source, through pleasures and pains, trials and errors, without cutting ourselves off from need—then we can come closer to the source of life, the archetypal infinite vessel which gives to each person the specialness of honouring his or her own desire and connects us all in the great community of seekers after the transpersonal true source.

The Feminine: The Challenge of Being

What is the value which the new Feminine finds itself called upon to reassert in the face of the patriarchal trends within and without? It is the very one which is the goal of the masculine search for the Grail; the vessel or magical cauldron of life's play and renewal. It is the self-experience of soul through subjective and personal feeling and intuiting in relation to the concrete here and now. What is valued is the feel of this moment in joy and pain, not the abstract ideas or remote heavens of unending, peaceful perfection to which the patriarchy was wont to aspire.

Patriarchy repressed the magical stratum, the fairy-world. In this global awareness, life and death were the peak and valley of one wave. Emotional oneness was experienced with group, clan, nature, and blood. Life was *known* through instinctual tides and rhythms, ESP communication, and yielding openness to whatever came along. In their archaic form, these tendencies are overly passive, fatalistic and hence regressive relative to our present level of consciousness. Integrated, however, with the best achievements of the mental phase and of patriarchal

ethics, and reality-tested in the here and now of self-experience and interpersonal relationships, they are to contribute a new step in the evolution of consciousness. The new femininity is to establish the value of
inwardness, and of affirmation (but also conscious clarification and
differentiation) of whatever *is*. It is open to—and able to integrate—
woundedness, pain, and ugliness, as well as joy and beauty. The sensuous is to be valued no less than the spiritual; the intangible no less
than the concrete. Finally, the patriarchal achievements of the past
must not be overthrown, but integrated into this new outlook.

The archetypal role of the new femininity is to stand as a priestess of
the fullness of life as it is, with its unpredictable pitfalls and unfathomable depths, richness and deprivation, risks and errors, joys and
pains. She insists on personal experiencing and personal response to
the needs of the human situation.

She may play and dance as Artemis, allure as Aphrodite, domesticate
as Vesta, or be maternal as Demeter. She may function as Athena by
furthering civilization and skills, or be concerned with comfort and the
relief of misery as Mary. These are but a few of the many faces of
the Great Goddess. They all aim at transforming the chaotic power of
the abysmal Yin, the Medusa, into the play of life. They mediate the
terrifying face of the Gorgon into the helpful one of Athena. Life is to
be lived and savored for its own sake, in sensitive interplay with earth
and cosmos as living organisms, rather than as dead objects of exploitation for the sake of economic or technological "progress."

Tomorrow's woman, if she is to meet as well as issue this challenge,
will need to be open and attuned to her own tides and instinctual directives. The awareness that hurts can heal us. The wound is inevitable.
Awareness of this allows her to risk involvement rather than opt for
avoidance. Particularly in subjective and personal encounters she will
be open to and accepting of facts, impulses and feelings—even though
they may seem ugly, destructive, and forbidden by traditional (as well
as her own) standards of esthetics and morality. This means nothing
less than receiving into consciousness and clarifying feelings, fantasies,
and desires regardless of their moral or esthetic implications. It also
means separating emotion and motivation from action. Traditionally
we have held that guilt lies in thought and feeling, no less than in action. We have held ourselves responsible for asocial or unconventional
desires, impulses, or fantasies because we have the sense that feeling is
equivalent to action. In the good world created and regulated by the
good King-God, any impulse or feeling contrary to his law must be an
expression of Satan, or of our own evil. Hence, we have learned to repress our "improper" wishes, feelings and fantasies. We do not allow
ourselves to admit, for example, that in a rage we might feel like break-

ing the neck of our own child. Such a feeling is too horrible for words, or even thoughts.

Yet even such an impulse is an expression of the life force. It shows us what feeling is actually there at *this moment*—regardless of what we may wish. Later we may feel differently again. The fantasy, if it can be contained, waited with, nourished, meditated on and listened to as a symbolic statement—no matter how awful or repellent the thought— may eventually reveal a hidden wisdom and open new avenues of energy. The urge to wring the child's neck may alert an all too lovingly sweet and cloying mother to the desirability of a different outlook. Symbolically, she may need to turn or *twist* the neck into a different direction, or *break* a too-rigid, *stiff-necked* stereotype in her indulgent attitude to herself or to the child. It is a challenge to think and feel through everything that may present itself, and wait for its hidden symbolic message, rather than to act out or sweep things under the rug and let sleeping dogs lie. The new woman (or the anima in a man) will have to champion and protect the need to live through and experience everything that (lest it threaten established order with chaos) has been repressed by the patriarchy. She stands not for abstract *oughts* but for emotional facts, however these may affect people in a given situation and moment of time. It is important to realize that when the woman (or the anima) allows this "night phase" of forbidden impulses to touch her she enters the realm of Medusa, the underworld of the dark Yin. It is like the Sumerian Inanna's descent into the underworld of death and terror to meet her sister, the black Ereshkigal. During this phase she is as though lost to the daily world of the living. Hence she must wait and refrain from acting upon her impulses. What she beholds is not yet fit for *this* life. For while in this phase she is related only to her own as yet unknown, puzzling, and even threatening depth, not to any person, as dear or close as they may be to her otherwise. She may feel utterly detached, indifferent, and devoid of warmth—even hateful—toward anyone who makes demands upon her. Like Inanna, in the legend, she is naked, impaled, and dead in the presence of Ereshkigal; devoid of external relatedness. This state can be extremely frightening to her and to those around her, needless to say. The temptation is great, therefore, to deny and repress the experience and *do something* instead. But whatever is done while in that state is likely to be the wrong, if not outrightly destructive, thing to do. On the other hand, the descent into the underworld presages a renewal of life, if consciously suffered through. Through waiting, and through listening to the images of the deep as to a child to be guarded and raised, a new phase of personal life can be gained. Risking the descent into "incubation" by the dark Yin for the sake of such a transformation and renewal necessitates a disregard, temporarily at least, for all oughts or shoulds and abstract notions. Only in the light of the raw personal experiences can new values be found and reality-tested.

If she can sustain the tension of this phase, a woman functions as a challenger in the service of unfolding life. She brings forth new patterns out of the depth of chaos, and demands that they be accepted and somehow integrated and valued, not only in their nurturing, but also in their potentially destructive implications. For a need can be life-sustaining yet, at the same time, shatter an already existing state. Change and transformation must do away with the established old. Hence the affirmation of the new is first for the sake of confrontation and internal gestation. Temporarily at least, it requires a renunciation of "I want" no less than of "I should." For the time being, the question of enactment of the fantasies or impulses is disregarded. Psychological acceptance, contemplation, and meditation come first. Then I often suggest that the images be woven into a semblance of a mythological play or ritual (see chapter 15) that could be enacted by mutual consent, for the sake of experiencing the emotional charge and symbolic significance. Now the wringing of the neck of the formerly mentioned fantasy may be transformed into a pantomime of clawing or tearing to pieces, or forcefully turning in a new direction; into an ecstatic dance or Dionysian frolic, for instance. A new life-myth can thus be found. It may be experienced, totally or in part, in ritual or psychodramatic enactment, and then be reality-tested in terms of what is possible or mutually acceptable in relationship. Only through this gestation period will new insights and a new conscience be born which, with the full consent of the "deep," can risk defying conventional rules of morality, should this be necessary. Prior to this process, all action carries the risk of acting out.

Such acceptance and protection of the urges of newly emerging life impulses require an attitude comparable to dealing with a little child. It involves a readiness to play and experiment, while ever concerned with relative safety, with whatever happens to be, for the sake of gentle disciplining, rather than repressing. This attitude is like dancing, an attentive and sensitive moving *with* the tides of being and happening, regardless of whether or not they fit in with what should be.

In thus gestating her feelings, impulses, and fantasies, the woman becomes a revealer, both of herself to herself and of others to themselves. For our motivations to action flow from our emotions and feelings, not only from our thoughts. Only through mobilizing feeling do thoughts motivate action. All too often, they merely rationalize feelings and emotional bias. We cannot understand ourselves fully without understanding our feelings and feeling-toned urges.

Like the moon, this gestating affirmation *reflects;* it has a mirroring and gently revealing affect. Not only does it reflect one's own being, it can help others experience their subjective reality as it emerges in a particular encounter. This kind of learning—far better than abstract explanations or precepts of how it *should* be—occurs through gradual revelation and experiencing.

It is a significant parallel that in our time also the new physics has discovered that all reality is subjective in so far as it grows out of the encounter between the observer and his interaction with and orientation toward a "you," the reacting object of the observation. What we have formerly considered objective reality we are now discovering to be subjective experience of encounter and relationship.

Such affirmative revealing contrasts with, but also complements, the masculine questioning, doubting, and criticizing that characterizes our intellectual tradition. The goal of the quest is a discovery of "faith." This means trust in the "river," the flow of life. This cannot be seen and touched in space, but can be discovered only through time and through experiencing its significance and value in one's own emotional self. For that reason, the feminine self has a greater difficulty than the male in feeling her a *separate* self. Hers is rather a *feeling with* selfness.

The feminine ego is more like an open channel, a flow in herself of emotions, feelings, and perceptions. She is not as rigidly will-and-conviction-determined as the male, but more open to finding natural order in what at first seems like chaos; namely, the flow of unstructured and unordered, nonrational dynamics and events. By empathizing with and nurturing, the feminine ego reveals and affirms the subjective experience of the moment as a new dimension of reality which extends not only in space, but also in the moving dimension of time. While opening a new capacity for psychological sensitivity through empathy, this relative ego plasticity, however, can also pose difficulties. This undifferentiated flow—not sufficiently sustained by her own Yang clarity, differentiation and assurance—can spell confusion, self-doubt, and dependency. The result is a need for affirmation, for being told by others, particularly men, that she really exists and that her revelations and subjective experiences are of value for others, not just for herself. That sensual and sensuous connectedness to whatever *is,* the sense of beauty, pleasure, enjoyment, and play has also tended to bring upon women the reproach of frivolousness (if not of being the tool of Satan) by the patriarchy.

The above by no means invalidates, but rather extends, the maternal and nurturing role, which is deeply and fundamentally an inseparable part of the feminine character. In some form or other, some tendency to mothering or being the daughter makes itself inevitably felt in every relationship encounter. A feeling for the other as a child, and of union with that child, is an intrinsic part of the nonseparative way of experiencing existence. The feminine, consequently, implies also a sense of conceiving and nursing, of caring for life, and of being in touch with one's roots in nature. It is important for a woman to be able to relate consciously to this dimension, lest it get out of hand in the form of suffocating or overbearing mothering, and also in case its conventional channels seem closed.

When pulling away from one's children or projects, and when the ego position feels threatened by the pressure of abstract *oughts* and *shoulds* which can make one feel childish, the necessity for self-mothering arises in men as much as in women. The one's own weakness and neediness calls for support from oneself, for tender comforting and protecting till one can rally oneself. When this need for nurturing is not satisfied, emptiness and depression are likely to set in. This applies as much if not more to self-mothering as to caring for others. Acceptance of this necessity is again in contrast with, as well as complementary to, the predominantly extroverted patriarchal tradition of the West, which one-sidedly stresses outgoing activity and "doing for others" in disregard of one's own needs and desires.

Caring for and respecting others in their true otherness is an indispensable first step of individualization. The next step fills and deepens this individualization through the emergence of the new feminine as the embodiment of inwardness which stands maternally in defense of inner values and of one's own uncertainties resulting from the untrustworthiness of outer rule and law. It expresses the need to gestate, patiently to listen into the time dimension, to let the tides rise and ebb until time brings forth the moment of birth.

Lastly, the intrinsic inward directedness of the Feminine ushers in a new form of relationship to—and experience of—the divine and of one's life as a transpersonally *given* individual pattern of destiny. With the exception of its mystical undercurrents (barely tolerated by ecclesiasticism and contemptuously dismissed by its heir, post-Renaissance scientism), the stress of Western patriarchal religiosity has been extroverted. God is depicted as a grim, self-righteous, and humorless male patriarch, in spite of all the protestations that "God is love." He has his abode somewhere "up there." Heaven and hell have been represented as localities in space. A religious life is taught in behavioral terms of omission and commission of certain acts regardless of individual needs and differences in obedience to God's law, as certified by church and state.

This extroverted religiousness taught us social consciousness. But in our time, it has reached its saturation point. It has degenerated into moralistic preaching and into a world view that can see only material and economic dynamics, devoid of any relevance to the mystery of existence. The resurgence of the Feminine, however, reopens the possibility of access to this mystery by revalidating the inward subjective dimension.

In the world of the Goddess, materiality is seen as a manifestation of spirit, rather than as something separate from it. Matter is but one form in which the ever-creative pulse of life, meaning, and evolving consciousness is perceived. It is the palpability and visibility of soul and spirit, as are our bodies. Hence the experience of the mystery of the "ultimate" is to be sought in the subjective, here-and-now experiencing of our problems, pains and joys, including those of our bodies. The unfolding of daily life—its personal and relationship conflicts, difficulties and discoveries—can become transparent with a meaning that aims to incarnate through the time dimension. Personal experience takes precedence over abstract reasoning and dogma. Joy and pain, beauty and ugliness, spirituality and sensuality are to be accepted and recognized as manifestations of transcendent power, hence as sacred and sacramental. They are the ways in which we experience the webs of our life's destiny, inner as well as outer. In accepting and embracing them we submit ourselves to the tests of growth and transformation. Through asking "What do they serve?" we can discover a dimension of meaning in our lives that points beyond ego limitations. Asking "What ails you?" (and also "What pleases you?") helps us toward awareness of feeling, toward becoming conscious of the depth and richness of our subjective emotional being.

Feeling now takes on a new orienting and validating function. In its subjective circular way (unlike the "objective" linear path of reason) it nevertheless contains its own objectivity in the sense of providing reliable intelligence. It is a new informational guide, largely undifferentiated and awkward as yet, to be refined and developed into a skill, in a way that is not unlike the way thinking evolved during the patriarchal epoch.

A new, inwardly oriented depth psychology is discovering in feeling new avenues to life decisions and existential orientations. Feeling qualities or attitudes are seen to be inherent in the web of life and cosmos, and need to be related to as objectively given and many-faceted, rather than just good or bad.

An example illustrates this new experiential attitude. A middle-aged analysand was wrestling with the problems posed by her traditional black/white morality. She had a hypnagogic vision or dream. In it she beheld a divine, creatorlike being holding the earth globe in its hands and, with amused detachment, watching and playing with conflagrations, wars, catastrophes and destruction on earth. Upon being questioned by the horrified dreamer, "Why do you let such things happen?" it answered: "Because it pleases me."

The shocked dreamer was confronted here with that aspect of the creative force which we have previously described as the transformative. In the West, this aspect (e.g., meting out destruction "because it pleases me") has been sundered from the patriarchal God image of absolute goodness and justice. In the older Goddess representations, such as the Egyptian Sekhmet, or the Indian Kali, we still find the complementary aspects of engendering life, love, and joy as well as revelling in suffering, destruction, and death. This duality of function emotionally encompasses the actual fullness of existence, the *no* phase of which we have repressed.

It is this very *no* phase that is to be revalidated in the new experience of the Feminine. The *feeling function* as a guide includes this *no* phase in the form of not caring, detachment, and even affirming destruction as a necessity, when the nourishing and supportive phase has run out and is no longer relevant to the given situation. For, in order to affirm, one must also be able to reject; in order to support, one must also be able to allow failure. The feminine instinct refuses to *have* to give, to be told how it *should* feel, that it *should* love and support when the actual feeling says no and calls for detachment and even rejection. This is a new lesson to be learned in the relationship between people and in one's way of being in the world.

Relationships, of necessity, contain varying degrees and timings of distance, noncommunication, and even rejection and dislike. These need to be acknowledged, tolerated, and affirmatively worked with if the connection between the participants is to be kept alive. The negative can give background to whatever attracts and holds the participants together. In the same way, a two-dimensional flatness is avoided in a painting by allowing dark/light contrasts. Likewise, dissonances in music intensify the emotional impact of their resolution in consonance. Without them, the result would be boredom. At other times, renewal of life which has run its course can occur only through death and destruction. This also calls for emotional affirmation.

Seemingly difficult, and painful *no* phases, when everything seems to go against us, are not just frustrating, waste periods. They express a purposeful, if negative, inward-turning phase. They manifest a special feeling aspect unfolding in the time dimension. They are just as vital in their messages and perceptions as the affirmative ones.

Dissolution of form, the ending of a cycle and the sense of loss and sadness, are inevitable phases of the total life process. Transformation and destruction are the inner and outer aspects respectively of the same process. This realization is vitally important for our feeling relationship to endings, collectively and personally. Endings are what we perceive as hopeless situations, deadlocks, depressions, feelings of wanting to give up, and finally death. Endings are terminations of particular phases and trends; they are indications of change due. What cannot be ushered in with our cooperation may rush upon us *force majeur*—externally or psychologically—in the form of obsessions. Suicidal or homicidal impulses also may represent an acting out of unrecognized or blocked transformational urges arising compulsively from the depth of the unconscious psyche. The recognition of such a constructive potential may make it possible to channel such impulses into psychological change rather than destructive action. Here again the Grail questions are to be asked: "What or whom does the impulse serve?" and "What is the nature of the suffering?" What, *inwardly,* is in need of being killed, destroyed, dissolved, or radically changed and overcome? Suicidalness is not helped by considering it merely repressed homicidalness. Both express the need for the dying of an obsolete self-image. The homicidal impulse wants to do away with complexes or qualities which are projected upon another person, a scapegoat.

Over and over again, the psyche seeks inner changes which need to be mediated through psychological understanding if acting out is to be avoided. Destruction is always the ending of a cycle, and is the indicator of a new beginning. It calls for creation rather than mere repression or paralyzing despair.

The Feminine is attuned to moving about more naturally than the masculine in the ups and downs of this dimension, in not expecting (indeed distrusting) perfection and semblance of permanent stability. Thereby it remains in touch with the mystery of becoming; of birth which equals death, of both the allure and the threat of the world-play as an unending process. It is in touch with the destiny aspect of the Goddess.

CHAPTER 13

Individuation and Destiny

Ducunt volentem fata,
Nolentem trahunt.
　　　SENECA

Behind the neurotic perversion is concealed vocation, destiny, the
development of personality, the complete realization of the life
will that is born with the individual. The man without "Amor
Fati" is the neurotic.

　　　　　　　　　　　　　　　C. G. JUNG*

Consciously accepting and honoring the Goddess in her time-destiny
aspect can bring forth a new attitude to life and existence in both men
and women. Also here, it is a matter of creative and responsible response to challenge and limitation rather than fatalistic or self-indul-
gent acting out.

To the illusory world which the patriarchal ego has built for itself the
idea of destiny is childish. True to our Cartesian schizophrenia, we believe on the one hand that matter is subject to absolute mechanical determinism, and on the other, that mind is "our" mind and by virtue of
"our" mind we are the sole makers of our lives' patterns. The mind's activity is purported to be free and unlimited.

Yet it is the very nature and evolutionary intent of our being—our
individual "historical process" of individuation—that limits our free-

* Collected Works, Vol. XVII, par. 313.

dom and prefigures our course through life. Thereby our individuality becomes also our destiny. As individuals we are genetically preprogrammed in terms of constitution, disposition, reaction patterns, drives, and motivations *in potentia,* namely as typical ways of response readiness which yet are specific and unique for each person. Through awareness, their effects can be modified to varying degrees. As long as we remain unconscious or deny their existence they become our "fate." They can be read as characterological predispositions primarily, but also, to a more limited extent, as probable—or at least possible—external patterns. For our personality attracts and responds to people and events selectively, tending to affirm and repeat its own built-in bias. Our idiosyncrasies become self-fulfilling prophecies. A self-pitying character creates its own catastrophes, the overly aggressive type its own enemies.

Jung called the sum total of our potential being the Self. He contrasted this larger Self with the smaller self, namely our conscious self-image, sense of personal identity and personal hopes and expectations. The Self operates as though generating an evolutionary will and intended pattern of its own, quite often at variance with the conscious ego personality. From the Self flow our "lower" instincts as well as our spiritual aspirations. It generates the individuation drive, the urge to become what we are as well as the genuine individual conscience which in its psychological significance is likened to *vox Dei,* the "voice of God." In this sense the Self operates like a transpersonal or indeed suprapersonal entity, a destiny, or *karma* which demands to be actualized or incarnated as best we can in terms of given possibilities and limitations of family, social, and cultural environment. The concept of destiny, hence, does not imply fatalistic determinism or Calvinistic predestination. It is a prepersonal yet individual pattern of an intended wholeness. It needs the cooperative attempt of conscious realization in concrete life, of fulfillment within the limits of the ego's capacity. Thus, destiny is the unfolding of the Self-archetype in time and space.

As children, our first task it to learn to orient ourselves in and adapt to our social environment. We must learn the law of cause and effect, and to control our wayward impulses and affects, so that we can will and act and be responsible for the effects of our actions. Having acquired that self-reliance and responsibility, however, later in life we need to discover the larger pattern within which our awareness and our being is contained. We need to discover the prepersonal intents which our personal intents are meant to give expression to: our destiny or *karma,* the plan or patterns of our greater Self.

The Sanskrit word *karma* means "doing," "conduct," and "result." It implies cause, pattern, and action as a dynamic unit: the prime causation of the Self manifesting through time evolution in space. It actualizes the potential nature of our being in the sequential flow of time's creation and destruction, by virtue of what happens to us and through us in the here and now. This wholeness of our being, consequently, can never be grasped adequately at a single point of time, but needs to be perceived as it changes, moves, evolves, and involves from birth to death and death to birth.

Whatever happens in our lives wants to be seen as our individual "that thou art" which implies equally "that thou art *not*." The butterfly must—and can only—fulfill its butterfly-ness; the oak its oak-ness. Just so, as individuals, do we respond to outer circumstances. Our nature is also our destiny. *Karma* and destiny are time and space manifestations of the quantum activity of Selfness, fulfillment of a potentiality to be realized along the time dimension in space and meaningfulness.

The popular notions of *karma* as reward or punishment for past virtues or misdeeds, or destiny as fatalistic determinism that justifies passivity or even inertia, rest upon a misapprehension of psychic dynamics. Such notions are based upon a materialistically decadent late medieval version of the Judeo-Christian mythologem, projected upon an originally much more psychologically sophisticated Eastern tradition. This Western mythologem features the somewhat arbitrary, though supposedly just despotic ruler "out there." He sits in judgment, enforces his laws, and dispenses benefits and penalties as he sees fit upon creatures whose only option is to submit, being forever guilty, deserving punishment, and unworthy of blessing.

As children of this tradition we readily confuse responsibility for our given life task with guilt and punishment for what we are, and for our inevitable shortcomings and mistakes. Mistakes are but stepping-stones in learning and developing; they are unavoidable. Instead of beating our breast in guilt for our faults and wrongdoings, it is more productive to accept responsibility for learning from past errors. Whatever task I set for myself, or is set for me, and left unfinished today, will be tomorrow's challenge or unfinished nuisance.

Whatever problems, difficulties, pleasures or possibilities our destinies happen to bring us can be just as much *in order to* help us to a new realization as they are *because of* what happened before. They are different ways to grasp the evolution of the Self in expansion and differentiation of consciousness through self- and I-Thou awareness.

Consciousness and differentiation of consciousness, in both the extroversion of relationship encounters and the introversion of self-confrontation, seem to be the universal human—perhaps even cosmic—goal toward which all destiny moves.

It is not to be wondered at that consciousness and conscious acceptance are also the universal factors that can and do modify the ways we meet our destiny, as well as the way our destiny meets us. "Him who is willing the Fates guide, the unwilling they drag," said Seneca.

Awareness and acceptance—not fatalistic passivity, but acceptance as a road map or thematic blueprint for individual creative activity—can modify adverse *karma*, adverse circumstances. In turn, unhappiness and frustration are states of the personality, parts of one's givens, ways in which we meet life and ourselves. These qualities cannot be simply explained as results of outer circumstances. If anything they are instrumental in creating or modifying outer circumstances so that they fit in with our expectations. It is always amazing to observe how, as insight and active acceptance of self and others grow, the outer circumstances also begin to change; even those accidental happenings over which one cannot possibly have any volitional control.

"Unsatisfactory" *karma* (and it is always unsatisfactory somehow or somewhere) is a call for consciousness to modify itself. The inevitable existential conflicts between good and bad, desire and necessity—indeed the very suffering that characterizes existence—are evidently the necessary inevitable criteria of value differentiation, the grindstones by which our consciousness is to be polished. The experimenting encounter with life and destiny occurs through conflict.

Consciousness is not to be confused with self-reflection, with mere thinking about oneself or reading books on psychology. It is that also, but it is more; consciousness is a state of bearing witness to our character structure and our life's pattern and becoming aware of how this structure and pattern are at variance with our ideals as well as the emerging blueprint of the Self. To be effective it needs to include an experiential awareness of our affects and instinctual drives, whether our mental conditioning approves of them or not; and an active experimenting approach to living that puts these insights to the test in real life and relationships. It means following one's calling, whatever that happens to be.

New energies and qualities that "want" to come into being as we evolve in time are often felt to be at variance with our moral and ethical principles. These principles, however, are of necessity conditioned by our past, individual and collective; by what is now the bias of yesterday's experience for our generation. We are always disposed to fight tomorrow's conflicts with yesterday's weapons. Neediness, wayward sexual impulses, anger, aggression, and the intrusions of mystical experience at variance with what is supposed to be real are the most frequent examples. We feel guilty about them and repress them or act them out defiantly when repression does not succeed. But either way we feel guilty. What I do not know and understand sufficiently—and guilt and repression deprive me of the capacity to know and understand—I cannot assign a suitable place. Yet to fulfill our appointed destiny we must allow somehow, somewhere, a relatively safe place for experimenting with such urges. The repression acting out circle can only be broken by conscious risk; cautious, deliberate *enactment,* if I am to avoid being dragged into unconscious, and then destructive, acting out. One must take a calculated risk of being a "fool" or "knave" and be prepared to pay the price in order to learn and find out about oneself, just as one needs to risk falling on one's face in order to ice skate or ride a bike. Whenever we experience desire or fascination in unison with guilt and fear—only then do we hear the voice of destiny. One must discover one's own way of expressing what wants to come to life, in a way that is in tune with the highest demands of a conscience frequently still to be discovered (hence overlaid with the fear instilled by old bias and habit). Blind necessity can be channelled into free will, at the price of conflict and tension, only when one is willing to try hesitant enactment rather than acting out of plain desire and base instinct. No wonder that Jung called this task, the task of individuation, the "Magnum Opus."

Self-experience and meeting one's destiny can never occur without a sense of insufficiency and guilt. At least twice in our lives we are all destined to encounter such guilt and insufficiency: first in encountering the collective conscience, the superego, and then in encountering our individual conscience, the call of the Self. The collective superego conflicts with the desire-motivated body ego. The genuine conscience flowing from the Self conflicts with the superego-conditioned ego. These basic conflict situations are like two guarded grand portals through which we must pass to find and fulfill our destinies. In the patriarchy the voice of God spoke mainly through collective standards. Conscience and superego were still largely identical. When a powerful individuality was pinned inexorably against cultural standards, tragedy was likely to ensue. Heloise and Abelard are well known examples.

In such tragedies, many destinies apparently have had to find their consummation. As we move into a new phase of psychological development, ego structuring initially occurs as it must, in confronting the collective superego which demands cultural adaptation. When this trial has been successfully met, however, it is discovered to be insufficient, and fraught with the danger of selling one's soul. Now a second call, the voice of the Self, the call of individual destiny, is heard and demands attention. The first adaptation, gained with so much difficulty, is to be transcended. A new Self-conditioned ego demands to be actualized.

Our first childhood conditioning, always traumatized to varying degrees by parents, school and environment, structures our superego. It constellates our shame and guilt feelings in traditional terms. When we have more or less succeeded in resolving this conflict by adaptation to external reality needs, usually in adolescence and early adulthood, we discover that we have had to force ourselves into molds at variance with our deepest innate urges and values. The conflict of our destiny now confronts us unavoidably from within.

Parents' and authority figures' needs and values, their unresolved strivings and urges, and their external adaptations inevitably modify the child's outlook, personality pattern, and reality adaptation in their way, not the child's way, thus diverting the child from being its own self. In our time at least, this is an inevitable aspect of human destiny. Alienated as we are from our deepest selves, a dim sense of guilt, existential guilt, is engendered. We are unaware as yet of the nature and demands of that hidden Self, so we mistake the nature of the call. We respond to it in terms of our accustomed value system. We explain the guilt as stemming from not giving enough value to parental and cultural standards, and of rebelling against them. More attempts at better conformity produce further alienation and guilt. A vicious circle entraps us here. It can create impasses and life crises that surpass the imagination of the most inventive playwright. It is as though the power of destiny were bent upon deliberately blindfolding us and setting us off in the wrong direction in order to stage a drama; the drama of the quest of self-discovery through trial and frustration. Indeed, for a playwright, this would be a most effective way to create dramatic tension. In order to have an arresting, meaningful play, a powerful impasse—a seemingly hopeless crisis—needs to be created. Hamlet's father is murdered by his brother; Cordelia, the loving daughter, is banished by King Lear. No impasse means no resolution, hence no play. Destiny is Lila, the world play of the Goddess, personalized into Selfhood.

Life as a dramatic play, as theater (*theatron* in Greek meant a "place for seeing," but especially, a "showplace for divine onlookers"), is an archetypal motif recurring over and over in dreams and poetry. The profoundly moving cathartic effect which dramatic art continues to exert through the ages may well be based upon its presenting us with a mirror of soul and life in the theme of men and women against their destinies.

In terms of dramatic meaning, our life histories may be viewed as the result of past conditioning and trauma. These past events, however, may equally be seen as necessitated by the plot, by the pattern of destiny, in order to produce or make possible those future impasses, events, and discoveries which are necessary for the content and meaning of the life play. What we suffered as children or adults, as the result of dis-

turbed (or even good) relationships with parents or other close associ-
ates, may be seen then not as regrettable accidents and misfortunes that
could have been avoided, but as destined emotional impasses essential
for staging our individual reality. The necessity for experiencing a particular conflict or trauma in childhood would shape the child-parent situation in such a way as to bring about the present or future impasse.

A dramatic evolution requires an awareness not only of the sequential chain of events, from exposition through crisis to *lysis* ("solution of
conflict") but also a comprehension of an underlying idea or meaning.
The naive observer, who identifies with the play as it is presented, is
moved in terms of material and effective cause and effect. In order to
provide motivation and engender involvement, the play must be presented in these terms.

While the staging of the tragic or joyful situation in act two seems to
be caused by the right or wrong action preceding it in act one, it is
equally true that this effect is a deliberate function of dramatic intent.
Awareness that the roles of the actors are indeed roles might also be
helpful; the villain may evoke anger or hate in the spectator, the hero
love and admiration. Only a naive spectator, however, would want to do
away with the villain. His or her presence is essential, and the por-
trayal of misfortune and injustice are integral parts of the drama. On
the other hand we also realize that if the battle is not joined against
those forces there will be no drama, no crisis nor *lysis*. Awareness of the
play as play is no excuse for inertia or fatalism. The attempts to overcome the villain, to resolve the injustice—whether successful or not—
are the called-for responses to destiny as a dynamic challenge. They de-
lineate the area in which our freedom counters destiny. Out of this encounter, growth and consciousness are born.

In one respect our life drama differs importantly from those we see
on stage. It includes the freedom to modify, if not alter, the script. It
includes the necessity to improvise. The patriarchal principle was:
"Thou shalt" (or "shalt not"). The Goddess says "You may—perhaps."
"It is for you to find out. Play with me, discover me." It is as though all
members of the cast had been coached except one actor, the ego. Perhaps
that which eventually becomes the ego has also been coached but (as
some myths and dreams claim) has forgotten the lines. More likely,
blank spaces have been left in the script—or only general instructions
have been given—in order to allow for creative expression. Thus the ego
is challenged to be alert for cues and take its chances on guessing and
improvising as the action unfolds. Herein lies our freedom, but also our
responsibility: not for the conflicts, unacceptable qualities, or mix-ups
we have gotten into—but for our performance; for how we respond to
these difficulties, how we use our talents. Contrary to what one might

expect, the destined evolution of the time pattern operates not as fatalistic compulsion but includes, even requires, the use of freedom. It
challenges us to create our own version, or at least modification, of the
script through creative improvisation.

The stern limitation of destiny includes freedom. This is the great
paradox of life: limitation and freedom are opposite poles on the axis of
self-discovery through creative responsiveness or responsibility. Freedom is not absence of restraint and limitation but a particular, imagi-
native way of responding to these limitations, or using them to discover
and invent. Nothing exists that is not subject to law and restraint. A
skipper may not in the name of freedom disregard wind, weather and
tides, or the goal of the journey. Likewise one may not assume that one
could walk to the moon disregarding gravitation. Equally one cannot
be the person one arbitrarily wishes to be, or live the life one wishes to
live, in disregard of a priori givenness. While these given factors cannot be disregarded, neither need we be victimized into inertia by them.
Wind, weather, and tides can be made use of in navigating; gravitation
is used in flying.

Freedom is the ability to be one's authentic self and to choose.
Therein lies its very built-in limitation. I can be only what is in accord
with my intrinsic nature. Our motivations are not subject to ego whim
but are functions of the a priori patterns in terms of which we evolve. A
feel for this inherency as destiny pattern, its possibilities and limitations, *amor fati,* makes it possible to fulfill ourselves.

An important aspect of this feel is also a sense of what we call timing.
Timing is an awareness of the propitiousness or unpropitiousness of the
particular time quality for a particular action. To be effective in bringing one's position to bear in the play requires not so much—or not
only—a forceful stance, but a sensitivity for the dynamics and rhythms
of the plot, and attention and responsiveness to the cues. One must
speak one's part and do one's deed at that point of the drama where the
play calls for it, or at least offers the most favorable opening to be effective. No purpose is served by the hero's delivering a rousing speech
when the potential listeners happen to be asleep or busy elsewhere. In
turn, missing one's cue may mean missing a chance.

The use of one's freedom demands a sensitivity to pattern and timing, a sense of *kairos,* of those moments when freedom is given and
choice is possible. Logic and reason may help, but intuition and feeling,
a quasi-artistic sense for the dramatic moment, is still better.

Probably it is just this, the developing of feeling intuition and timing, that is one of the challengers of the next phase of consciousness development. Analytic rational and logical thinking alone cannot bridge
the gap between ego and Self, cannot make us Self-motivated. Nor can

it bridge the gap between person and person, individual and collectivity and world.

The significance of conscious development of feeling and empathy, not only for ourselves but seemingly for our culture and the collective is intimated by the experience and dream of an elderly woman. As late as her early sixties this woman still had to wrestle with her childhood trauma, her sense of feeling rejected and abandoned in personal relationships. This she traced back to her hurt feelings of not having been valued by her rather cold and impersonally remote mother. That feeling came to a head in a most traumatic fashion when at age eight she was suddenly hospitalized with pneumonia. She felt confused, bereft, and abandoned when her mother failed to visit her.

After reliving these memories in therapy she dreamed of a man lying on a pallet with a deep wound in his side. She, the dreamer, was kneeling by his side and sent healing to him by radiating her feeling onto him in meditative concentration. Here the dreamer is shown ministering to the archetype of the wounded man, an entity beyond her personal self. We are reminded of the image brought before us in the poem of the Knight of the Grail (see head of Chapter 11). "And in that bede ther lythe a knight/ his wounds bledying day and nyght/By that bede ther kneleth a may/ And she wepeth both nyght and day."

But in this dream she no longer weeps helplessly like the maiden in the poem. Instead she radiates healing through her feeling that is now consciously directed. The implication is that through conscious acceptance of our wounds, healing can occur, not only to us but also *through us.* Our consciousness of feeling helps the Corpus Christi, the wounded embodiment of the spirit in man. This way, apparently, we can contribute our share to the healing of mankind and offer redemption to the redeemer.

CHAPTER 14

Ethics

Two things fill the mind with an ever increasing wonder and awe, the more often and the more intensely the mind is occupied with them: the starry heavens above me, and the moral law within me.

KANT

Before there was the law of a pope or his trouble
Each one made love
Without blame to his loved one.
Free and easy enjoyment will be without blame
Well has May made houses of the leaves
There will be assignations, beneath trees, in concealment
For me, myself and my dear one.
            Red Book of Hergast, 13th–14th Century Welsh*

Some day there will be girls and women whose name will no longer signify merely an opposite of the masculine but something in itself, something that makes one think not of any complement and limit, but only of life and existence: the feminine human being.

This advance will (at first much against the will of the out-stripped men) change the love experience, which is now full of error, will alter it from the ground up, reshape it into a relation that is meant to be from one human being to another, no longer of man to woman. And this more human love (that will fulfill itself, infinitely considerate and gentle in binding and releasing) will resemble that which we are preparing with struggle and toil, that love that consists in this, that two solitudes protect and border and salute each other.

RAINER MARIA RILKE, *Letters to a Young Poet**

* Poem quoted in A. R. B. Reese, *The Celtic Heritage* (London: Thames & Hudson), p. 287. Rilke, trans. M. D. Herter Norton (New York: W. W. Norton & Co., 1954), p. 59.

Ethics are value regulations of human relations. For an individual living alone, if such were to exist, no question of ethics would arise. Ethics grow out of the individual's awareness of being a separate entity concerned with how he or she relates to others and the community as a whole. Ethics in our sense, with its good-bad valuation, arose with the ego. For a sense of individual responsibility presupposes the sense of *I*.

We have seen how the magical prepatriarchal communities presumably regulated behavior by taboo rather than by ethics. This orientation sought to avert danger to the community and its members. The criterion was practical, not moral. It was based on survival needs, not on feeling values.

The height of achievement of all patriarchal ethics is the Golden Rule, "Love thy neighbor as thyself." It was, according to a legend, considered the very essence of Judaism by Rabbi Akiba, who remarked that "everything else is but commentary."

The Golden Rule legislated concern for one's neighbor by equating his needs with one's own. The rights of a separate other as a personality are thereby explicitly recognized as requiring individual concern, for the sake of group survival. "You shall not take vengeance or bear any grudge against the sons of your own people, but you shall love your neighbor as yourself" (Lev. 19:18).

On the other hand, while the patriarchy brought about individual differentiation, each person was given value primarily as *homo faber,* doer of deeds who would work upon, manipulate, and help control the external world. Individuality was defined in terms of external values. Actions were acceptable (good) if they were socially useful. Otherwise they were unacceptable (bad). Individuals were valued by what they did, not by the kinds of people they were. On that early, still prepsychological, level of evolution, emotions, needs, and motivations operated compulsively; they tended to result in predictable action. There was little distance between emotion and acting out. One can see still that situation in little children; anger leads to aggression, desire to attempts at possession. On that pre-ego level, emotion and action are one. Action can be prevented only by inhibiting emotion through superego-induced fear, shame, and guilt. This step toward reasoned self-control, moreover, had to be learned slowly and painfully. The discipline of using will and reason to adhere to a code of conduct regardless of one's predominant feeling was the highest personality achievement at which the patriarchy aimed. Feelings and emotions were judged only in terms of the actions which, in a deterministic and uninhibited way, they were likely to produce. As such, feelings were suspect as likely to interfere with reasonable acts. Reasoned obedience was valued more highly than feeling.

From antiquity on, and during the Middle Ages up to the Renaissance, the cultural trend worked towards the differentiation of separate individual consciousness. However, this goal was accomplished by virtue of collective, group discipline. In antiquity, the individual and individually separate positions were of no account. The word *privacy* is derived from the Latin *privatus* which means "deprived." The corresponding Greek term was *idiotes* from which we have derived not only *idiosyncrasy* but also *idiot*. Individual lives were cheap and expendable. The only individuals who were given value in this system were the group's heroes, the leaders who embodied and fulfilled the collective ideals through their excellence. *Excellence* is derived from the Latin *excelere*, which means "to outrun others." Successful battle led to public esteem. The hero was a conqueror. In turn, individuality and individual behavior (what we now tend to call ego strength) were developed by exerting willpower to repress impulses, instinctual needs, desires and hurts. In short, individual feelings and behavioral motivations were channelled toward compliance with the culturally approved value system. Virtue was defined as braveness and self-control in obedience to God's law, as promulgated by church, state, and community. Christianity affirmed the idea of an individual soul and of individual conscience, but only in the abstract. The real test of the value of each soul was to be its obedience to the collective code. *Extra ecclesiam nulla salus:* "outside of the church [and its laws] there was no salvation." Ego strength came to mean self-control in terms of the patriarchal, androlatric value standard of doing, achieving, controlling, separating, commending, forbidding and denying one's needs. "Thou shalt" and "thou shalt not" were enforced upon the recalcitrant, natural and spontaneous instincts and emotions. Virtue and goodness, which would lift and exalt a person over the masses, were to be based upon training one's will to enforce compliance with the general, collective law. Subjective, hence individual, emotions and feelings were considered arbitrary and interfering, and were ruthlessly suppressed.

Action was judged by the standards of law, and by rules of behavior. Even love was made a rule: "Love thy neighbor as thyself." "You shall love the lord your God with all your soul, and with all your might" (Deut. 6:5) and "This I command you, to love one another" (John 16:12, 17). Will and reason were to overrule spontaneous emotion, and to enforce obedience to the collective rule of behavior. By setting up regulations for the expression of aggression and of Eros, law became the social equivalent of aggression-inhibiting ritual in animals, and of the taboo of primitive magical society. The law of *agape* was imposed upon Eros and Ares. Eros represents natural need and passion, desire-arousing and potentially destructive because he is the son of the dark Medusa mother, and is allied to the seductiveness of Aphrodite. In the world of law, he is an unruly disturber of the peace. Hence in late antiquity and the early Middle Ages, passionate involvement was usually held to be a calamity, rather than a great emotional experience. Consequently, Judeo-Christian culture imposed the "law of love" instead of an unruly Eros who was to share the exile of Pan-Dionysus. Later he was castrated by sweetening and sentimentalizing. *Agape,* the love of the Golden Rule, is caring and reasonable concern for the other person and his or her lawful needs. Commanded by law it is to be imposed by willed obedience and to operate regardless of actual feeling. "Everyone who looks at woman lustfully has already committed adultery with her in his heart" (Matt. 5:28, 29). "If your right eye causes you to sin, pluck it out and throw it away. It is better that you lose one of your members, than that your whole body be thrown into hell" (Matt. 18:9).

The very same repressive discipline of the superego over the self is demanded of the other person as well. In keeping with this conviction—honestly and sincerely held—the Inquisition tortured and killed heretics as an act of Christian *agape;* for the salvation of their immortal soul. For the same reason, the ordinary individual was expected to mortify his or her body in order to conquer the temptations of the flesh and thereby reach ultimate goodness.

Human existence was conceived as intrinsically fallen and evil, to be atoned for with grim usefulness and hard labor: "Cursed is the ground because of you; in toil shall you eat of it all the days of your life . . . In the sweat of your brow you shall eat bread until you return to the ground . . ." (Gen. 3:17–19). Play and playfulness became increasingly devalued throughout the period of patriarchal mental development beginning with Plato and Aristotle, the fathers of modern thought, and carried on, chiefly, by Christian theology.

As the natural urges were devalued for the sake of reason and willed obedience, they ceased to be regarded as expressions of the divine. Yet the secularization of nature led also to a secularization of matter. The result was the satanization of pleasure and the divinization of work and achievement; in short, the Puritan work ethic. Eventually work itself became secularized—with the death of God—and matter became nothing but dead matter.

The patriarchal ego ideal rested upon the three basic pillars of

(1) willed efficiency—"I can," and "Where there is a will there is a way"; (2) possession—"I own"; and (3) honor, fame, rank, and esteem in the hierarchy of the community—"I am approved and respected." The sense of "I can" is the sense of being able to accomplish, to have an effect upon objects, other people, and the environment. It spells strength, effectiveness, accomplishment, and self-confidence. It creates identity through applied will, manipulation, and force exerted over the object; in a word, aggression. Possession extends, anchors, and secures the sense of identity through assimilating the object, thereby creating comfort and security. Honor and fame affirm that *I am* through the approval of others. The child's dependence upon approval and affirmation, and the loss of security and self-esteem through rejection, demonstrate how much we still depend upon the approval of others, and of the community. On this level, the *I am* bases its self-esteem and self-confidence on winning honor and fame and avoiding guilt and shame. We must, of course, pay the price of repressing our socially unacceptable needs and feelings.

The need for a nurturing and supporting environment is so basic that its absence interferes with the physical development of children. This "deprivation syndrome" has been demonstrated even with monkeys.[1] Lack of nurturing acceptance is at the bottom of self-rejection and of inferiority feeling. It concretizes the general human feeling of being lost in a strange cosmos by making one feel helpless and bereft also in one's family or group. Therefore it is probably the very substratum for Adler's "organ inferiority," which results in the psychological inferiority complex and its compensating power drive.

Taken together and maximized, these three factors tend to produce an ego ideal which is based upon aggressive strength, possessiveness, and acclaim. Carried to extremes, they lead to belligerence, greed, self-righteousness, and ruthless power play. For, in the superego-dominated collectivity, which does not allow for nonconformity, the nascent and ever-growing urge to separation and individuality can express itself only in *more of*—not in deviation from—the permitted qualities. The only alternative is total rebellion and refusal to participate. Chronic need-denial undermines one's sense of self-esteem and leads to a sense of personal inadequacy, and compensatory excessive envy, greed and hunger for power when the assertive capacity is too weak. A sense of lacking approval makes one feel unreal as a person; not having enough of one's own leads to a sense of emptiness and insufficient trust in one's capacities. It leads to a sense of impotence. When maximized and not successfully compensated by successful emotion and individual power achievement, the sense of unreality, emptiness, and impotence calls forth envy. They arouse the atavistic, deep urge to destroy a world that cannot be made one's own and in which one feels threatened, crowded, outclassed. The striving for excellence and aggressive competitiveness springing from power or possession urges were encouraged as virtues in the patriarchy. Nonconformity, deemed evil and vicious, makes for heresy and dissent, for antisocial behavior, and for identification with— or acceptance of—the scapegoat role. The dissenting and disturbing emotions, instincts, and needs are generally subject to repression. They are replaced by a self-righteous, holier-than-thou sense of security in being in the right with God and community, as proved by one's honor and possessions. The disowned qualities and tendencies are then projected upon the heretic, enemy, Jew, Black, woman, or whoever is assigned the role of scapegoat. He, she or they must then be conquered, exterminated, or at least kept in their place lest they undermine and pollute the goodness of the community. Since the compliment is usually returned by the other side with equal fervor, this phase of ego-development pits man against man, and nation against nation. In the epoch of nuclear power, projection of this kind poses a serious threat of total extermination.

In this legalistic frame of reference, certain acts of commission and omission have been classified as good or bad in themselves, regardless of circumstances or motivation. The taking of life, for instance, is a criminal act, even when the victim suffers extreme pain from an incurable illness, unless it is legalized by the claim that the victim is an enemy of society or of the state. Adultery, "unnatural," and premarital sex were, until recently, classified as mortal sins. Obedience to authority was deemed praiseworthy, no matter how immoral the commanded act.

An example of law enforcement from the past, grotesque as it may seem to us, serves to illustrate this fact. In France in 1750 a certain Jacques Ferron was hailed into court and tried on charges of felony: sodomy with a she-ass. After a formal trial, he was pronounced guilty and sentenced to death by hanging. This, to our minds, extreme verdict, was not at all unusual. We have records of court proceedings in which death penalties were carried out even for "unnatural" (oral) sexuality among married spouses. In one case the husband was executed and the wife, who had denounced him for committing the crime of fellatio, was banished from the country as an accomplice in the crime.[2] So also in Ferron's case, there was an additional defendant. The animal was tried, along with Ferron, as a coconspirator in the crime. If convicted, the animal also faced execution by hanging or burning in the public market place. In this case, however, the witnesses, among them the Prior of the convent and some of the leading citizens of Verviez, testified that they had known the she-ass for several years and that she always had shown herself to be virtuous and well-behaved at home and abroad. They jointly signed an affidavit that she had never given occasion for scandal to anyone, and that she was "in word and deed," and in all her habits of life, a most honest creature. The testimony and affidavit were persuasive with the court. It was found that she had not participated in the crime of her own free will, and had been the victim of Ferron. She got off with a verdict of not guilty.[3] The above may merely make us smile, yet its seeming absurdity should not deceive us into underrating the possible serious conflict of conscience between law-observance and individual urge. Indeed, it is in this area of established law and tradition versus individual feeling that the conflict between the new ethic of the emerging individual conscience and the old ethic of communally approved law emerges most vividly in our time. The fact is that our own sense of values is still largely superego determined. Our nonconformist views all too often hide traditional convictions under a veneer of modernistic terminology. We are sexually liberated but need to justify sex by calling it recreation. We want to really know ourselves but are ashamed of what we discover.

The oppressive power of our guilt feelings, when we find ourselves at variance with traditional religious beliefs about sin, shows how strongly we still tend to equate right or wrong with those traditions. In our upbringing "sin and guilt ... cannot be derived from something more basic, such as depressive states, or psychological imbalances. The concept of guilt is fundamental for theology, for theology deals with God and with his word towards man. This word, which addresses the totality of man, declares man as sinner before God. [Guilt is] a *no* against God and against his will."[4] The most excruciating conflict of values arises when the individual conscience cannot say yes to traditional morality.

During the Second World War, for instance, the battle of France stood in the balance while the commander in chief of the Western German armies struggled to decide whether to follow the feeling of his individual conscience and join the conspiracy against Hitler, or abide by the traditional officers' code and his pledge of fealty to the Führer as head of the state. Unable to reach a decision, he committed suicide. The opportunity that might have shortened the war was lost. Count Stauffenberg, facing the same conflict, sought spiritual advice from the Bishop of Berlin before planting his bomb in Hitler's headquarters. Supposedly, the Bishop sympathized with him personally but said that the church could not condone his act, nor give him absolution.[5] The Bishop found himself in the same unsolvable conflict between church law and the word of God speaking to the individual. At the Nuremberg trials, it was judicially stated for the first time that obedience to the law was no excuse for the commission of deeds that are abhorrent to the judgment of (Judeo-Christian) conscience and morality. This was the first time in history that legal sanction was given to disobeying a law because it violated individual moral and feeling values. Before this, the very idea that there could be a difference between the moral experience of an individual and the law of the community, or the teaching of the church, was anathema to the Christian tradition, as it still is to modern totalitarianism.

It is at this juncture that the new myth points the way to the comprehension of the new ethos. The cosmogony, by means of a personal God who made the world, and set up its rules and laws, has lost its credibility. Externally imposed law is no longer a *numinosum* to us. For better or worse, increasing numbers of us are asking Parzifal's question. We want to know whom or what it serves.

The new Aquarian world view, ushered in by twentieth-century physics, no longer thinks in terms of discrete objects; rather it conceives of a continuous flux of process, vibrational fields, quantum pulses of an undefinable, nonmaterial substratum. This is a universal consciousness, perhaps, yet prior to what *we* call consciousness. Prior to energy and matter, it results in both. It is a self-directed flow that gives form. The dynamics of our world, in the view of the modern myth, do not flow from a maker or director outside of it, who manipulates it like an object. The world is inner or self-directed, an immanence groping for self-realization in the three dimensions of space, and in the fourth dimension of time as well. Consciousness and conscience now discover self-direction. They find themselves in relation to the newly emerging Feminine—the Yin—as inner-directed awareness, with its growing transformative aspect—time. The new holistic consciousness perceives human existence as an aspect of a unitary, cosmic organism. From that perspective, conscience is an inherent potentiality which underlies existence, rather than a quasi-accidental byproduct of man-made culture. The new conscience functions by virtue of being sensitive to what wills to be born anew in any new situation or time movement. Out of the depths of the dark abyss, it is sensitive to patterns in events, to the outpouring from the Aquarian *amphora*, or to the directives of the Grail.

Here we are at the beginning of a new vision which is likely to lead to new insights as yet unimaginable to us. To a superficial view, there may seem to be scant difference between Self-directed ego and personal whim or arbitrariness. Yet the inner voice can be differentiated from inner caprice. It speaks to the ego from the depths of the unconscious psyche, as a subjective experience, just as formerly a like power addressed itself to the individual through the collective God-given law. It must be remembered, however, that the "law of God" was not literally handed down from heaven, nor was it directed by a divine or angelic person. It was the perception of a transpersonal (if you will, divine) necessity and made part of the collective psyche through the awareness of outstanding individuals such as Hammurabi, Moses, Muhammad, and Jesus. Superego demands are precipitates of collective psychic developments to which the individual psyche relates as branches to a tree. During the magical, mythological, and mental phases, which precede our change of consciousness, those individual parts were not sufficiently aware of inner dynamics, nor sufficiently differentiated psychologically, to discover the source of the ethical demands as arising through their own psyche. Hence these commands were experienced as coming from a god outside, one who dealt mostly with social rather than individual needs.

Now this is beginning to change. The seekers after the Grail set out together from Arthur's court, but each chooses his own individual and separate way for the search. The inner conscience which now wants to be discovered is individual. Its values and demands may vary from person to person. Such values may or may not agree with ego and superego standards. An individual yet autonomous steering center arises from the unconscious psyche; Jung called this the Self in order to differentiate it from the familiar ego conscience. It makes itself felt in modern man's psychology like a newly emerging instinct and need. This center, the Self, is concerned with our ethical or moral attitude to existence. Rather than arising from personal ego urges or from collective demands, it addresses itself to the ego in dreams and in emotional and intuitive urges and resistances. It is like an individual yet nonpersonal conscience, and demands a psychological orientation towards individual meaning and purpose in life. The capacity to feel responsible for ethical wrong is an aspect of this archetypal need for meaning, and it differentiates human from animal psychology. This individualized ethical sensitivity insists upon, and opens one to, the experience of conflict, because it demands individual choices in conflict situations. After having learned to control ourselves by the exercise of will, and by adhering to the rule, we have now to learn to make individual choices at our own risk. Conscience, the inner voice, is a new dimension of meaning whose demands upon the ego are no less significant than were those of the superego and of collective morality. Individual ethics and collective morality are *both* part of the social and cultural web; they arise in the human psyche rather than being imposed upon it by an external culture. The relationship between individual and collective psyche is now a dialectical one of complementary polarization. The individual's uniqueness is to be found through discovering his own synthesis between the thesis of superego demands and the antithesis of intrinsic values and needs; of the inner voice. Through this dialectical tension between individual and collective values, the search is conducted for the Grail, for one's life meaning, one's selfness.

These individual antitheses to the collective themes are the challenges that will eventually bring about an evaluation and renewal of collective standards. As the ego becomes increasingly Self- rather than collectively determined, it consciously modifies the superego standards rather than unconsciously accepting them as in the past. These new standards will become the superego demands for following generations, to be complemented, opposed, and restructured in their turn, by new antitheses of individual consciences.

Inasmuch as ethical choice is subject to the scrutiny of this autonomous inner voice, it is experiential. The dilemma, choice, or even simple situation to be judged, must be experienced—as must the response of the conscience. They cannot be anticipated or prejudged by legalistic means. Experiencing, however, implies the possibility, if not the necessity, of risk-taking. Innocence maintained by shunning risk and error is simply a way to avoid discovering one's own conscience. What in the past was considered virtue and goodness begins to look like mindless conformity, even moral cowardice, if based upon avoidance of the risk of individual experience, mistake, and feeling.

In order to be in touch with the conscience-coordinating calls of the Self, a new skill has to be acquired by rational consciousness. It has to learn to receive and decipher the urges and warnings of the Self which arise from the nonrational, hitherto unconscious sources. A first step in this direction has been initiated by Jungian depth psychology, particularly in terms of deciphering the messages of dreams, fantasies, and active and guided imagination. To give technical details of this methodology would lead us too far afield. Some pertinent points, however, can be stressed.

The understanding and interpretation of dreams or fantasies is made considerably easier and at times is possible only with the help of another person who serves as a sounding board, challenger, or questioner. This is someone who is able to bring an outsider's view to aspects that the dreamer cannot see even though understanding the message of the dream theoretically. In current psychotherapeutic practice, this part is filled by the therapist or fellow group member. However, any sensitive and trusted friend who is touch with the unconscious dimension can be of help. The way is to ask questions, elicit information and associations, and give reactions. Such verdicts, of course should not be accepted uncritically, not even from a therapist. One's own "Aha!" feeling is the best guide.

The second point to consider is that the voice of the unconscious is neither a reflection of ego wishes nor an internalized superego. It does

not tell us what to do or what not to do, but confronts us with the
images of where we are. It shows us the nature of our dilemma and the
likely result if we follow our motivations. It shows those qualities in
ourselves, which guide or misguide us, and which we do not see clearly.
The unconscious presents all this in the language of symbol and metaphor, leaving us to draw our own conclusions. A new faculty, which I
might call ethical intuition, is being trained in this fashion.

One example would be a dream of one of Jung's clients who, while
considering a particular business venture, dreamt that his hands were
covered with black mud. This dream drew his attention to shady aspects
of the intended venture which he previously had preferred to overlook.
He now realized that he was about to get his "hands dirtied," and chose
to withdraw.

Usually, of course, our dreams confront us with more involved dramatic representations of our inner dynamics. It helps to keep in mind
that they can be perceived as dramatic presentations which speak to us
in terms of *as if*: "Your situation or (more frequently) inner attitude—which you fail to see adequately but need to understand—is as if
. . ." Now follows the image or message. And they always address themselves to our blind spots. Since most of these messages are concerned
with the evolution of awareness they are likely to correct one's view of
self, rather than of external factors. Most of our dreams make little
sense when applied to external situations. This is particularly important to keep in mind when a dream seems to confirm a position or conviction already strongly held by the conscious ego. A dream warning
me, for instance, of the treacherousness of X, might indeed point to an
external situation I should know about. This is more likely, however, if
I am unaware, or at best only vaguely aware, of the situation. Should I,
however, be fully conscious, or heavily suspicious of X's real or imagined treachery, the dream message is more likely to show me my
projection upon X. It then confronts me with that side of myself which,
to me, resembles the picture that I have of X, namely my own treachery.

The messages, then, are best understood by feeling or meditating
ourselves into the dramatis personae and situations of a dream or fantasy, and experiencing them as dynamics of oneself. Some examples
may help. A dream: "I am driving uphill, but the road is blocked by a
rider on horseback. He makes progress next to impossible and might
cause an accident if I do not slow down." In seeing himself as the horseback rider, the dreamer experienced great impatience. He felt himself a
knight in shining armor, full of pride and high-flown idealism. The
message is that the dreamer's progress is blocked by his unrealistic ide-

alism and inflated pride. Indeed he is endangered by his impetuosity and impatience. The driving would refer to pursuing his life goals.

In another dream this man saw himself as a passenger in a black car driven by a Mr. A and assisted by a Miss B. After meditating on it, the dreamer remarked, "It cannot end well. I better get out fast. I'm too fascinated with Miss B." The black car was felt as depressive or funereal. Mr. A was felt to be a ruthless perfectionist, and Miss B, a sulky, moody "princess." The dreamer's pessimistic way of proceeding through life (automobile equals that which moves under its own power) and his "funereal," depressive attitude are shown here as determined by an unrealistic perfectionism, accompanied by a sulky, moody way of responding when his expectations are not met. This cannot end well, but he is too much in love with his princesslike attitude to be able to get out of it.

Another dream: "Mr. Y wants to withdraw into a sand castle on the beach." Mr. Y was felt to be an impractical idealist who had difficulties in getting along with people. As a child, the dreamer had often built sand castles when playing on the beach, populating them, in his mind, with soldiers, knights, kings, and monsters. Sand castles are obviously too small to harbor a real person. Hence the impractical idealist is shown as tending to withdraw into a child's fantasy world.

The above dreams aim essentially at confronting the individual with the existential situation which he fails to understand. A more direct statement of a moral dilemma and the voice of conscience may be illustrated by two dreams of two different individuals in comparatively similar situations.

The first one had decided to leave his wife and children in order to marry a wealthy girl, many years his junior. After he made this decision he dreamt that he was about to set off on a trip to an out-of-the-way destination. Rushing off hurriedly, he passed a group of respectable-looking elderly men, who shook their heads at him disapprovingly. He disregarded them, however, and pushed on. Suddenly, from out of the clouds, a huge hand appeared, grasped him, and shoved him right back to where he had started from.

This dream showed that the dreamer was about to do something "out-of-the-way" of his accustomed moral standards. He is able to disregard these collective superego standards, depicted here also as the disapproving elders. But something else, a more powerful force he has overlooked so far, reaches down from heaven and will not allow him to proceed. We may call this power the inner judge or conscience, the moral integrity of the personality, or the hand of God. We are merely using different words or concepts for an essentially unknowable power which nevertheless is capable of creating serious psychological difficulties when overlooked.

One may be justified in questioning whether this dream does not confront the dreamer with his own wish to "cop out," by offering a rationalization in religious terms. At times, such a rationalization may be the case, and the wish to "cop out" would then be the moral problem which demands a decision. Most often, however, the dream presents a point of view quite at variance with or even unacceptable to the dreamer's conscious views and desires. It thus presents a dilemma that calls for a choice, where the conscious view has seen only a simple decision. In this case, the one-sided readiness for risk-taking is opposed; the conscience allies itself with the superego.

Our other example demonstrates the opposite situation. A young man dreamt that a policeman tried to stop him from entering a beautiful orchard. Enter he did; however, when he was about to pick a piece of luscious fruit, he was scared off by a snake coiled around the branch of the tree. In terror he pulled back, and thereupon the snake struck.

Here the dreamer's tendency is to play safe, to avoid the risk of the serpent of paradise, who offers knowledge of good and evil at the cost of disregarding the divine injunction of the collective taboo: "Thou shalt not." Knowing (the growth of consciousness) must be paid for by travail, and even suffering; in any event through losing one's paradisal innocence. The dreamer's resistance to risking himself in a more courageous way of living is shown here to arise from two sources—the policeman, the guardian of the collective superego, whom he manages to bypass, and his fear of the snake, which proves fatal. The superego by implication says "Stay away," but the life-will, represented here by the snake, which could be likened to the genuine conscience, says, "Take a risk." The dream shows that his fear of taking risks, of actually testing out his defiance of accepted standards (from which he considered himself liberated), leads to the very troubles which he fears and hopes to avoid.

Ordinarily, when not bothered, a snake will not attack. In this dream, however, it was the very attempt to escape from the situation that brought on the attack, contrary to what one would expect. And therein lies the dramatic message of the dream. Throughout all cultures prior to the Judeo-Christian tradition, the snake, as a symbol for healing and renewal, represented poison as well as medicine. Avoidance of confronting the danger brings out its destructive side, as in this dream.

The guidance center thus expresses itself *as if* it were an authority that requires acceptance and fulfillment of a personal myth, and of a destiny. It calls for the discovery of meaning and of ethical significance (at the risk, always, of error) rather than the automatic blind following of a preestablished, safe, moral system. We finally are leaving the substitute garden of Eden in which the superego kept us, in a fashion, until now. The unconscious guidance system rarely, if ever, tells us what we should or should not do. It does not confront us with law or compulsion. Rather, it confronts us with the probable effects and the implications of what we are about to do, and leaves the decision to us. More often than not, this choice is between mutually exclusive emotions or moral obligations.

What seems to matter to this depth center is not so much doing the right deed by following the rules, but the quest per se; the awareness of what is happening and its implications. The awareness of dilemma and conflict, and thereby the training of feeling discrimination, empathy, and moral intuition, are intended.

Only when a consensus, or at least a compromise, has been reached among the conscious standard or intention, the unconscious desires and fears, and the unconscious "voice of God," of ethical affirmation, can a decision be made that authentically involves and affirms the whole person. That process implies the necessity of waiting until a reconciling image or fantasy arises from the depths. It cannot be forced or invented by the ego. The answer is gestated, and the ego attends it like a midwife, waiting and suffering until the appropriate time. Formerly, the Golden Rule was to be obeyed as an external command. Now it can be authentic only if it arises as an inner imperative from the depth of feeling. We can act in real sympathy ("suffering with") only by first accepting and working through our aggressions and rejections.

Under patriarchal rule, the magical level of consciousness had to be buried. As we now rediscover it, we also perceive that whatever we do to our neighbor we are simultaneously doing to ourselves as well. Thus, in our time the ethic of the Golden Rule is no longer just a social necessity. Our psychological growth, our human stature, and the integrity of our feeling depend on it. How we feel about ourselves and treat ourselves, we "do unto others." We admire and cherish in them what we desire to make our own qualities. We hate and fight others for those defects, whether real or imagined, which we detest in ourselves and project outwards. Attempting to destroy the other, we destroy growth potentials in ourselves. The scapegoat we are trying to exclude is in ourselves and waits to be redeemed in ourselves.

Formerly, in applying the Golden Rule the question was asked, "Who is my neighbor?" (Luke 10:29). Now we need to ask, "Who am I?" and "How do I love myself?" For thus I am bound, willy-nilly, to love my neighbor. Alas, the patriarchy has taught us precious little love for ourselves. Indeed self-love and attention to our own neediness were deplored as weakness, egotism, arrogance, vanity, narcissism (even in early psychoanalysis!). We were taught always to be only "selfless," to distrust, disregard and repress our own desires and needs, foremost among them those of bodily, sensual, and feeling nature—all for the good of our souls, of course, and in obedience to the collective laws of conduct. As we were taught to repress our own nonconformist inner reality, so we learned to suppress our fellow human beings; to fight them, whip them into shape—for goodness' sake. To preserve democracy, social justice, freedom, or what not, we would destroy the enemy—and ourselves in the process. But if we are ever to live in peace with one another, we will first have to find ways to be at peace with ourselves, to affirm and live with the enemy or scapegoat within. We will have to learn to be good also to ourselves and to accept, even though not indulge in, our weaknesses and vices. First we need to discover them, then to perceive that they are indeed hindrances to growth and adequate relations, but are not evil or sinful as such. They are to be transformed, not repressed. Psychic "hygiene" rests upon self-discovery and self-acceptance. For unconscious forces under repression tend to erupt compulsively and destructively and thereby interfere with good intentions. It is vital, therefore, not to confuse repression with consciously willed discipline and the inhibiting of acting out. Deliberate inhibition of action that is deemed inappropriate is a function of human consciousness; it divides man from beast. Repression, on the other hand, is loss of awareness, an instinctive denial in ourselves of what we judge as bad. It does not inhibit action but attempts to annihilate emotion. But emotion cannot be eliminated. The attempt to do so merely drives it underground: it continues as motivational impulse, but now unconsciously. Instead of informing us about our inner state it impels us to do what we do not *mean* to do.

No impulse or motivation, however, is good or bad in itself. How we handle it in a given situation makes it so. Anger and hate are frustrated and potential assertiveness. Avarice bespeaks a need to take hold of life and world, to take hold of and hold on to one's *own*. Pride shows self-respect is lacking or misplaced. Destructiveness expresses an instinctual urge for change and restructuring. Behind laziness hides an undisciplined need for meditative waiting and maturing before acting. Gluttony is a primitive exaggeration of the longing for sensual enjoyment and affirmation of our existence as physical beings.

When such hidden urges are simply repressed as vices they become personal and social stumbling blocks. Defined, disciplined, and felt in context as well as in terms of their consequences, they can be stepping-stones to growth. If anything is absolutely evil, it is the willed refusal to cooperate with the growth and maturational demands of life, one's own as well as others', and the deliberate conscious intent to destroy or hurt for personal satisfaction. Yet even here it is possible that life is being served in a way we are as yet unable to fathom.[6]

Jung remarked:

I call a certain fact bad, often without being sure that it really is so. Some things seem to me bad though in reality they are not ...

Where do we get this belief, this apparent certainty that we know what is good and what is bad? 'Ye shall be as God, knowing good and evil,' only the gods know, not us. This is profoundly true in psychology. If you take the attitude: 'This thing may be very bad—but on the other hand it may not,' then you have a chance of doing the right thing. But if you already know in advance, you are behaving as if you were a god. We are only limited human beings and we do not know in any fundamental sense what is good and bad in a given case. We know it only abstractly. To see through a concrete situation to the bottom is God's affair alone ...

We know only the surfaces of things, only how they appear to us, and so we must be very modest. How often have I wished to get rid—so it seemed to me—of some absolutely harmful tendency in a patient, and yet in a deeper sense he was perfectly right to follow it. I want, for instance, to warn somebody of the deadly danger he is running into. If I am successful I think this was a fine therapeutic achievement. Afterwards I see—if he did not take my advice—that it was just the right thing for him to run into this danger. And this raises the question: did he not *have* to be in danger of death? If he had dared nothing, if he had not risked his life, perhaps he would have been poorer by a supremely important experience. He would never have risked his life and so would never have gained it.

So in the matter of good and evil, as a therapist one can only hope that one is getting the facts straight—though one can never be sure. As a therapist I can not in any given case deal with the problem of good and evil philosophically or theologically, but can only approach it empirically. *But because I take an empirical attitude it does not mean that I relativize good or evil as such.* I see very clearly: this is evil, but the paradox is that for this particular person in this particular situation at this particular stage of development it may be good. Conversely, good at the wrong moment, in the wrong place, may be the worst thing possible. If it were not like this everything would be so simple—too simple.[7]

Good and bad are feeling valuations coming to us from the depths of the psyche. But there are no fixed standards that would enable us to predict rationally of any given situation whether it would constitute good or evil.

The feeling verdict or the unconscious reaches us as our conscience. But our perception of conscience may be deceptive; we may confuse conventionalized standards with the profoundest judgments coming from the unconscious foundations of the personality.

What remains then, for us, is to accept as did Gawain or Parsival, the challenge to the quest of discovery; to experiment and experience at our own risk. There is no safe and assured set of rules which can protect us

from avoiding evil and guilt. Only by getting to know our shadow qualities, by daring to risk and experiment with ourselves and with the situation at hand, can we discover what is right or wrong for us, in that particular situation and at that particular time. Our motivations are
always mixed, selfish and unselfish, constructive and destructive. Only
through taking risks and being ready to take on responsibility for our
acts and errors can we discover and scrutinize the nature of our motivations. We do not have to answer for what we are, but we *must* answer
for failing to *recognize* what we are, and for what we can do with what
we are. Freedom of will is to be found in discerning our human situation, and in finding an attitude, not of grumbling resignation, but of
consenting acceptance; consenting to the challenge of creative transformation. In resignation, one admits the fact of the situation, but claims
an inability to do anything about it, owing to what is felt as constrain-
ing or overwhelming circumstances. The intent is to escape or to give
up. The attitude is of protest or grudge, inertia or self-pity. One feels
oneself, and identifies with, the scapegoat.

Consenting acceptance, on the other hand, uses the facts of the situation, inner and outer, good and bad, as the raw material for a work of
experimentation, self-expression, and initiative. This is like the attitude
of the player who applies his skill and enterprise to the cards which the
game has dealt him, instead of bemoaning and feeling helpless because
fate did not deal him a better hand. The skill and joy of the play of life
is to be found in testing one's skill with poor cards, qualities, situations,
partners, and relationships as well as with good ones. Alas, this is more
easily said than done.

Yet, of course, such a sense of self-responsibility can degenerate into
ego spasm and self-aggrandizement if one feels that one can handle
every possible situation, and can handle it alone. We all have our
limits. We find these only through failure: through the experience of
having tried too hard, or not hard enough, risked too much or too little,
and indeed even through having become stagnant by holding onto the
middle position. Trying to achieve a perfect balance burdens us with
immobility and rigidity, and is, in the end, impossible. It is merely an
attempt to stave off life. Only the living balance, swaying not too much
or too little, can see us through. What is too much or too little we discover only by hindsight: by trying, risking, testing, intuiting, and feeling; by exerting our capacities to the utmost, and thereby discovering
our abilities and limitations. We need our friends and enemies to show
us what we cannot see, and our friends to support us in our inevitable
mistakes.

It is conscientiously living up to the challenge of the quest that earns
us the blessing of the Grail in this new phase of human consciousness.

Previous generations lived under the protective illusion that destiny could be controlled and life mastered by right action, and that misery is but a malfunction which, in principle at least, could be righted if given the proper approach. The task set for us, however, seems to be to look straight into the abyss and learn to affirm it without losing composure and compassion. We have to learn to live with the abysmal and to embrace it. One is reminded of the parable told by Buddha of the man who, pursued by a hungry tiger, hangs on to a wild vine over an abyss. He sees another tiger waiting below, the hungry tiger above, and two mice, one white and one black, gnawing away the vine he is holding onto. The man sees a luscious strawberry near him. Grasping the vine with one hand, he plucks the strawberry with the other. How sweet it tastes! To commit oneself to living, to say yes to life even in the face of the harshest reality might be the new hero's task. Thus play and playing take on new values in our time, after having been proscribed and trivialized by the patriarchy.

Play is ritual and exploration; it is also experimentation. It is at its best when performed for its own sake, not for any purpose or achievement other than itself. Play is self-discovery in the here and now. It is spontaneous, yet has its own discipline. It is light, yet potentially passionate. It is discovery, and it is enjoyment of one's own and of others' possibilities, capacities, and limitations. Most, if not all, great discoveries, even in science, have been the result of intense effort along with playful curiosity and joy of exploration on the part of the discoverer.

Joy in play grows from the capacity to savor the intensity of the unfolding pattern of time. The player discovers not only meaning, but also feeling; discovers personal values, joy and pain, success and disappointment. An enormous range of affect is elicited in the interplay of *I* and world, and of I and Thou. Play is the Yin side of exploration, just as exploration, experimentation, and discovery comprise the Yang side of play, enjoyment, and feeling.

We have already discussed how the emerging new psychological archetypes of the Yang will take the form of exploration and experimentation, rather than judging and achieving. The new archetypal direction of the Yin lies in the caring for, and insistence upon, differentiation of personal and interpersonal feeling values and playful interaction, rather than in submissive receptivity.

In the patriarchy, life was to be serious and grim. Play required special sanction, either as preparation for life or training in the martial arts, or for recuperation in order to be more efficient at one's work tomorrow. As a way of life itself, as a formal relation to the body—one's own or another's—play was proscribed. At the most, *fore*play has been recommended as an aid to more effective sexual performance. Yet in gynolatric cultures the relationship between the sexes tended to include the freedom of body play, an openness to sexuality as a sacred way of living. Women were active not only as priestesses of the Goddess who mediated the mysteries of life and death through bodily experiencing, but also as administrators, givers, and preservers of standards of interpersonal conduct. I believe, in fact, that the possibility of working out human relationships on the basis of mutual trust and acceptance, individually and (as a far hope) also collectively, rests on mutual affirmation in the face of superior forces that cannot be altered but only accepted, worked and played with.

The fact is that our character structure is given and can be modified only by playing with it, and thereby discovering its potentialities, rather than by consciously warring against it in the hope of trying to better ourselves. We are all vulnerable. When we begin to recognize that fact, we can be of mutual and sympathetic support to one another, rather than reproachfully saying, "You should have known better," or, "Why didn't you?" Once accusatoriness is removed from a relationship, one can begin to explore what one is up against. Together, compatibilities and incompatibilities can be felt for and adjusted to, as may be the case.

To use one's vulnerability consciously for search and quest rather than for scapegoating, accusations, and vendetta, may point to the new human equivalent of the animal surrender ritual. It may be the new way of channeling aggression. Such a process requires self-searching, self-affirmation, and acceptance of one's less desirable qualities and needs for what they are and perhaps could be. It also means extending the same courtesy to the other to the limit of one's capacity to share, tolerate and trust. Not because one should—but from the realization that the other is as helpless, when it comes to willing her or himself into a better person, as I am. It requires trust in one's own and the other person's ability to risk pain without retaliation: trust in one's own ultimate worth and in the other person's caring. Then the questions can arise, "What can we or can we not do together?" "How do we feel about what we are up against together?" and "To what extent is it desirable, joyful, bearable, or unacceptable?" Then only can viable forms of interrelating be mutually worked out, regardless of convention and expectation, solely on the basis that "anything goes" between consenting adults. Such mutual acceptance and affirmation in a relationship is equivalent to what we earlier described as a consensus between outer collective standards and demands, ego desires, and the inner voice. In both forms, it requires listening, searching, sharing, affirmation, playing, and experimenting. The increasing trend toward analytic and gestalt enactment in encounter groups seems to me a step in this general direction. It is important, however, if these group endeavors are to be maximally helpful, to be attentive to the problem inherent in all group formations; namely, of establishing a collective group normality which, like a new superego, tends to want to become a supreme compelling authority. I say to be attentive to this, not to try to avoid it, for *avoid,* one can not. The development of superego authority is an inherent, archetypal, evolutionary principle of collective dynamics. It cannot be bypassed, but only lived through and transcended. Every individual, couple, and group, therefore, needs to examine its a priori expectations of what should be in terms of individual versus group authority, so that these preconceptions can be tested against the given reality. Genuine individuality needs the other person and the group as much for sharing and support as for the sake of discovering one's own genuine nature in the process of differentiating one's own position from, and even against, the other.

All these forms of sharing interplay rest largely on "checking out" and differentiating one's feeling reactions. Intellectual and conceptual understanding surely is called for, but it does not suffice for genuine experiencing of one's own and the other's reality. Feeling is an evaluating function. It evaluates in terms of emotional and affect reactions. Hence a differentiating feeling evaluation requires a differentiated awareness of the qualities of one's emotions and affects, the latter of which include and largely express themselves, in bodily reactions, tensions, and gestures. In my opinion the acceptance and differentiation of emotion, feelings, and needs as a means of reality orientation and of mutual communication, will be as significant for the centuries ahead of us as was the differentiation and training of the thinking function through late antiquity and the Middle Ages. A new dimension of world orientation is in the process of development here.

Whereas thinking is largely abstract, feeling and the expression of need are concrete. They are object- and body-connected. Feeling, which has its own logic, is no less objective than thinking. They are really both subjective, yet thinking bases its claim of objectivity upon generally accepted common trends and standards.

However, whereas abstraction pushes away from the object, feeling reaches out to it. It touches and is being touched. Feeling communication and exploration, therefore, of necessity include body contact and body explorations of varying degree; as much as can be acceptable between consenting adults. Whereas the androlatric value system created distance and separation, the integrative trend of tomorrow will create and demand contact and nearness, both metaphorically and concretely.

Just as physics has discovered that the slightest event affects the whole cosmos, so we begin to discover in our collective life that no man is an island, that life on this planet rests upon mutual interdependence, and that any event, any place—no matter how isolated—may have communal and international reverberations. We can no longer dismiss what happens in China or Africa as of no concern to ourselves.

I would not speculate on the extent to which the ways of interacting described above can be applicable and helpful to the political life of one country or of the world. The basic polarities are undoubtedly the same in the sense that here also the autonomous archetypal factor of evolutionary time operates as historical process, requiring affirmation and active working with by individuals and groups. Indeed, the study of one such autonomous historical process, the change from the predominance of Yang to the greater Yin influence, has been the object of this book.

It seems to me, however, that unlike the individual issue of unconscious versus conscious, the conflict of mass dynamics versus personal dynamics is incomparably more heavily weighted in favor of the power of the collective, at least now. The individual has had little chance so far. There is no question, however, that individual awareness and responsibility are modifying factors, and are likely to become more so. Yet, it must not be forgotten that individuality and individuals are like leaves and branches of a tree. The survival of the tree depends upon their health and functioning, but compared to each single leaf, the tree as a whole carries immeasurably more weight and power. Also, within a given community, the level and degree to which consciousness has evolved varies from individual to individual. Some people are modern, others still Victorian, and some hardly yet even medieval. Hence the integrative capacity described in these chapters may not be applicable to a great majority of people as yet.

Consequently, convulsive conflagrations and conflicts may have to be accepted by the individual, at least for now, as being an aspect of his destiny or *karma*. It is another factor (that we can do little or nothing to change) which asks to be affirmed and explored.

CHAPTER 15

On Ritual

The essence of man can be found and determined only as play if
man is seen in terms of his ecstatic openness to the ruling world
... the world plays, plays as the Dionysian god which brings forth
the Apollonian world of appearance.

F. NIETZSCHE*

The wounder shall heal.
DELPHIC ORACLE

Can we find rituals analogous to those instinctual rites whereby animals inhibit and transform aggression? How would such rituals embody and serve the new ethic? Let us first examine what ritual is and
how it works.

Through ritual, energy is incarnated and the passage from one state
to another is enacted. The dynamics of archetypal powers are integrated so as to be available for collective or personal needs.

Any affect or emotion which in its raw and unaltered form is too intense to be controlled by will alone may need its ritual. Without ritual,
such energies may inundate the ego and force it into acting out or into
obsessive behavior. Ritual brings about containment and acceptance,
control of intensity, and "dosage." The conscious personality can learn

* Eugen Fink, *Nietzsches Philosophie* (Stuttgart: Kohlhammer, 1963), p. 188.

to disidentify itself from the affects evoked while at the same time relating to them. A pattern of wholeness is found that enables one to endure the tensions of mutually opposing emotions and to balance affects
with ego intents and needs. Ritual offers us an alternative to repression
for dealing with potentially overpowering affect.

All affects are autonomous "powers," grounded in instinct and drive.
Though not of our own making, they are capable of making or unmak-
ing and dominating us. They may need, indeed demand, their own rituals. The ancients knew this. The Greeks considered it dangerous hubris,
likely to invite retribution, to serve only one god. Dependency, need,
desire, aggressive violence, sexuality, depression—these are but special
instances. While we have been concerned primarily with violence, what
is said in this chapter applies to any other affect as well.

The traditional rituals of the past mostly served collective needs. Except perhaps for individual healing rituals, they concerned the individual only in order to help him integrate his functioning into collective
norms and needs. This was accomplished by propitiation and evolution
(or redirection), the two basic ingredients of ritual. The former is exemplified, on the animal level, by the surrender gesture of the weaker
partner, and the partial blockage of the aggressive impulse by the
stronger one. The latter we observe in the redirection of a part of the
original aggressive energy, i.e., the killing and eating of the god to a
more desirable or higher form of expression, such as the Mass. In the
more primitive and prepsychological forms of ritual, the energy to be
extinguished is projected upon and carried by a sacrificial victim, a
scapegoat. In the new contemporary rituals, the partner will have to be
recognized as representing and playing a part of ourselves. The objects
of propitiation, sacrifice, and evolution are our own impulses, desires,
and urges, even though we (at first) confront them through a partner.

By virtue of propitiatory inhibition and redirection, ritual helps
sublimation. It has been serving as a civilizing and acculturating factor
in transforming raw and brutal energy into humanly cooperative
forms. In the past this sublimation served collective superego needs exclusively. As a result, blockage, displacement and splitting off prevailed over transformation. The new impulse is toward individuality as
an integrated whole. It aims at reintegrating what formerly was repressed. Hence it will give a relatively greater space to transformation
than to blocking and splitting.

On the animal level, a purely behavioral pattern seemingly suffices
for an effective ritual. Not so for the human being. The element of
meaning distinguishes man from the animal. Consciousness of meaning
must somehow be woven into the fabric to the utmost; the ritual must be

felt to be meaningful. When this sense of meaning is absent, the ritual does not speak to consciousness and cannot transform.

In turn, when a particular ritual has fulfilled its purpose, personally or culturally, its stock of meaning becomes exhausted. It becomes devoid of psychological effectiveness. A new step on the path of differentiation and evolution may require a new ritual form.

One may liken this state of affairs to the image of a pipe which has served to channel a particular vital liquid for collective use. Once the composition of that liquid changes, in response to new and different needs, the old pipe may no longer serve. Perhaps the new compound corrodes it, or requires a wider pipe. This new impulse is the return of the repressed; the Goddess and Dionysus-Azazel.

Our past rituals have expressed the overruling demands of superego and patriarchal values. They addressed affect primarily in order to aid repression. The strength of the patriarchal ego was gained by repression and splitting. The ritual of the Mass is meant to help us carry out our *imitatio Christi* as the sacrificed scapegoat. Through the mortification of the body and desire, we can fulfill the law and appease the wrath of the father as judge and lawgiver for the sinful state of humanity. This concept no longer speaks to us; it does not help us any more. The newly arising trend, coming from the depth of the unconscious, nonpersonal psyche, moves beyond keeping away the dark and sinful side for the sake of collective superego standards. The new Self-motivated ego demands an integration in terms of coexistence rather than of repression. "Ye shall not resist the evil" is taking on a new meaning for us as a psychological reality; it poses formidable demands upon our capacity to suffer crucifixion. In psychological terms, this means a conscious enduring of the conflict of opposing and seemingly mutually exclusive demands, needs, affects, and feelings. The sacrifice demanded of our generation is the willingness to endure the discipline of conscious enactment and responsible experimentation, rather than the seemingly easier (because more familiar) way of repression and acting out, while blaming others. We need to endure the struggle of searching for answers from our own personal conscience regardless of collective approval, and to pay the price for our errors. For this, new rituals are required. This is the reason that the traditional rites have lost their power. E. Neumann assumes the new rituals are to be only intrapsychic, rather than including external action.[1] However, this would not suffice.

Indeed, for the modern ego, the Self speaks not only from within but also from without; also the modern ego is psychologically as well as physically dependent upon the community of which it is a part. It is precisely in order to establish the new and different position of a Self-motivated ego, in relation to a *Thou* and to a group, that appropriate interpersonal and group rituals are needed. Indeed, in our time the need for ritual may be greater than ever before.

As the old channels no longer serve to contain and direct the affects, those energies break loose; they charge the psychic field with disruptive forces that generate a sense of anxiety and crisis. In our time, the new impulse toward a Self rather than a superego-directed ego and conscience has corroded the old channels of the legalistic system. Self-motivation which is not yet adequately channeled leads to irresponsible, utopian selfishness. Thus we are confronted, individually and collectively, with an increasing contempt for, and disregard of, law as a regulatory system of ethics and social change. The response to this threat, in turn, is a backlash in the form of increasing stress on legalism. The outdated attitudes are stiffened and intensified. The vacuum left by the increasing distrust in church and ethical standards, in international and social agreements, and in the rites of judicial procedure, is filled with yet more legalistic and ritualistic proceduralism and moral protestation that no one really believes in. A vicious circle ensues in which ritualism replaces meaningful ritual. Unwittingly we tend to regress to the animal's level of acting out and will continue to do so until such time as the new meaning has found its new ritual form.

From the sacrifice of the royal God-King or substitute (prisoner of war, *pharmakos* or scapegoat) to the judicial legal procedure of the patriarchy, the control of aggression changed from a nature-bound, magico-mythological system that dealt with power by propitiation to an ethically responsible sense of personal freedom and choice. The superego knew good and evil, dealt with right and wrong and held the ego answerable to a higher judge (god, king or state) above its own needs and desires.

The next step seems dangerous indeed as do all new steps. To vest the authority for the use of aggressive or self-assertive energy in an inner judge carries the danger of arbitrariness and disregard for the needs and rights of others. Hence it is precisely the regard for the other person and persons—the regard for the non-*I* in the depth within, as well as for the needs of Thou and We without—that will have to be emphasized and differentiated.

In addition to the aggressive impulse itself, aggression-enhancing factors need to be contained in the new regulatory channels. Foremost among these violence-promoting factors stand the following: a sense of inability, real or imagined, to have an effect on others and to make oneself seen, heard, appreciated, valued, or cared for; an inability to have one's needs, physical, emotional or sexual, validated and satisfied; an inability to influence events, hence a sense of depersonalization and dehumanization, of being a mere object, a cog in a wheel in a large machine devoid of sense or meaning.

This sense of impotence and alienation, the absence of personal significance and of a living connection with a containing organic field—be it social group, nature, or cosmos—is surely the distinguishing psychological characteristic of our time, fostered by the prevalent religion of the last two hundred years, better known as science. Impotence and alienation, moreover, are accentuated by the effects of city culture, crowding collectivization, and technology—all of which have tended to reduce the social organism to a state of herdlike numbness. In addition, the dehumanizing effect of these developments has been magnified by weapons and communications technology, which have made aggressive encounters and warfare into statistical and administrative abstractions. "Statistics don't bleed," said Arthur Koestler.[2]

The emotional feedback that would occur in a direct personal encounter with an adversary (through directly witnessing the effects of one's violent act) is avoided when you drop nuclear bombs from ten thousand feet. Potentially painful emotion can be avoided and denied. The perception of human suffering is repressed. The *other* is but a cipher, but so also is the sense of one's own individuality, the feeling awareness of one's own deed and one's responsibility for it.

A further dehumanization is brought about as this lack of direct seeing the other is aggravated by our prevalent patriarchal scapegoat psychology, which tends to produce a strong inclination to paranoic projection. One sees others as instruments of Satan, parasitic exploiters, enemies of society, state, or mankind; hence, bad humans, subhuman or inhuman.

These shadow aspects of patriarchal legalism are further fueled by the subtle effects of the repressed—but for that matter no less living—magical stratum. This layer of the psyche is highly responsive to group affect and emotion and to group fears and panic. It tends to confuse wish or fear with reality, and is obsessed with an urge to control and direct.

Also on the magical level operate the fundamental sadomasochistic urges described in a previous chapter, the *Urlust,* or primal ecstasy of annihilation of self or others for the sake of renewal, the rapture of merging in the oceanic mystery of the maternal nonself. This is as much a component of aggressive violence as it is of sexuality. It is also a part of the child's world of play and of being contained in maternal oceanic all-oneness. "Becoming and passing away, a building and destroying of every moralistic calculation in ever eternal innocence (which) is possessed in this world only by the play of the artist and of the child. And as the child and the artist play, so plays the ever living fire, building up and tearing down in innocence; and this is the game Aion himself plays."[3]

These energies are no longer (not yet) contained and regulated by viable cultural safeguards. As a result, like fiery lava and noxious gases from a volcano believed dormant, they threaten to poison the air and to destroy the land. The individual psyche is endangered by what Jung has called "psychic infection"; by those free-floating impulses from the magical layer. The danger is in direct proportion to the individual's suggestibility and unawareness of this suggestibility and of the workings of the magical dynamic. The effect is a state of intoxication and invasion by the collective affect: the fears, paranoia, and lynch-mob spirit of his group, of which he deems himself free. This may be made manifest in family vendettas, and social, national, patriotic, or religious fanaticism.

These then are the powder charges waiting to be ignited by the sparks of the torches of the returning Dionysus and his menadic retinue. They cannot be rendered harmless by good will or by mere abstract or reflective meditation. They require a medium that can regulate and rehumanize the magical affect dynamic in terms of direct relationship encounters. The factors or themes which the new rituals will have to contain and help integrate into new forms of human relations are familiar enough: impotence, alienation, helplessness, despair, emotional and sexual frustration, unsatisfied need for affirmation and affection from others, envy, depersonalization, paranoic shadow projection and sadomasochistic frenzy in the encounter between individual and individual and between individual and group. These problems cannot be dealt with by social or political measures alone. They are psychological predispositions as well. Unless dealt with in their own terms, through psychological awareness and ritual, they will continue to create and re-create those external conditions which validate them in a reciprocal relationship, and which we naively assume to be their external causes.

Ritual, fundamentally, is psychodrama; it is a conscious, earnest and devoted play. Yet what is play? Many definitions have been attempted since Huizinga's brilliant demonstration of how the play element underlies most, if not all, human activities as an unconscious determinant.[4] Instead of attempting the impossible—namely to define elemental experience in abstract terms—I shall attempt to characterize it by way of descriptions.

Play is an activity of testing reality in a symbolic and quasi-experimental fashion. There are rules in play which one must obey. But the rules are flexible; they serve the needs of the particular activity, and can and should be changed as the sense and intent of the activity require.

The rules serve rather than determine play. They are not a priori laws of truth. There is seriousness and commitment, winning and losing in play; but for it to remain playful, winning and losing cannot be ends in themselves. At best, they are merely criteria, stimulants, and direction-setters. The commitment is to the activity as such and this, in a spirit of pleasure, not to the useful result. Winning or losing is never final; one may always start all over again. Play, then, never gets trapped in the doomsday notion of irreversible finality. Every ending calls for a new beginning. Human play is a deliberate, microcosmic, *as if* restaging of life's flowing dynamic—its changing patterns, discoveries, beginnings, endings, and new beginnings. In play, fantasy, and practicality complement each other; mind measures itself, and experiments with existence. Play mobilizes and structures the powers of the unconscious psyche. It gives form to raw energy; it civilizes. Through its symbolic, *as if* enactment play moves and transforms the player (and to a lesser degree) the involved spectator.[5] Hence the cathartic effect of the symbolic enactment of the "life play" in the theater, the original patron being no other than Dionysus himself. This god appeared, variously, as playing child to be cared for; raving mad power; Lord of Life and Death; and empty mask, appearing and disappearing.

Ritual, then, is a deliberate play or enacting, within a formalized context, of affect-charged impulses, feelings, and archetypal visions or fantasies. By virtue of seeking and creating a formalized context these energies are safely contained; they can be propitiated, invoked, and confronted. To an extent they can even be controlled. Animal rituals, as well as the play of children, have shown us that on the most elementary instinctual level, those play activities not only contain and safely direct aggressive and sexual impulses, but also serve as means of communication between the participants. Our human courtship rituals and adult games serve the same purpose. Ritual also bridges the gaps and difficulties of personal relationships, by offering a formalized, readily available, nonpersonal (hence safe) channel. Ritual opens doors of communication to others, but also to the *other* within; to one's own self. It connects with one's inner roots and inherent powers. This latter fact is illustrated by the effects of psychodrama or the solitary rituals of yoga or Tai Chi and even by the unassuming trivial game of solitaire. Ritual, then, is psychodrama; psychodrama, a form of ritual.

When it comes to the question of what makes ritual effective, we have to stop and step out of the trap which our mental habits have created for us. The Cartesian mind-body dichotomy—the culmination of the separative trend of the late mental epoch—has brought about a split in the understanding of human activity. Physical, concrete action is reserved for the outer, "real" world of space and physically tangible objects. Reflection belongs to the mind—that which is inner, subjective, hence not quite real. (This, despite Descartes' claim to personal identity based on his dictum *Cogito ergo sum.*)

With this mind-set, mental activity is held to have no direct effect upon the world of things, except when translated into physical action. In turn, physical action—doing something with objects and things—is not expected to have a direct transforming effect on the mind except perhaps in a general way through the moral and health-improving effect of good works and exercise. In the light of this bias, any ritual activity appears senseless.

Yet we are currently discovering that this artificial dichotomy is totally arbitrary and does not correspond to observable facts. The study of synchronicity and psychokinesis shows that in quite an unexplainable way,[6] thoughts, emotions, affects, and intents do have a direct effect upon the behavior of animals as well as even inanimate (if there be such a thing) matter. Moreover, we can learn from psychodrama and bioenergetics—as well as the thousands of years of experience of yoga, Tai Chi, and Sufi dances—that bodily activity has direct effects upon psychic dynamics.

The body ego is the earliest form of self-experience. It operates in terms of the magical stratum of the psyche, on a level of symbiotic field identity with what later we divide into a within and without. This ego operates in magical all-oneness in which what we call a part, or partial event, contains, mobilizes and affects the whole. This (for our traditional reasoning) strange and unimaginable concept has only recently been demonstrated again in terms of the hologram, where each fraction of the pattern, when broken up, continues to present the whole image. Karl Pribram of Stanford University has proposed that we can understand the functioning of the brain in terms of the hologram.*

By connecting with body activity, then, we link our awareness with the activated magical dimension of the unconscious psyche. That means we mobilize and channel primitive and undifferentiated (potentially obsessive) affect energy into form. Simultaneously, conscious awareness expands. What we have come to call an altered state of consciousness ensues whenever emotionally charged imagery connects with bodily experience or activity. This "magically" altered state of consciousness can bring forth changes on the biological and psychological level which could not be accomplished by mere willing or reflecting.

* "Holographic Memory." Interview with Karl Pribram, by David Coleman. *Psychology Today,* February 1979.

Examples of this are the anesthesia or immunity to heat (walking on glowing embers) brought about through hypnosis, meditation, or in ecstatic conditions; and the recall of forgotten (or never consciously experienced) events under hypnosis or in meditation as well as under the influence of mind-altering drugs.

In a hypnotic state deep enough to bring about such profound changes, however, and under the influence of mind-altering drugs, conscious and deliberate ego activity and rational judgment are reduced in favor of the altered state. Ego participation is limited in varying degrees: more so with drugs, and minimally in the lighter forms of hypnotic trance or guided imagination, which operate by means of image-body ritual.

It should be noted, however, that while the bypassing of ego participation may be therapeutically called for in specific situations, this will always call for expert professional supervision. Habitual use of mind-altering drugs has long-range deteriorative effects and can seriously weaken the ego, as our knowledge of drug addiction has taught us. Such drug-induced experiences are not necessarily integrated, and therefore do not balance the magico-mythological with the mental level in terms of continuous working coexistence.

Ritual enactment techniques as well as formal meditation practices bypass the above dangers; addiction is avoided by the fact that ritual induction requires a conscious ego effort. As a result, full daylight consciousness coexists along with the altered state in a paradoxical and simultaneous dialectic.

A similar coexistence of both states has also been aimed for by the sexual practices of Tantra— and probably also of courtly love—which we have referred to previously. The aroused sexual energy brings about an alteration of consciousness which, with appropriate meditative approach, can be experienced consciously. It can be directed into a devotional, formalized enactment by giving full attention to an extended and contemplative playing while withholding ultimate climax, at least temporarily.

The experience mediated by body-enactment participation highlights the difference between knowing *about* and directly knowing something. This difference might be compared to the difference between reading about a particular place or country in a traveler's guide and actually going there; or by reading a menu versus actually eating the meal. Quite frequently patients, particularly women, have spontaneously remarked to me that an insight or understanding is not real to them unless it is also experienced bodily in some way.

The hidden wisdom of our language knows about this fact. The root words for "knowing"—*kennen* and *können* ("being able to") in German; *ken* in Gaelic; *gnosis* ("knowledge," "wisdom") in Greek; and *gnosco* in Latin—are the same ones we find in such words as *genus, gender, genital, genetic,* and *engender.* Knowledge and creativity are sexual as well as spiritual. When the Bible tells us that Adam "knew" his wife, it likewise expresses this experiential, creative meaning of knowing that includes the body.

The subsequent devaluation—indeed the abhorrence—of the body and bodily experience which took place during the reign of the patriarchy was part of the rejection of the magical and feminine dimensions. It culminated in the Cartesian mind-body dichotomy, and became the basic dogma for positivistic science. The concept was the starting point for psychology and psychoanalysis and effectively severed our conscious mind from awareness of the magical transformative dimension. In consequence of this fact, ritual, in the course of patriarchal development, gradually and increasingly became ineffective and meaningless.

The essential elements of ritual can be summed up in the formula purportedly spoken by the initiate at the Eleusinic Mysteries: "I saw," "I said," "I did." This formula lays down, the ingredients of transformation: image perception and assimilation of form and symbol (I saw); expression by means of word, sacred formula, *mantram,* sound, or even deliberate silence, all charged with power, awareness, and meaning (I said); solemn enactment (I did).

The effect of a rite is a transformation of the pattern of events. Sometimes this takes place in the outer world, as in the following description by Frobenius of a primitive hunting ritual:

> In the early dawn, a picture of an antelope was drawn on the ground; as the first ray of the rising sun fell on the drawing it was struck in the neck with an arrow. Then the actual antelope hunt began. After several hours, the hunters returned with a killed antelope; the animal had been struck by their arrow in the precise point of the neck in which, earlier, the arrow had struck the drawing. Now that it had fulfilled its purpose of exorcizing hunter and animal, the arrow was removed from the drawing and the drawing erased, with a certain ritual, to divert the effect of the committed murder from the hunters. The whole rite, drawing, hunting and erasing, took place in absolute silence.[7]

After the animal was eaten, the unused parts were returned and buried with appropriate ceremonies and thanksgiving.

In the hunting ritual described above, the image foci are antelope, sun ray, and arrow; the appropriate verbal expression for the hunt is silence; the enactment is shooting at the drawing.

In other instances, the inner nature of the participants is transformed, as in rites of passage, the Christian Communion, initiation or puberty rites, or in the Eleusinic Mysteries, or Extreme Unction which prepared the participant for eventual death. An intensely affect-charged enactment of an image pattern transforms behavioral and event patterns in such a way as to modify them by way of analogy, similarity, and synchronicity. The effect of symbolic representation and enactment rests upon the fact that, by availing itself of analogical vision, consciousness can grasp and, in part at least, direct the flow of energy.

Power becomes available to consciousness and as a result, responsible use becomes possible. Without conscious awareness of power and its particular quality, there is no possibility of choice or decision, hence no question of responsibility.

In the patriarchal world the use of power was the right and privilege of the appointees of collective authority: king and church, military and police forces, or, within the limited scope of home, the *paterfamilias*. Power—used to rule, conquer, repress, and punish—was forbidden to the ordinary person. The deliberate use of psychic power was condemned as magic, sorcery, and heresy—to be risked only under penalty of the sword and the stake.

Small wonder then, in view of this heritage, that the idea of power has for us become suspect, even reprehensible. We associate power with misuse and, psychologically speaking, the word *power* is mostly used pejoratively: "power trip," "power mad," "power hungry." We still automatically associate power with danger, hubris, repression, and suppression. In our frame of reference power is seen as predominantly destructive. Correspondingly, the idea of yielding, submitting to or serving power, smacks of shame, dishonor, and the giving up of human responsibility. Existential guilt is the result. The notion of power as a positive force is scary to most of us: the power of need, of sexuality, of assertion. Even power felt as transpersonal divine energy, working in us and through us, requiring of us conscious channeling and responsible use of its intents, is still suspect to most of us. We may theoretically consider such a possibility. But to take the risk of deliberately trying to live with and serve such a power in our personal lives frightens us. The result is that power is left to be used by those who claim it for their personal satisfaction and who are largely unconscious of their selfish motivations. It is the irresponsible use of power by dictators, do-gooders, fanatics or greedy entrepreneurs which gives it a bad name and seems to confirm its intrinsic evil.

Yet power is a manifestation of natural energy, the creative force of the world play, shaping and dissolving form. It is the life process itself, in which the human *I* experiences its own nature, its vitality and motivation. Life is power at play, Shiva or Dionysus dancing.

Dionysus, however, must now accommodate Apollo and Jehovah. The play is to be structured into form, into new ethics and responsibility. In order to separate power from oppression we have to learn to use it consciously and responsibly; not for self-aggrandizement and ego inflation at other's expense. We have to affirm and respect our own personal selves and also practice the Golden Rule as part of this personal reality: namely, that whatever I do to the other, I do to myself. Whatever I project onto the other, I can and need to find in myself.

We shun our human task as much when we refuse to use power as when we use it irresponsibly. The former is the introvert's, the latter the extrovert's fallacy. The introvert tends to refuse to risk himself and play his part in the external world play. He declines to experiment with and discover his needs, desires, power wishes, and fears in interpersonal situations, lest he risk his innocence. The extrovert, conversely, who perceives life as his plaything and people as his pawns, may be so fascinated by the effect he discovers he has upon others (or should have, according to his expectation) that he fails to notice the corruptive effect of his inflation or fears upon his own personality.

Ritual and ritualization can help remedy this double danger. It allows the introvert to play with his reluctance and the effect he has upon others and they upon him. It enables the extrovert to discover himself as the player who is being played with. In this way we discover ritual as a modality of significance for personal life, as well as interpersonal relation.

Past rituals in our culture have been predominantly transpersonally and collectively oriented, endeavoring to connect the individual with a sense of the divine, and reconciling him to collective standards. Consequently, they were administered by the powers of impersonal collective authority: church and state.

In contrast, the ritual to come is likely to be primarily concerned with the individual handling of power and relating to the transpersonal through finding one's individual way. It will connect and integrate individuals with their inner stirrings and the implications of these for self and others. It will connect the individual to the life of the containing group organism, and to personal and collective destiny. Ritual enactment fosters awareness of the fact and quality of the power surge in ourselves and as a result delimits it and gives us a chance to direct the ecstatic onrush.

Suppose, for example, we allow ourself to fantasize our hidden wishes, desires, and fears of how we would really like to treat a friend or foe, or would like or fear being treated by that person. If we then explore these fantasies to the limit of our imagination, we get a much better idea of what we really feel, as well as of what is possible or desirable, and what the effects would be upon the other as well as upon ourselves. For instance, to enact symbolically one's fantasies of death or destruction on someone hated brings one face to face with the victim's reaction and suffering. This is particularly true if the action is replayed, with roles reversed. Now one becomes the victim and experiences the torments engendered for him or her. The all-out enactment of dependency wishes or fears, to use another example, may bring home the truth that beyond a certain limit of what one previously has considered an insatiable wish to be cared for, one begins to feel hemmed-in. As the roles are reversed, one may feel contempt for that helpless "baby" who clamors for all that caring. One may now feel openly the previously hidden contempt for one's own dependency which made one secretly clinging or exploiting.

In a group setting, ritual enactment promotes confrontation and relatedness between individual and group. It helps one to discover and define one's own scope and standards, and to hold one's own against group compulsion and suggestibility. In the I-Thou context, ritual enactment may clarify such conflicts as care versus aggression or closeness versus distance.

In limiting drive power by channeling it into acceptable form, ritualization also limits fear of being swallowed and dehumanized by one's affects and impulses. Ritual propitiates the dread of the demonic side of affect by helping us discover its built-in limitation; like the safety valve of a boiler, it reduces the danger of explosion.

Ritual can humanize and personalize violence and aggression into assertiveness by something akin to an immunization process. The noxious element is first objectified and externalized; it is sent away like the scapegoat, and meditated upon (incubated like a bacteria culture). As the second step it is reintroduced ("reinjected") by means of enactment; it is acknowledged and received as one's own. It cannot be made to go away by wishing or willing, but has to be used responsibly, under appropriate circumstances and timing. Surprisingly, as the result of this conscious integration, the impulse itself changes character: its obsessive, destructive potential diminishes; its helpful aspects become available. Dionysus-Azazel, welcomed back under these conditions, gives us new depth. Through conscious integration we are no longer helplessly and obsessively at the mercy of the affect. "The wounder heals."

How is a new ritual to be arrived at? A genuine ritual, like a living symbol or a religious experience, cannot be fabricated; it can only be discovered. Some ritual forms may in time become collectively valid. Initially their discovery will have to occur by virtue of individual search. Like the seekers after the Grail, each one will have to set out on a separate path through the unknown land to find the common goal of the search. The new consciousness is psychologically oriented and concerned with each individual's revelation and discovery, rather than in-

sights revealed to an outstanding personality or culture hero like
Moses, Jesus, or Muhammad, who would then hand down the truth to
the many. Blind and uncritical submission to a guru's words gives us
the feeling of psychological regression now.

Yet, since the individual psyche is not a totally separate entity but,
like a leaf, is part of the tree of the collective psyche, the communal
pattern will, of necessity, sooner or later emerge out of the shared elements of the many individual searches. In the same way, new social or
political solutions can only work in proportion to the psychological maturity and self-awareness of their advocates. The wild-eyed fanaticism
of such "world-improvers" as Hitler, Lenin, and today's urban guer-
rillas helps them to act out their own unassimilated rage and paranoia.
This may, alas, be unavoidable for tearing down obsolete existing
structures. Perhaps times of transition need God's scourges. But in
order to develop viable forms for tomorrow, greater depth and psychological insight into personal motivations are needed.

Since the new integrational ethic is to be affirmative and inclusive,
rather than rejective and exclusive like the patriarchal ethic, the new
ritual will be based upon incorporating whatever happens to be, including our worst and ugliest aspects or tendencies. Gawain transforms
and redeems the bewitched castle by suffering the onslaught of the devouring lion; he saves Arthur's realm by embracing the repulsive hag
and undergoes his ordeal of transformation by responsibly and consciously playing with what ordinarily and traditionally is forbidden.
As a result, he makes it possible that at the right time the right question
which restores the power of the Grail can be asked: "What is wrong?"
"What end or meaning does it serve?"

Affirmation requires prior discovery and validation of what *is:* of the
ingredients of a particular psychological situation, and of one's motivations, urges, and feelings, whether or not they are to one's liking or in
accord with one's own or the community's standards. This value given
to discovering one's desires, feelings, and motivations contrasts with
our cultural heritage, which valued only what one *did,* not what one
was, or why one acted as one did. A person was measured by how his or
her action conformed to the collective value standard.

The new ritual, then, calls for exposure of the bad with the good, the
ugly with the beautiful. Along with all the positive qualities and feelings, such as faith, hope, love, and charity, it will also have to include
(and, possibly, first work through) loneliness and despair, defeat and
fear, want and need, resentment, hate, envy and greed and lust for violence. The whole gamut of childishly dependent and destructive urges
will have to be recognized as well as all the polymorphously perverse
contents of the magical stratum. These were denied and rejected

through the preceding ages; therefore they became numinously fascinating. Only after these have been acknowledged and assimilated can we reach a genuine and trustworthy relatedness.

The content of the ritual, then, is experimental play with—and trying to answer such questions as—"Who" and "How am I?" "What makes me tick?" "What turns me on" or "off"? "Thus am I." It is a ritual for partners, as well as for the solitary Self: "Who" and "How are you?" "What makes you turn on" or "off"? "Thus are you." "What do I; what do *you* desire?" "How much and what can you and I tolerate?" "What do we desire?"

It is a testing-out, confronting, validating, and experimenting with what motivates the partners, a giving of space to playing, testing, trying. It is a willingness to experience intensely, and without bias, whatever in a given situation, at a particular moment of time, happens to come to the fore within and between me and you.

In one way or another, most of these elements have been used in various psychotherapeutic approaches and modalities, such as encounter groups, psychodrama and Gestalt psychology. Yet so far there has been little awareness of their archetypal implications. For through or behind the personal experience operates also a transpersonal guidance factor bent upon shaping a new significance and relation to self, other, and world. A new structuring of communality and consciousness is under way.

In the following pages I shall describe the steps which I suggest to my patients or clients in order to help them to discover their individual rituals. These are no more than first attempts to apply the above guidelines; by no means do they pretend to offer anything like final or general answers or prescriptions.

The first indispensable step is to allow into awareness one's hitherto unacknowledged (or only shamefacedly acknowledged) fantasies, fears, and wishes. These include the whole gamut of desires, through expressions of destruction and violence; whatever fascinates and arouses energy, particularly if it also inspires fear or revulsion. Indeed, it is that very combination of simultaneous attraction and fear which characterizes the energy pattern that needs to be integrated as an intrinsic aspect of the unfolding of one's individual potential. An example is a person thinking about a major career change. If the new career looks like the answer to all life's problems, if it promises to remove all frustrations, if contemplating it arouses no doubt or fear, then this is probably an escape into fantasy. On the other hand, if the positive attraction is coupled with legitimate fear of possible failure and risks, then this is probably a genuine potentiality. The attraction-fear combination marks the call from the transpersonal Self; it also signals the need for the ego personality to translate such calls into a viable and acceptable form of expression. The creative artist faces a similar task in translating his vision into what is possible in terms of available materials, and esthetically acceptable under given circumstances. To present the vision in the raw, uncritically and without working it through, or to refuse to present it at all, would in either case be a bungling of the task.

Lovers and married couples can channel their affects by utilizing sexual play. For often the material in question is of a sexual nature, or at least has sexual overtones. Particularly relevant are masturbation fantasies with contents that have traditionally been adjudged perverse. We need to stop here and give some consideration to the archetypal and symbolic significance of sexuality. Sexuality is more than just nature's way of assuring reproduction of the species. It is also more than just pleasure and recreation.

Sexuality, as Freud correctly intuited (but owing to the positivistic bias of his epoch was unable to grasp fully), is a fundamental expression of psychic energy. It is an undifferentiated channel of basic force, of cosmic fire. It pulses into rapturous identification with the life force itself, with its flood and ebb tides. It moves us through elementary upheavals. It is a channel of power, of self-realization, of ecstatic transcendence, surrender of self, and renewal. The pagan sexual rites, then, were not merely agricultural or gynecological fertility procedures. They were also celebrations of death and renewal, mysteries to experience the Great Goddess and her son, the master of death and rebirth. Without that understanding we cannot fully understand their orgiastic and frequently violent character.

It is only when one starts with the utilitarian bias of sexuality as nothing but pleasure or a way to reproduce the species that one arrives at defining as proper or normal the most simple or effective methods of fertilization. Having done so, one can then judge other forms, the play of aboriginal rapturous lust, for example, as deviant and perverse. Yet, any and all of the so-called perversions—sadomasochism, homosexuality, oral and anal sexuality, fetishism, voyeurism, transvestitism—are fundamental and, in their own ways, meaningful patterns of energy as it plays at creation and development. They express basic, unconscious, and often unacknowledged urges which aim at compensating and balancing too one-sided a conscious position. They are archetypal in the sense that they express the call of basic power of an essentially religious and numinous character.

Sadistic urges express the unacknowledged and unchannelled need to be more assertive. One finds a predominance of sadistic trends usually in weak, frustrated, and unassertive personalities who feel limited, ineffective, and relatively impotent. Masochism, in turn, compensates the over-assertiveness of leaders, bosses, top executives, and other domineering, powerful, and successful personalities. Often one side may predominate physically and the other psychologically: a sense of physical helplessness or weakness compensated with a sadistic urge, and a sense of mental or emotional dominance compensated for masochistically. Aggressive assertion, even violent conquest, and self-effacing surrender are often pivotal aspects of sexual play. They pertain equally to the dynamics and needs of both sexes. Aggressive and assertive needs occur in feminine fantasies, and surrender urges in masculine ones. They need to be acknowledged and affirmed, particularly in view of the fact that the traditional roles have tended to repress sexual aggression in women and passivity in men.

Oral sexuality expresses a dependency need and often represents the unacknowledged worship of phallic power or of the dark mystery of the *yoni,* the abysmal ground of the Feminine. To have one's *yoni* or phallus orally "worshipped" is to have it validated in oneself. To offer cunnilingus or fellatio to the other is to make her or him feel that power within and through her or his body.

Anality is a form of needful ego expression or control. Homosexuality expresses an urge for an as yet inadequately realized fulfilling of one's own sexual gender; for a more adequate validation of one's femininity or manhood.

"Fetish" is a derogatory term for a cult object foreign to one's own recognized (hence "true") religion. Cult objects, whether a statue of the Holy Virgin or of a god, a splinter of the true cross or the representation of a tribal spirit, are symbolic representations of power embodiment. They mediate power to the one to whom they speak, who is touched by them. This power can of course also be manifest sexually particularly when the instinctual, earthy side has suffered repression. Fetishism, then, is an unconscious urge to worship those particular qualities which the fetish embodies to the fetishist. The foot or shoe worshipper, for instance, is driven to give reverence to the lowliest or most earthly aspect of personality; to heed a call for more submissiveness or acceptance of the feminine, for instance, since most shoe or foot fetishists are men. Of course, the specific personal associations of meaning of the particular fetish will have to be elicited in every case before an interpretation can be made.

Voyeurism is the sexualized form of the *theatron,* the beholding of a vision of a godhead. It represents a need for direct conscious confrontation and acceptance of something one did not want, or was afraid, to see: the lustful ecstasy of the sexual power, the divine quality of the sacred energy shining through the sexual object as acknowledged in the Tantric sexual ritual. Voyeurism may frequently compensate for an attitude which depreciates the sexual act as nothing but an animalistic urge or the partner as merely an object to be used.

Transvestitism was an established custom in the worship of Kybele (Goddess of caverns, of wild nature, worshipped on mountain tops), and other Goddess cults as well as among shamans. Even now the ritual garment of a Catholic priest is skirtlike. Wearing the clothes of the opposite sex bespeaks the urge to identify with the Goddess, the Great Feminine, the need for more assertiveness of their feminine selves in women ("wearing the pants"), more expression to feminine qualities in men.[8]

Sexual expression and sexual play, moreover, include varied patterns: of aggressor and victim, violence and surrender, caring, nourishing and need-fulfilling, as well as fear and loneliness. All these facets are constellated in the dimension of self-transcendent sexual ecstasy. Through ecstatic sexuality, pagan ritual acknowledged the presence of suprapersonal power as well as its capacity to influence human behavior in mutual assertion and surrender. In turn, by depriving sexuality of its place in consciously experienced religious ritual, the religions of the Book deprived themselves of one of the most vital vehicles of transformative power and mutual influencing. Sexual fantasies mobilize and reveal some of the strongest motivational urges. Meditatively enacted in Tantric play and within the limits of mutual acceptability, or translated into a formal ritual, such fantasies can provide some of the most powerful ritual forms.

The first step, then is the acknowledging and elaborating of one's desire, need, and fear fantasies, with no holds barred, and regardless of how immoral, destructive, scary, immature, dirty, unesthetic, childish, or sentimental they may seem.

The next step calls for their acculturation. The dramatist or stage manager must take over. The fantasies are now to be made stageworthy. They are to be molded into a play. Their suitability for the stage is judged by whether they are performable yet still maintain this fascinating power. The flaming breath of a dragon, for example, may have to be represented by an analogous symbolic act or gesture by a human participant. A fantasy of strangling someone would have to be expressed by a less dangerous action or gesture. It is essential, however, that the substitution maintain a genuinely symbolic character, that it be the best possible vehicle for the intensity of the affect that is to be expressed and experienced. The limits of safety and acceptability will have to be stretched to the utmost if the play is not to lose the intensity of the affect.

This entails discussing the scenario of one's play with one's partners, and getting their consent to its performance. Optimally, such a consent is reached when the fantasies of the partners match and complement each other. Second best is the assistance of partners who are not themselves touched by the particular fantasy, but are willing to help by role playing. In any event, the mutual acceptability of roles and actions assigned is to be established beforehand, and limits are to be set in order to avoid physical harm. A "stop" signal is also to be agreed upon as a safety measure in the event that the intensity of affects, deliberately aroused by the enactment, should prove too much for a participant.

By virtue of these arrangements, particularly of the "stop" option, the intensity of the ecstasy and exposure are limited and made assimilable. Too great a fear of the aroused affects can be prevented by knowing that any moment one can call a halt.

Now, its broad outlines agreed upon, the play is to be improvised. The general trend of action is to be blocked out. But the specific actions and/or verbalization are to be spontaneous, as in the *commedia dell'arte* format. Reactions and impulses that arise in the course of the action are to be given free play. It is frequently helpful first to enact the script nonverbally by gesture, motion, and pantomime only. Words introduced too soon often detract from emotional and bodily experiencing. They promote the safety of abstraction and siphon away the affect experience. Later, when the affect has been experienced, and particularly when the core action that most adequately expresses the affect has been established, words may help to intensify or structure the dynamic. This run-through of the play, then, establishes the particular form of the ritual. It is that enactment of the fantasy which proves meaningful and worthy of repetition for the sake of helping one get in touch with the powers of one's life needs.

It is important here, to recall once more the difference between enactment, which we advocate, and acting out. By acting out we mean a willful expression of one's impulses for "kicks," for immediate satisfaction of an urge, or an involuntary—often unconscious or compulsive—blowing off steam. One simply does what one wants, no matter what the consequences. Such behavior is often rationalized and justified with such explanations as, "I couldn't help myself," "I don't know what came over me," or "I didn't mean to, I'm sorry." Acting out is a way of using a safety vent or directly defying a superego inhibition. Temporarily, at least, acting out serves to relieve tension and anxiety. It helps little, if at all, in integrating drives, and its effects—undesirable at best—can be downright destructive at worst.

Enactment, on the other hand, as referred to in working on a psychodramatic ritual, strives for a symbolic rather than a literal expression of problematic, unacceptable, or dangerous impulses. It utilizes a relatively controlled, safe, and conscious form in order to bring about assimilation and civilizing transformation. It is symbolic in seeking a "best possible" expression within the limits of safety and acceptability. This means expressing a part of the drive directly in order for the other part to be altered into a positive growth or relationship factor. Enactment, consequently, occurs in terms of *as if*. It deliberately attempts to generate powerful affects in the service of connection, communication, and awareness. As a result it initially increases tension and anxiety. Its long-range effect, however, is constructive and supportive because the cooperation of a consenting partner or partners is required. Enactment is not meant for "kicks," but should be done in a spirit of respect for the right and needs of the partner and of attention and reverence for the energy it releases. Enactment, properly understood, is part of the quest to discover the secret of the Grail.

Meditating together upon the task, before and after the action, may be helpful for the participants. Only after that is done are discussion, sharing, and interpretation desirable. The value of repeating the enactment—and in what form—will need to be discussed. Role change or reversal should be instituted for every participant to experience the energy from all its aspects.

Aggression and violence, fear and need, affect us both actively and passively. The victim carries an aggressor in himself; the aggressor hides an unacknowledged victim in his soul. Frequently our needs are unfulfilled because of a rejecting part of our selves. We dare not ask or try for satisfaction because our superego or self-rejecting animus deems us unworthy and forbids us to look for relief or satisfaction. Also our fears are to a large extent the monsters, ghosts, or punishing superego authorities of the past, projected onto the people and situations we must deal with today. The more unrealistic and obsessive these projections are, the more we are unable to cope effectively with the person or situation in question. The sense of being uncared-for corresponds to an unwillingness and inability to care for and value ourselves, which we were taught by not truly being cared for as children.

As a general rule, the aggressive urge in overtly weak and nonaggressive victim personalities tends to be introjected and turned against themselves. It appears as self-depreciation and self-hate, which result in depressiveness and a sense of impotence. Deep down, the compensatory fantasies on the often repressed sexual level show a predominance of sadistic elements. Beneath the surface of timidity and nonassertiveness smoulders a dark fire of resentment and hate which eventually may give rise to explosions of violent destructiveness. Enacting the aggressor or tyrant helps such a person connect with that side of her- or himself. Equally, the habitually overbearing hero-conqueror harbors an unacknowledged surrender urge, and may identify with the victim by paranoic rationalizations of the violent urges: everybody is "trying to do me in" or "taking advantage of me." This encirclement or exploitation phobia, which easily becomes a self-fulfilling prophecy, has led to much disastrous violence in national and international conflicts, as well as in personal relationships. The unacknowledged surrender urge may also operate as an unconscious impulse to self-undoing through drugs or drink, workaholism, accident proneness, or overreaching oneself into a blundering that invites destruction by self or the now sufficiently aroused others. Our personal—as well as collective—histories abound with examples of this Napoleon or Hitler syndrome.

In the ritual enactment of such powerful urges as aggression it is important, therefore, for both sides to enact both poles of the constellation; to experience fear, diffidence, helplessness, and uncared-for loneliness as well as the feelings of conquest, strength, effectiveness, and even the capacity to destroy. Experiencing the power of the most negative as well as the most positive feelings is necessary if one is to find the eventual balance within oneself.

An example of a simple enactment in a group setting will help to illustrate my points. Two members of the group, a man and a woman, were constantly at each other's throat, regardless of the issues involved; they seemed totally unable to get at the roots of, or resolve, their antagonism. They were asked to meditate on and envisage their respective wishes and fears in approaching each other. They were then instructed to place themselves at opposite ends of the room and, walking toward each other, to enact nonverbally whatever arose in themselves as an expression of their fantasy and in response to each other's approach.

The man began by slowly plodding toward the woman. She remained rooted to the spot. As he came nearer, she began moving her body in a sinuous dance, in a highly suggestive fashion. When he came close enough to reach out to her she abruptly stopped and turned her back on him. As he tried rather clumsily to turn her toward him by force, she flew at his throat—as though to strangle him. At once, they were in vicious combat, wrestling and rolling on the floor. The angry fighting, they said afterwards, had clear erotic implications. With the discovery of this ambivalence they stopped and began to sort out what had happened. It had become obvious to onlookers as well as to the participants themselves that the woman's motivation was to arouse the man's aggression at any cost to herself. She would risk violence, perhaps even desire it, in order to be noticed as a woman in her own right. She felt uncared-for and inferior as a woman, and had to prove to herself that she could attract men, at least physically. Yet when she had succeeded on this level she was unwilling, and indeed unable, to face up to the implications of her "come-on." She wanted to be taken notice of as a person, not just a body, and the direct physical approach which she constantly (albeit unconsciously) provoked only increased her inferiority feeling and made her angry.

The man, in turn, was afraid of women. He felt inferior because of his notion of men as conquering heroes, a model he felt unable to emulate. He ought, he felt, to be a breaker of hearts. Consequently he went about proving his manhood by a show of plodding, even brutal, strength. This "macho" response, however, was only a flimsy disguise to cover up his inferiority feelings, which burst into desperate fury when he felt himself seduced, deceived, and trapped by woman's guile and trickery.

The roles were then reversed. Each replayed and copied the other's part. The woman was now the clumsy "macho" and the man the "vamp" woman. The man now got a sense of how her attitude found an echo in himself. In playing her role, he discovered that in spite of himself he liked something about it. He now began to see his own seductiveness and desperate wish to attract attention. The woman, for her part, discovered and connected with the brutality of her judgmentalness, which decreed the inferiority of feminine values and deemed herself in particular to be worthless. All of this she had previously projected onto men, not realizing it really came from her own harsh superego.

Recognizing what had happened through their mutual experience and feedback helped both of them to see their own problems and also to begin to understand and sympathize with their partners. An avenue to communication and mutual helpfulness was opened where before there had been only mutual resentment.

In working this way with the fearsome strangers, dangerous beasts, and helpless waifs in one's soul, one always, sooner or later, comes across the resistances, rejecting judgments, prejudicial thou shalts and shalt nots, and self-destructive limitations that emanate from the potentially castrating patriarchs in one's own mind. Indeed, each new discovery of hitherto unacknowledged urges brings with it the discovery of an injunction which has inhibited and prevented it from unfolding and finding a suitable place in the overall pattern of things. In the process we discover both the self-righteous superego judge and the rejected scapegoat in our psyche. This discovery offers us a chance to integrate both and to begin to see ourselves more realistically; to accept our limitations, weaknesses, and inabilities, and to find growing space for the rejected problem child.

When we work on our personal problems we mold the stuff of which our lives are made. Enacting rather than acting out our personal complexes enables us to become conscious and cooperative participant-spectators rather than unconscious victims of the drama of our lives. Through such consenting action participation we can become witnesses, *martyroi* (the Greek word *martyros* means "witness"), of the drama of our own *tragodia* and *comedia* of the song and dance of the goat god in ourselves; of our own painful and often funny evolution. No longer need we then be involuntary, unconscious, or self-styled martyrs, victims of lives that are felt as forever putting us at a disadvantage. Neither need we continue to project the scapegoat upon our neighbors, friends, and enemies.

As the martyr discovers himself and becomes witness to his feelings, he changes his questions from "Why me?" "How did I deserve that?" to the Grail questions: "What is the meaning of this?" "What can it lead to?" "What can it teach me?" and "What is it to serve?"

References

Introduction

1. William Butler Yeats, *The Collected Poetry of W. B. Yeats* (New York: Macmillan Co., 1956), p. 309.
2. E. C. Whitmont, *The Symbolic Quest* (Princeton, N.J.: Princeton Univ. Press, 1978), p. 197.

Chapter 1—A Modern Theophany

1. Dionysus was the consort of Ariadne, the Goddess of the Cretan Labyrinth, the place of mystery, of the dance of life and death (the bull dance). He was the son, lover, sacrificial victim, and reborn consort of the ancient Great Goddess, mistress of heavens and dark power of earth, whose worship and culture preceded the patriarchal religions and culture. And he was a sexual and phallic god, a phallus in a basket, like a little child and a phallus torn off by the maenadic women to be restored to the realm of the maternal goddess to be born of her like Osiris-Horus of Isis.
2. E.A. Wallis Budge, *The Gods of the Egyptians,* Vol. 1 (New York: Dover, 1969), p. 515.

   Massey identifies her as the Great Mother of Mystery (later denounced in the biblical Book of Revelation as "Babylon the Great, the mother of Harlots and of abominations of the earth"). She is "higher than all the gods and is the only one who stands above her father." (Gerald Massey, *Ancient Egypt,* Vol. 2 [New York: S. Weiser, 1970], p. 698.)

Chapter 2—Desire, Violence and Aggression

1. Exodus 20:13, Martin Buber's translation. See also *The Torah. A New Translation according to the Masoretic Text* (Philadelphia: Jewish Publication Society, 1962), p. 134.
2. Carl Gustav Jung, "The Meaning of Psychology for Modern Man," *Collected Works,* Vol. 10, Bollingen Series XX (Princeton, N.J.: Princeton Univ. Press, 1964), p. 137.

3. *Deuteronomy* 13:12–16.
4. A *daimon* is a divine or semi-divine guiding spirit in ancient Greek terminology. A *demon* is an evil spirit in medieval language.
5. Erich Neumann, *Das Kind* (Zurich: Rhein Verlag, 1963), pp. 175ff.
6. Stanislav Grof, *Realms of the Human Unconscious* (New York: Viking Press, 1975), p. 123.
7. Irenäus Eibl-Eibesfeld, *Liebe und Hass* (Munchen: Piper Co., 1970), p. 15.
8. Paul D. MacLean, *The Triune Brain.* The Neurosciences: Second Study Program, ed. F. O. Schmitt (New York: The Rockefeller University Press, 1970).
9. *Liebe und Hass,* pp. 40ff.
10. Personal communication to the author.
11. Abdul Hussein, M.D. and Seymour Tozman, M.D., "Psychiatry on Death Row," *Journal of Clinical Psychiatry,* no. 3, March 1978, pp. 183ff.
12. William Blake, *The Portable Blake* (New York: Viking Press, 1974), p. 114.
13. Other examples include the Orphic and Eleusinic or Samothrakean mysteries, the Christian Eucharist on the one hand, and the bloody Bacchantic orgies or those of Cybele, the ancient scapegoat ceremony, on the other.
14. Konrad Lorenz, *On Aggression,* trans. M. Letzke (London: Methuen & Co., 1967), p. 40.
15. *Ibid.,* p. 148.
16. *Ibid.,* p. 117.
17. Anthony Storr, *Human Aggression* (New York: Atheneum, 1968), p. 118.

Chapter 3—Myth and Psychological Functioning

1. Viktor Frankl, *Man's Search for Meaning* (New York: Washington Square Press, 1959).
2. For more detailed information, the reader is referred to the writings of C. G. Jung and J. Campbell as well as to the relevant chapters of my *Symbolic Quest.*
3. Miguel Serrano, *C. G. Jung and Hermann Hesse* (New York: Schocken Books, 1966), p. 85.
4. Joseph Campbell, *Myths to Live By* (New York: Viking Press, 1972), pp. 214–215.
5. C. G. Jung, *Memories, Dreams, Reflections* (New York: Pantheon Books, 1961), p. 11.
6. *Satan,* ed. Bruno de Jesus Marie O.C.D. (New York: Sheed & Ward, 1952).
7. Whitmont, *Symbolic Quest,* p. 20f.

Part 2—Consciousness in Evolution

1. Paul D. MacLean, *The Triune Brain.* The Neurosciences: Second Study Program, ed. F. O. Schmitt (New York: The Rockefeller University Press, 1970). By the same author, *On the Evolution of Three Mentalities,* Laboratory of Brain Evolution and Behavior (Bethesda, Maryland: National Institute of Mental Health).

2. Erich Neumann, *The Origins and History of Consciousness* (New York: Harper & Row, 1962).

3. Jean Gebser, *Ursprung und Gegenwart* (Stuttgart: Deutsche Verlagsanstalt, 1949).

4. Frederick A. Van Scheltema, *Die Geistige Wiederholung* (Bern: Francke Verlag, 1954).

Chapter 4—The Magical Phase

1. Gebser, *Ursprung und Gegenwart*, pp. 73–171.

2. John Michel, *The Earth Spirit* (New York: Crossroad, 1982), p. 4.

3. A. Van Scheltema has cogently shown that there are also close parallels between paleolithic behavioral patterns and the behavior of the newborn up to three; between neolithic and bronze period patterns and the child from three to twelve; between the antique iron epoch and its heroic world and puberty; and between the medieval period and adolescent mentality.

   Apparently, the movement of consciousness does not occur at the same pace among various cultures or even among the different social strata of one culture. In Imperial Rome the intelligentsia had, by and large, already reached a mental level while their masses as well as the Germanic and Gallic people that were their contemporaries still functioned on mythological and magical levels. In Western Europe mental functioning did not begin until the onset of the second millennium and even to the present day many strata of peasantry, European and South American, still function mythologically, and parts of the indigenous population of Africa, Asia, and Australia, magically.

4. J. C. Pearce, *The Magical Child* (New York: E. P. Dutton, 1977), p. 58.

5. *Ibid.*, p. 156.

6. *Ibid.*, p. 151.

7. Jakob von Ucxkull, "A Stroll Through the Worlds of Animals and Men" in *Instinctive Behavior*, trans. and ed. Claire H. Schiller (New York: International Universities Press, 1975), p. 11.

Chapter 5—The Mythological or Imaginal Phase

1. The assumption that power, soul, or soullike qualities, when ascribed to an object, must of necessity originate and belong to the observer, and hence rests on projection, follows the metaphysical assumption and bias that the nonhuman, object world cannot have mind or soul; that matter is dead. This was the general position of scientific knowledge in Freud's and Jung's day. It is, however, a gratuitous a priori assumption. It is the particular bias of the postmedieval mind, not supported by any evidence and increasingly contradicted by gradually accumulating evidence to the contrary.

2. Laurens Van Der Post, *A Mantis Carol* (New York: William Morrow, 1975), p. 110.

3. Karl Kerenyi, *The Religion of the Greeks and Romans* (New York: E. P. Dutton Co., 1962) p. 108.

4. K. Lorenz, *On Aggression*, p. 148.

5. K. Kerenyi, *Dionysos*, Bollingen Series LXV 2 (Princeton: Princeton Univ. Press), p. 238.

6. Walter F. Otto, *Dionysus* (Bloomington, Ind. & London: Indiana Univ. Press, 1965), p. 140f.

7. *The Gospel of Sri Ramakrishna* (New York: Ramakrishna-Vivekananda Center, 1969), p. 884.

8. Dylan Thomas, *Collected Poems* (New York: New Directions, 1971), p. 128.

9. Martin Buber, *Good and Evil* (New York: Charles Scribner's Sons, 1953), p. 89.

10. William Butler Yeats, *The Collected Poems of W. B. Yeats* (New York: Macmillan, 1979), p. 286.

11. Lao Tzu, *The Tao Te Ching*, trans. C. N. Wu (Jamaica, New York: St. John's Univ. Press, 1962).

Chapter 7—The Divine Kingship

1. The Christian *agape*, the injunction to love one's enemies, does not correspond to a spontaneously aroused feeling. It seeks to impose a new civilizing ideal upon resistant, natural love and hate urges.

2. The story goes that Rabbi Hillel, a leading Pharisaic authority of the first century A.D., when asked by a Roman soldier under threat of death to define Judaism in the time one can stand on one leg, answered: "Love thy neighbor as thyself, everything else is commentary." Thus Jewish tradition points to the command of the Golden Rule as the heartpiece of its culture.

3. Genesis 1:2, quoted after Robert Graves and Raphael Patai, *Hebrew Myths* (New York: McGraw-Hill, 1966), p. 2.

4. *Ibid.*, p. 31.

5. "In the history of the beginnings of consciousness we can discern successive phases of development during which the ego frees itself from containment of the unconscious, the original uroboric situation, and finally, at the end of the process, having become the center of modern Western counsciousness, confronts the unconscious as a separated system in the psyche. *During this development,* leading to a liberation from the ascendancy of the unconscious, the symbolism of consciousness is masculine and that of the unconscious, *in so far as it stands in opposition to the emancipation of the ego,* is feminine, as we learn from mythology and the symbolism of the collective unconscious." Erich Neumann, "On the Moon and Matriarchal Consciousness," *Spring,* 1954, p. 83, italics mine.

6. The great invocation of Israel, Sh'ma Yisroel.

7. Status comes from the Latin *stare*, "to stand," specifically, where one has been placed or made to stand.

8. To be discussed below.

9. St. Augustine, quoted in Julius Evola, *Metaphysik des Sexus* (Stuttgart: Klett Verlag, 1962), p. 251.

10. This is a mythical motif which is still operative in modern history, in Japanese tradition, in the British "white man's burden," the Germanic *am deutschen Wesen wird die Welt genesen* ("through German ways the world will

recover"), and in the American notion of "keeping the world safe for democracy."

11. Tatian, as cited in *Collected Works of C. G. Jung,* Vol. 9, Part II (Princeton, N.J.: Princeton Univ. Press), p. 46, par. 81.

12. George P. Fisher, *History of Christian Doctrine* (New York: Charles Scribner's Sons, 1902), p. 85.

13. "Sin and guilt are aboriginal phenomena for theology. They cannot be derived from something else more basic such as depressive states or psychological imbalance. They are not a form of psychic illness even though they might be interwoven with it . . . The concept of guilt is fundamental for theology, for theology deals with God and with his *word* toward man. This word which addresses the totality of man decrees man to be a sinner before God . . . Guilt is a 'no' against God and against His will." From Karl Rahner, "Schuld und Schuldvergebung" in *Angst und Schuld in theologischer und psychotherapeutischer Sicht,* ed. Wilhelm Bitter (Stuttgart: Klett Verlag, 1962), p. 54. Essay appears also in *Spring,* 1974.

14. P. Tournier, *Guilt and Grace* (New York: Harper & Row, 1962), p. 10.

15. The Bishop to John Wesley: "Sir, this pretending to a special revelation of the Holy Ghost is a horrid thing, a very horrid thing." Cited in Charles Williams, *Witchcraft* (New York: Meridien Books, 1960), p. 110.

16. Aquinas, *Summa Theologia,* 1 A, 1 act 8.

17. *Ibid.*

18. John Wesley as quoted by Stephen Hobhouse in *Selected Mystical Writings of William Law* (Sharon Hill, 1938).

Chapter 8—The Human Exile

1. Symposium held at School of Theology, Claremont, Calif. Apr. 1970, cf. *New York Times,* May 1, 1970. E. B. Fiske, reporter.

2. Colin Turnbull, *The Forest People* (New York: Simon and Schuster, 1962), p. 272.

3. Yeats, *Collected Poems,* p. 293.

4. The figure of Mary as the intercessor for man is but a feeble shadow of the grand figure of the triple goddess whose major expressions were nature-mother-virgin, creation and destruction, wise old woman, witch and harlot.

5. According to Christian doctrine, "God is in all things not as part of their essence nor yet as an accident or attribute, but as an agent is present to that on which it acts." Fisher, *History of Christian Doctrine,* p. 236.

6. R. H. Tawney, *Religion and the Rise of Capitalism* (London, 1948), p. 267.

Chapter 9—The Scapegoat

1. At Mentes in Egypt the goat of Memphis symbolized the ithyphallic Kheu, the dark, a mummy, representing the hidden male power of nature. It was also called Min, the ruler, a form of Amon or Amen, the potter with the wheel fash-

ioning the primal egg of generation (I 72, II 390). The ancient Jews still accused the Samaritans of saying that a goat had created the world (II 154). Volume and page references are to J. G. R. Forlong, *The Encyclopedia of Religion* (New Hyde Park, N.Y.: University Books, 1964).

2. Commentary on Matthew, Homily, cited in Hugo Rahner, *Man at Play,* trans. B. Bottlershaw and E. Quinn (New York: Herder and Herder, 1967), p. 98, quoted in D. L. Miller, *Gods and Games* (New York: Harper & Row, 1970), p. 108.

3. Disidentification rather than repression (i.e., distorted by later interpretation as a call for repression) is possibly also the implication of the saying of Jesus. "If your right eye cause you to sin, pluck it out and throw it away.... And if your right hand cause you to sin cut it off and throw it away" (Matt. 5:30, 31).

4. J. W. Goethe, *Faust I,* trans. Charles E. Passage (Indianapolis & New York: The Bobbs-Merrill Company, 1965), p. 71, verses 2049–2050.

5. *New York Times* of June 8, 1980, p. 45.

6. Paul Tournier, *Guilt and Grace* (New York: Harper & Row, 1962), p. 92.

7. C. G. Jung, *Collected Works,* Vol. 10, p. 454, par. 856.

Chapter 10—The Feminine and Its Repression

1. Jane Harrison, *Prolegomena to the Study of Greek Religion* (New York: Meridian Books, 1922), p. 285.

2. Ernest Jones, *The Life and Work of Sigmund Freud* (abridged) (New York: Doubleday, Anchor Books, 1963), p. 368.

3. *Ibid.,* p. 367.

4. *The Malleus Maleficarum,* trans. Montague Summers (New York: Dover Publications, Inc., 1971), pp. 43, 44, 45, 48.

5. Paul Tabori, *Secret and Forbidden, the Moral History of Mankind* (New York: Signet Books, The New American Library, 1971), p. 204.

6. Helen Diner, *Mothers and Amazons* (New York: Julian Press, 1965), p. 156.

7. Raphael Patai, *The Hebrew Goddess* (New York: Ktav Publishing Inc., 1967), pp. 25–28.

8. Clement of Alexandria, *Stromata* II, quoted in Robert Graves, *King Jesus* (New York: Farrar Straus & Cudahy, 1946), p. 2.

9. Robert Ornstein, *The Psychology of Consciousness* (New York: Harcourt Brace Jovanovich, 1977), p. 37.

10. First Epistle of John 4:16.

11. *Areios*—devoted to Ares
    areious—better than, stouter, braver (comparative to good)
    arete—goodness, excellence
    aretao—to thrive
    ari or *eri*—(equivalent prefixes) strengthen the sense of a word, e.g.,
       erikoos—sharp of hearing
    erizeo—to strive
    eromai—to inquire, ask after or for, to petition
    eros—desire or love

12. Erich Neumann, *"On the Moon and Matriarchal Consciousness," Spring,* 1954. (Trans. from *Zur Psychologic der Weiblichen,* Zurich, 1953.)

13. Sylvia B. Perera, *Descent to the Goddess* (Toronto: Inner City Books, 1981), pp. 15–34.

14. Esther Harding, *Women's Mysteries* (New York: Pantheon Books, 1955), p. 102ff.

15. See also Goethe's "Selige Sehnsucht," *West-Östlicher Divan:*
    Tell it no one but to sages
    For the crowd spurns the desire
    I extol what through the ages
    Has aspired to death by fire.

16. Erich Neumann, *The Great Mother,* Bollingen Series XLVII (New York: Pantheon Books, 1955), pp. 293–94.

17. Toni Wolff, *Structural Forms of the Feminine Psyche* (Zurich, 1956). Privately printed.

18. See also E. C. Whitmont, "Reassessing Femininity and Masculinity" *Quadrant,* Vol. 13, no. 2 (Fall 1980), pp. 109–122.

19. I would only in passing draw attention to the obvious logical contradiction between the contention that unconsciousness is feminine and seeing the animus as representing the feminine unconscious; we have conveniently avoided confronting this contradiction or have explained it away.

20. In the past this practice has frequently led to such terminological absurdities as "animus of the anima": or to calling a man dominated by mother's animus or a woman by father's anima in order to avoid admitting the bona fide animus or anima dynamic as it operated in the person's own psyche.

Chapter 11—The Grail

1. John Matthews, *The Grail: Quest for the Eternal* (New York: Crossroad, 1981), p. 5.

2. *Ibid.,* p. 10.

3. *Ibid.,* pp. 5–7.

4. Emma Jung and M. L. von Franz, *The Grail Legend* (New York: Putnam, 1970), p. 121.

5. C. G. Jung, "Psychology and Alchemy," *Collected Works,* Vol. 12, p. 179.

6. Joseph Campbell, *The Masks of God: Creative Mythology,* Vol. 4 (New York: Viking Press, 1968), pp. 410–412.

7. *Ibid.,* p. 373.

8. Joseph Campbell, *The Masks of God: Occidental Mythology* (Baltimore: Penguin Books, 1976), pp. 10–14.

9. *Ibid.,* pp. 13–14.

10. *Ibid.,* p. 14.

11. Buber, *Good and Evil,* pp. 83–84.

12. Francis King, *The Secret Rituals of the O.T.O.* (London: C. W. Daniels, 1973), pp. 14–16.

13. Wilfried Daim, *Der Mann der Hitler die Ideen gab* (Vienna: Institut fur Politische Psychologie, 1958), p. 202.
14. *Ibid.*, p. 142.
15. *Ibid.*, p. 12.
16. *Ibid.*, p. 56.
17. *Ibid.*, p. 140.
18. Strabo VII, 2, as quoted in J. Markale, *Celtic Civilization* (Paris: Gordon and Cremonesi, 1978), p. 41.
19. King, *The Secret Rituals of the O.T.O.*, p. 162.
20. In *The Symbolic Quest,* I have described this method of substituting "I" for "she" or "he" for the purpose of clarifying the nature of a projection. Whenever one is gripped by a strong affect in response to another person or persons, this substitution infallibly reveals the nature of the unconscious content in individual no less than collective situations (p. 61).
21. Teilhard de Chardin, *Phenomenon of Man* (New York: Harper Torch Books, 1959), p. 248.
22. A. Coomaraswami says: "We hold with J. L. Weston that the Grail story is not . . . a product of imagination, literal or popular. At its root lies the record, more or less distorted, of an ancient ritual having for its ultimate object the initiation into the secret sources of life, physical and spiritual. In this of course the application is equally the story of the green knight and for 'ancient ritual' we should read 'ancient myth and ritual.' " A. Coomaraswami, *Selected Papers,* Bollingen Series LXXXIX (Princeton: Princeton Univ. Press, 1977), p. 121.
23. Roger S. Loomis, *Wales and Arthurian Legend* (Cardiff: Univ. of Wales Press, 1956), pp. 35–36, 154.
24. *Ibid.*, p. 62.
25. *Ibid.*, pp. 184, 62.
26. *Ibid.*, p. 291.
27. After Heinrich Zimmer, "The Indian World Mother," *Spring,* 1960.
28. Coomaraswami, *Selected Papers,* p. 108.
29. Loomis, *Wales and Arthurian Legend,* p. 355.
30. *Ibid.*, pp. 221, 229.
31. Zimmer, "The Indian World Mother," p. 71.
32. *Ibid.*, p. 61.
33. Evelyn Sullerot, *Women on Love* (New York: Doubleday, 1979), p. 7.
34. *Ibid.*, p. 44.
35. Philip Rawson, *The Art of Tantra* (Greenwich, Connecticut: New York Graphic Society, 1973), p. 9.
36. *Ibid.*, p. 11.

Chapter 14—Ethics

1. B. Slay, E. Hansen, and H. F. Harlow, "Mother–Infant Separation in Monkeys," *Journal of Child Psychology,* Psychiatry Three, 1962, p. 123.
2. Paul Tabori, *Secret and Forbidden* (New York: New American Library, Signet, 1971), pp. 205–208.

3. E. B. Williams, *One Man's Freedom* (New York: Atheneum).
4. K. Rahner, *Schuld und Schuldvergebung, Spring,* 1974, p. 7.
5. C. Fitzgibbon, 20 July, New York, 1956, pp. 150, 152, quoted in W. L. Shirer, *The Rise and Fall of the Third Reich* (New York: Simon and Schuster, 1960), p. 1048.
6. "Good must needs come, but blessed is he by whom it cometh; in like manner also evil must needs come, but woe to him by whom it cometh." Logoi of Jesus; G. R. S. Mead, *Fragments of a Faith Forgotten* (New Hyde Park, N.Y: University Books), p. 594.
7. C. G. Jung, "Good and Evil in Analytical Psychology," *Collected Works,* Vol. 10, pp. 861, 862, 865, 866.

Chapter 15—On Ritual

1. Erich Neumann, "The Psychological Meaning of Ritual," *Quadrant 9* (Winter 1976), 27–34.
2. Arthur Koestler, "On Disbelieving Atrocities," in *The Yogi and the Commissar* (New York: Macmillan Co., 1945).
3. Friedrich Nietzsche, *Collected Works,* ed. Karl Schlechta, III, p. 376, quoted in E. Fink, *Nietzsches Philosophie* (Stuttgart: Kohlhammer Verlag, 1963), pp. 40–41.
4. J. Huizinga, *Homo Ludens* (New York: Roy Publishers, 1950).
5. "As far as I know, ethnologists and anthropologists concur in the opinion that the mental attitude with which the great religious feasts of savages are celebrated is not one of complete submission to illusion. There is an underlying consciousness of things 'not being real' " (*Homo Ludens,* p. 22).

   "The mask in a primitive festival is revered and experienced as veritable apparition of the mythical being that it represents—even though everyone knows that a man made the mask and that a man is wearing it. The one wearing it, furthermore, is identified with the god during the time of the ritual of which the mask is a part. He does not merely represent the god; he is the god" (Campbell, *The Masks of God,* Vol. 1, p. 4).
6. One might ask if these phenomena really require explanation any more than, let us say, gravitation, which we can only observe but not explain. The fact is that we take gravity for granted, but have paid no attention to—or even refused to consider—synchronicity or psychokinesis since they do not fit in with our bias.
7. Leo Frobenius, *Kulturgeschichte Afrikas* (Vienna: Phaidon Verlag, 1933), p. 127f.
8. In the *Hysteria,* orgiastic festivals of Aphrodite in Argos, men wore women's garments and women men's clothes.

Index

Aaron, 106
Abel, 108, 157
Abélard, Pierre, 64, 209
Abraham, 62, 66, 94, 117
Achilles, 13, 188
Actaeon, 58
Adam, 85, 124, 157, 244
Adler, Alfred, xi–xii, 94, 119
Adonis, 33, 55
Aeneas, 64
Ahriman, 61
Ahura Mazda, 61
Akiba, Rabbi, 215
Albigensians, 159
Alger, Horatio, 152
Allah, vii, 79
Amargon, 156
Amazons, 122
Anath, viii, 122
Aphrodite, xiv, 129, 131, 136, 177, 197, 217
Apollo, 6, 50, 57–58, 60–61, 63, 65, 82–83, 107, 131, 235, 245
Apuleius, 41
Aquarius, 152, 156–158, 166, 172, 186, 221
Arabic poetry, 153
Ares, 13, 17, 129–132, 217
Aries, 61
Aristotle, 50, 60, 70, 72–73, 217
Armanentum Armandom, 161
Artemis, 32, 174, 197
Arthur, 123, 152, 154, 168–170, 173–174, 178, 191–192, 222, 248
Aryan myths, 161–162
Astoreth, 126
Athene, viii, 135, 140–141, 186, 190, 197
Attis, 6–7, 33, 55
Augustine, 124
Austria, x, xii–xiii, 160, 162

Azazel, 6, 21, 58, 61, 63, 106–110, 112, 118–120, 177, 237, 247

Baal, 126
Babylon, 126
Bachofen, J. J., 139
Baigant, M., 160
Baphomet, 159, 164
Basho, 37
Bast, 7–8
Bellona, viii, 122
Beowulf, 65
Berkowitz, David ("Son of Sam"), 18
Bhagavad-Gita, 11, 174
Black Masses, 139
Blake, William, 19, 82, 85
Blavatsky, Elena, 159
Boccaccio, Giovanni, 64
Bohu, 83
Bors, 154
Botticelli, Sandro, 160
Boyle, Robert, 160
Brahma, 11, 171
Bronze Age, 42–43, 50–51
Brunhilde, xi
Buber, Martin, 62
Buddha, 231
Budge, Wallis, 8
Bushmen, 52–53

Cain, 62, 110, 114, 157, 172
Calvin, John, 206
Cambodia, 54
Campbell, Joseph, vii, 30, 156–158
Canaanites, viii, 61, 126
Cancer, 61
Carter, Jimmy, 33
Catholicism, 32, 88, 124, 184
Celtic myths, viii, 122, 153, 155, 161, 174
Ceres, 152, 197

Cerunnus, 155, 161
Chaldeans, 83, 155
China, x, 1, 128, 143
Chlysts, 139
Chrétien de Troyes, 149, 156
Christ, *see* Jesus
Christianity, xii, xiv, 8, 12, 15–16, 24,
  32–33, 51, 53, 61, 63–65, 74, 79–82,
  87–88, 91, 93–95, 98, 100–101,
  105–107, 110, 139, 152–155, 159, 164,
  167, 184, 195, 207, 216–217, 221, 226
Chrysostom, 109
Cocteau, Jean, 160
Columbus, Christopher, 51, 152
Constantinople, Council of, 101–102
Cordelia, 210
Crowley, Aleister, 159
Crucifixion, 153, 155, 172, 195
Crusades, 159–160

Daim, Wilfried, 162
De Die, Beatrix, 176
Debussy, Claude, 160
Decalogue, 15, 53, 63, 74, 81, 87–89, 100,
  126
Delilah, 184
Delphic Oracle, 188, 235
Demeter, 152, 197
Depression, Great, 20
Descartes, René, 69, 71, 205, 241–242,
  244
Devil, *see* Satan
Diana, 32
Dido, 64
Dionysus, ix, 6–7, 12–15, 21–22, 30–34,
  49–50, 57–59, 61–64, 83, 85, 96–97,
  105, 107, 118–120, 131, 135–136,
  138–139, 144, 149, 155, 159, 163,
  165–166, 174–175, 177, 217, 235, 237,
  240–241, 245, 247
Dumuzi, 6–7, 141, 155, 157

Ecclesiastes, 181
Eckhardt, Dietrich, 165
Eden, 156–157, 172, 227
Egypt, ancient, viii, 6–8, 61, 122, 126,
  203
Eichmann, Adolf, 96
El Salvador, 12
Eleusinic Mysteries, 244
Eliade, Mircea, 98
Enlightenment, 74
Episcopalianism, 52
Ereshkigal, 134–135, 138, 140–141, 155,
  198
Eros, 17, 19, 24, 59, 64, 82, 129–133,
  140–141, 191, 217

Eskimos, 44–45
Eucharist, 153, 176, 236–237, 244
Euripides, 57, 139
Eve, 124, 157, 183
Extreme Unction, 244

Fates, 208
Ferron, Jacques, 219–220
Fisher King, 154–156, 167, 170–171, 178
Flannel, Nicolas, 160
Fludd, Robert, 160
Foster, Jodi, 33
France, 13, 219–220
Franz Ferdinand, 162
Frauja, 162
Frazer, James, 33
Freud, Sigmund, 9, 14, 56, 59, 81, 103,
  123–124, 150, 160, 250
Frobenius, Leo, 244

Galahad, 154
Galileo Galilei, 88
Garuda, 170–171
Gaul, xiv
Gawain, xiv, 154, 156, 167–172, 174–175,
  177–178, 186, 192, 229, 248
Gebser, Jean, 39, 50
Gemini, 61
Germanic myths, xi, 83, 122, 161
Germany, ix, xi–xiii, 12, 18, 29, 48, 163,
  220–221
Goethe, Johann Wolfgang von, 110, 152,
  160
Golden Age, 100, 150, 152, 156–157
Golden Dawn, Order of, 159, 164
Golden Rule, 87, 89, 178, 188, 215, 217,
  227, 246
Gorgon, 135, 197
Grail myths, ix–xiv, 29, 58, 74, 118, 123,
  128, 135–136, 149–179, 186–187,
  191–192, 195–196, 204, 213, 221–223,
  230, 247–248, 254, 257
Graves, Robert, 49
Greece, ancient, viii, xiv, 6–7, 11, 15, 51,
  55, 57–58, 61, 67, 70–71, 79–80, 82–83,
  87, 91, 101, 109, 122, 129–130, 135,
  155, 236
Green Knight, 168–169, 175, 177
Grillparzer, Franz, 13
Grof, Stanislav, 17–18
Gromar, 170
Gromoflanz, 167

Hades, 31, 58, 135, 155
Hamlet, 210
Hammurabi, 222
Harrison, Jane, 122

Hathor, 126
Hebrews, *see* Judaism
Helen of Troy, 64, 154
Héloise, 64, 209
Hera, xiv
Heracles, 86
Heraclitus, 11
Hermes, 6, 160
Hinckley, John, 33, 164
Hinduism, viii, 6, 11, 59, 125, 168,
    170–172, 174–176, 203, 206–207
Hitler, Adolf, ix, 12, 48, 118, 158–
    159, 161–166, 172, 188, 220, 248,
    255
Hölderlin, Friedrich, 183
Holocaust, 54, 166
Holy Roman Empire, 88
Holy Spirit, 130
Homer, 60
Hrabanus Maurus, 130
Hugo, Victor, 160
Huizinga, J., 240

Inanna, viii, 121–122, 133–134, 140–141,
    198
Indian myths, *see* Hinduism
Indra, 171
Industrial Revolution, 20, 74
Innocent VIII, 124
Inquisition, 88, 139
Iran, 12, 48, 81
Irish myths, viii, 122, 174
Ireneaeus, 91
Iron Age, 50–51, 66
Isaac, 62
Ishtar, viii, 167
Isis, 7, 126
Islam, vii, 79, 81
Isolde, xi, 64
Israelites, *see* Judaism

Jacob, 8, 25
Jehovah, vii, 8, 15, 58, 61–62, 66, 72, 74,
    79–85, 87, 89–90, 98, 103, 106,
    108–110, 112, 131, 144, 194, 245
Jesus, 49, 74, 86, 88–89, 105–106,
    153–155, 160–162, 164, 172, 213, 222,
    248
Job, 108
Joseph of Arimathea, 153
Judaism, x–xi, 5, 8, 16, 29, 53, 61, 65, 74,
    79–85, 87–88, 91, 94, 101, 105–110,
    126, 161–163, 165–166, 184, 207, 215,
    217, 221, 226
Judas, 153
Jung, C. G., ix–x, xii, xv, 3, 6–7, 14, 23,
    28–29, 31–32, 40, 45, 60, 81, 83, 86,

118, 128, 130, 142–143, 183, 187, 193,
    205–206, 209, 222–224, 229
Jupiter, 7, 79

Kali, viii, 203
Kant, Immanuel, 214
Kenge, 99, 102
Khomeini, Ruhollah, 12, 48, 163
Krushchev, Nikita, 70
Klingsor, 162
Knights Templar, 159–161, 164
Koestler, Arthur, 239
Krishna, 6
Ku Klux Klan, xii
Kundrie, 135, 167
Kybele, 252

Lancelot, 154
Lao Tzu, 147
Last Supper, 153
Lear, 210
Leigh, R., 160
Lenin, 248
Leonardo da Vinci, 160
Libya, 81
Liebenfels, D. Lanz von, 160, 162,
    164
Lila, 140–141, 186, 190, 210
Lilith, 157, 184
Lilly, John, 101
Lincoln, W., 160
Longinus, 154
Lorenz, Konrad, 22–24, 55
Lucifer, 63, 155, 166
Lueger, Karl, 162
Luna, 140–141

Mabinogion, 167
MacKellar, Jean, 44
Maclean, Paul D., 39
MacLeish, Archibald, 77
Malcreatiure, 155–156
Manu, vii, 125
Marduk, 65, 83
Mars, 129–130
Marx, Karl, xii, 29
Mary, Virgin, 154–155, 184, 197, 251
Mary Magdalene, 160
Masons, 159–160
Mass, 176, 236–237, 244
Maximillian von Hapsburg, 160
Medusa, 135, 138, 140–141, 155, 171, 190,
    197–198, 217
Mephistopheles, 110
Merlin, 154
Merovingians, 160
Mesopotamia, viii, 156–157

Middle Ages, 74, 80, 88, 94, 116–117, 153, 216–217, 233
Mimir, 157
Minoan civilization, 55, 57
Mithraic rites, 7–8
Molière, 99
Montsalvat, 159
Montsegur, 159
Morgan le Fay, 167, 169–172
Morrigan, viii, 13, 122
Moses, 222, 248
Moslems, *see* Islam
Mowat, Farley, 44–45
Mozart, Wolfgang Amadeus, 160
Muhammad, 222, 248
Murray, Margaret, 150

Napoleon Bonaparte, 255
Nazism (National Socialism), ix, xi–xiii, 12, 18, 29, 33, 163–166, 172
Neolithic period, 42–43, 50–51
Neumann, Erich, 39, 45, 83, 133, 140, 237
Newton, Isaac, 160
Nibelungenlied, xi, 49
Nietzsche, Friedrich, 235
Norns, 157
Norse myths, 49, 51, 155, 157

Odin, 49, 155, 157
Odysseus, 50
Oedipus, 42, 62, 173, 195
Ootek, 44–45
Ordo Templis Orientis, 159, 164
Orgeluse, 155–156, 167, 178
Original Sin, 100
Ornstein, Robert, 128
Orpheus, 6
Osiris, 6, 61
Otto, Walter F., 58–59
Ovid, 47, 64, 66, 157

Pallas Athene, viii, 135, 140–141, 186, 188, 197
Pan, 6–7, 32, 34, 63, 68, 98, 177, 217
Paris, 64
Parsifal (Parzival), xi, xiv, 154, 156, 162, 166–168, 175, 177–178, 186–187, 189, 192–194, 221, 229
Pearce, J. C., 44
Pentheus, 7
Perera, Sylvia B., 133, 135
Perl, Fritz, 193
Persephone, 58, 152
Perseus, 86, 135
Persia, 61
Philosopher's Stone, 152

Phoenecians, 51
Plato, 217
Plutarch, 98
Pluto, 155
Poland, xiii, 12
Polo, Marco, 51
Pribram, Karl, 242
Prieuré de Sion, 160
Proserpine, 58, 152
Protestantism, 96, 104, 124, 184
Puritans (Puritanism), 51, 72, 95–96, 104, 112, 217
Pygmies, 99
Python, 65, 83

Ragnell, Lady, 167–169, 174, 177
Rahn, Otto, 159
Reagan, Ronald, 33, 164
Renaissance, 60, 70, 74, 216
René d'Anjou, 160
Revelation, Book of, 63–64, 126
Rhea, 58
Rilke, Rainer Maria, 214
Rome, ancient, viii, xiv, 15, 51, 54, 65, 70–71, 79, 82, 109, 122, 129–130, 155
Rosicrucians, 160
Rousseau, Jean-Jacques, 21, 47
Rumi, 37

St. George, 65, 83, 86, 94
St. John, 63–65, 105, 126, 130
St. Matthew, 65, 77, 109
Salome, 184
Samson, 13
Satan, vii, 9, 21–22, 32, 58, 61, 63, 85–86, 100, 103, 109–110, 118, 155, 159, 164, 183, 197, 200
Saturn, 129, 131
Schopenhauer, Arthur, 150, 162
Sekhmet, viii, 7–8, 13, 122, 203
Seneca, 205, 208
Seth, 61
Shakespeare, William, 210
Shakti, 176–177
Shaman, 155, 164
Shiva, 13, 171, 174, 245
Siegfried, xi, 65, 83
Socrates, 43, 60, 70
Solomon, 64
Sphinx, 155, 173
Stalin, Joseph, xi, 163, 188
Star of David, 5–6
Stauffenberg, Count, 220
Steiner, Rudolph, 159
Stone Age, 42
Storr, Anthony, 26
Strabo, 163

Sufi thought, 153, 242
Sumer, viii, 58, 122, 134, 155, 198

Tai Chi, 241–242
Tammuz, 6, 33, 55, 155
Tantric rites, 175–177, 186–187, 243, 252
Tao, 67, 147
Taurus, 61
Teilhard de Chardin, 106
Telephos, 188
Templars, 159–161, 164
Ten Commandments, see Decalogue
Thanatos, 59, 131
Thule, 160–161
Thyr, 13
Tiamet, 65, 83
Tohu, 83
Tournier, P., 114
Tristan, xi, 64
Turnbull, Colin, 99–100

Uexkull, Jakob von, 45
Uganda, 44
Ulfila, 162
Urak, 122

Valkyries, 122
Van der Post, Laurens, 52
Van Scheltema, Frederick, 39, 51

Venus, 129, 155, 167
Vesta, 197
Victorians (Victorianism), 9, 14–17,
    112, 151
Vietnam, 12, 54
Vincent de Beauvoir, 121
Virchov, Rudolf, 70
Virgin Mary, see Mary
Virgo, xiv
Vishnu, 170–171

Wagner, Richard, xi, 158–159, 187, 189
Waste Land, 154–156, 170–171, 173–174
Watts, Alan, 101
Wesley, John, 96
Wolff, Toni, 140–141
Wolfram von Eschenbach, xiv, 155–156,
    159, 166–167, 175, 177
World War I, 18, 54, 162
World War II, 46, 54, 220–221
Wotan, vii

Yeats, William Butler, v, xii, 63–64, 69,
    100, 159, 181
Yin and Yang principles, x, 15, 50,
    60–61, 128–133, 142–144, 151, 189–190,
    197–198, 200, 221, 231, 234

Zeus, 7, 58, 79